*Twayne's English Authors Series*

EDITOR OF THIS VOLUME

Sylvia E. Bowman

*Indiana University*

*John Milton: Poetry*

TEAS 242

Gul. Faithorne ad Vivum

Delin. et sculpsit.

Joannis Miltoni Effigies Ætat: 62.
1670.

John Milton

# JOHN MILTON: POETRY

### By DAVID M. MILLER

*Purdue University*

**TWAYNE PUBLISHERS**
A DIVISION OF G. K. HALL & CO., BOSTON

Published in 1978 by Twayne Publishers,
A Division of G. K. Hall & Co.
All Rights Reserved

Printed on permanent/durable acid-free paper and bound
in the United States of America

*First Printing*

**Library of Congress Cataloging in Publication Data**

Miller, David M
John Milton.

(Twayne's English authors series ; TEAS 242)
Bibliography: p. 189–94
Includes index.
1. Milton, John, 1608–1674—Criticism and interpretation.
PR3588.M47      821″.4      78-18800
ISBN 0-8057-6724-X

For Garth, Dain, and Joanne

# Contents

# About the Author

David M. Miller received his academic training at the University of Minnesota (B.S., M.A.) and the University of California, Davis (Ph.D.). He is the author of *The Net of Hephaestus: A Study of Modern Criticism and Metaphysical Metaphor* (The Hague, 1971), and of critical articles on Milton, Faulkner, and Tolkien. In 1966 he joined the English Department of Purdue University where he teaches Milton, Seventeenth Century Poetry, and Science Fiction.

# Preface

Whenever the literary game of ranking our greatest authors is played, Shakespeare heads the list, but John Milton most frequently is next. Only Shakespeare and the Bible have received more critical attention than Milton, for he is both the most learned and the most ambitious of our major poets. A brief work on such a figure requires hard choices, and I have made them with regret. There is no room to trace Milton's relationships in thought and technique to his great predecessors or to examine the love-hate complexity engendered by Milton's long shadow in poets from John Dryden to John Keats to T. S. Eliot. The great prose that shows Milton's passionate involvement in the political and religious upheavals of his age must be left for a second volume.

With Milton, the temptations and rewards of literary history and biography are great, but I have chosen to examine his art, not as the record of a great man fitted for the demands of his country, nor as a supreme effort in the evolution of English literature; rather, I examine his poetry as the most successful attempt in our language to meld the contrary demands of spirit and flesh into a vision congruent with the paradox of human freedom existing within divine omnipotence. Over and over Milton indicates that such was his purpose. Always he strove to subdue the pride of art to the glory of God, and it is remarkable that, in pursuing the second, he so often achieved the first.

This study is a "spiritual" reading of the seven great poems which comprise the center of Milton's esthetic accomplishment; but, for Milton, "spiritual" is a much more capacious word than it is for many modern readers. In seeking first the kingdom of heaven, all the world of art can also be gained; hence, we should not expect to find bloodless piety in retreat from the carnal realities of earthly existence but a strenuous attack upon life. Milton's spirituality enabled him to have life more abundantly; it heightened, rather than dulled, his senses and his intellect.

My first chapter sets Milton in his age and notes some of the forces which produced his complex personality. The next four chapters discuss the greatest of his early poems and trace the emergence of his central vision as he works his way from the "minor" genres of elegy and ode to the major genres of tragedy and epic. Despite the accomplished genius of the 1645 poems, Milton regarded them as preparation for a greater work. Even "Lycidas," which some find the greatest English lyric, was considered by the poet to be an apprentice poem.

The most complete statement of Milton's vision is, of course, *Paradise Lost,* and my discussion of it in chapter 6 comprises the bulk of this study. Since Milton wrote his epic in the pursuit of truth, I concentrate on the nature of truth as Milton attempted to express it. Despite his efforts to prove art the servant of God, Milton does not minimize the conflict; and, in my last two chapters, two quite different problems in applying the vision of *Paradise Lost* to human existence control my discussion of *Paradise Regained* and *Samson Agonistes.* E. M. Forster found Beethoven's music trustworthy because beneath divine harmony the demons always rumbled. Milton, too, is to be trusted because, in illuminating the timeless dilemma of humanity, he never forgets that we are infinite in imagination and finite in deed.

This study of Milton's art is for two kinds of readers: the student reading Milton seriously for the first time, and the nonspecialist who wishes a companion voice as he renews acquaintance with Milton's genius. To record my debts to previous scholarship and criticism would require inordinate space, and so I have silently (and gratefully) incorporated the scholarship that seems most useful for the purpose at hand. Chapter notes indicate critical works of immediate interest to my discussion, and the reader wishing further guidance will find it in the studies and bibliographies listed at the end of my text.

I wish to thank the Odyssey Press for permission to quote from Merritt Hughes's *John Milton: The Complete Poems and Major Prose* (all citations are from that edition), the Purdue English Department for generous support, and most of all those students who each semester continue to prove that Milton's poetry is a monument to living ideas.

DAVID M. MILLER

*Purdue University*

# Chronology

1608   December 9, John Milton born in Cheapside, London.

1615(?)–Attends St. Paul's School; tutored by Thomas Young.

1625

1625   Enrolled a lesser pensioner of Christ's College, Cambridge.

1626   Expelled for disagreement with tutor, William Chappell. Readmitted with new tutor, Nathaniel Tovell.

1628   Anne Phillips, niece, dies. "On the Death of a Fair Infant Dying of a Cough."

1629   Bachelor of Arts, Cambridge. "On the Morning of Christ's Nativity."

1631(?)–"L'Allegro" and "Il Penseroso."

1632   Master of Arts, Cambridge. Settles with parents in London for private study.

1634   September 29, *Comus* performed at Ludlow Castle.

1635–   Intensive private study at Horton, near Slough, Bucks.

1638

1637   *Comus* published by Henry Lawes.

1638   "Lycidas" published with other elegies for Edward King. Milton leaves for Continental tour.

1639   August, Charles Diodati, friend dies. Milton returns home.

1640   *Epitaphium Damonis* ("Damon's Epitaph"), Latin elegy for Charles Diodati.

1641–   Involved in antiprelatical movement. Three pamphlets: "Of

1643   Reformation in England," "Of Prelatical Episcopacy," and "Animadversions."

1642   "The Reason of Church Government" and "An Apology for Smectymnuus." Marries Mary Powell; wife leaves him.

1643   First divorce tract, "Doctrine and Discipline of Divorce." "Areopagitica."

1645   Divorce tracts, "Tetrachordon" and "Colasterion." Takes "great house" in Barbican. First volume of poems, *Poems of Mr. John Milton, Both English and Latin*, registered for publication.

1646 July 29, first child, Anne, born. Royalist inlaws take shelter with Milton.

1647 Milton's father dies. London occupied by Roundheads.

1648 Second child, Mary, born.

1649 January 30, execution of Charles I. "Of the Tenure of Kings and Magistrates." Named latin secretary; chambers in Whitehall. "Eikonoklastes" written to refute "Eikon Basilike."

1651 *Pro Populo Anglicano Defensio* (A Defense of the English People), in response to Salmasius's *Defensio Regia, pro Carolo I* (A Defense of the Reign of Charles I). Milton's health poor, eyesight failing. Third child, John, born.

1652 Totally blind. Granted an assistant in secretaryship. Daughter, Deborah, born. Mary Powell Milton dies. Son, John, dies.

1653 Oliver Cromwell's *coup d'etat*.

1654 *Defensio Secunda* in response to Peter Du Moulin's *Regii Sanguinis Clamor*.

1655 Slaughter of Protestant Waldenses prompts Milton to write "On the late Massacre in Piedmont." Relieved of chief duties; salary granted for life. *Defensio pro Se*.

1656 Marries Katherine Woodcock.

1657 Andrew Marvell appointed Milton's assistant. Daughter, Katherine, born.

1658 Katherine Woodcock Milton and infant daughter die. Sonnet 23 ("Methought I saw my late espoused Saint").

1659 "A Treatise of Civil Power in Ecclesiastical Causes" and "Considerations Touching the Likeliest Means to Remove Hirelings Out of the Church." Cromwell's son, Richard, abdicates. Rump Parliament restored.

1660 General Monk enters London. *The Ready and Easy Way to Establish a Free Commonwealth* published. May 29, Charles II takes the throne. Milton dismissed from office, arrested, fined, and released.

1663 Marries Elizabeth Minshull.

1667 *Paradise Lost. A Poem Written in Ten Books*.

1670 *The History of Britain* published.

1671 *Paradise Regained* and *Samson Agonistes*.

1673 Enlarged edition of the 1645 poems issued.

1674   Second edition of *Paradise Lost* (twelve books). November 8(?) Milton dies of gout; survived by three daughters and widow.

1754   Elizabeth Foster, last known decendant, dies.

CHAPTER 1

# Introduction: Life and Times

BECAUSE John Milton was deeply involved in the political and religious upheavals that vexed the seventeenth century as they prepared the ground for modern England, and because he believed that not only his work but also his life should be an artistic creation, dedicated to revealing the ways of a stern and loving God, the details of his life are much more fully known than those of his early contemporary, Shakespeare, or of his great predecessor, Spenser.[1]

Milton's father, also John Milton, was an educated, talented man who made a comfortable life for himself and his family after he had been rejected by his Catholic father for having read an English (hence Protestant) Bible. John Milton senior was a scrivener, a combination of notary and businessman, who also gained an international reputation as a musician and composer. In an age when parental tyranny was the norm, he was remarkably understanding of his brilliant but often opinionated son. Not only did he enroll John at St. Paul's School, he also hired private tutors to work with the boy after hours; and tradition has it that John early invited blindness by studying far into the night. One of John's tutors at St. Paul's was Thomas Young, a radical Puritan, who undoubtedly gave the boy an opportunity to develop his taste and skill in religious polemic. At St. Paul's, John learned Latin and Greek; in later life, he added an astonishing number of other languages. By the time he was thirty, his Italian verse was good enough to draw praise from the Italian cognoscenti in Florence.

In 1625, at the age of sixteen, Milton entered Cambridge University to study for the ministry. We may imagine the hopes of his proud father, for John's brother, Christopher, was later to become a lawyer. But John found Cambridge a difficult place. St. Paul's School, harsh enough by our standards, was essentially humanistic,

but Cambridge was still depending upon authority and rote learn-
ing, just as the scholastic Aristotelians had for generations. The
conflict between Milton and his tutor must have been serious, for in
1626 he was "rusticated" (expelled). As a boy at St. Paul's, Milton
had formed a friendship with Charles Diodati, whom he idealized
and with whom he carried on a carefully literary correspondence.
From a letter to Diodati, we can sense the defiance with which
Milton responded to unfair disciplining. However, Milton was
readmitted the same year and continued at Cambridge through the
master's degree.

## I   *Early Poetry*

Milton's early poetry, in Latin and English, is that of a talented
amateur in love with learning. The most substantial is a poem oc-
casioned by the death of his niece in 1628; "On the Death of a Fair
Infant Dying of a Cough" shows both talent and wide knowledge of
various literary traditions. The following year (1629) Milton pro-
duced the first of his great poems. "On the Morning of Christ's
Nativity" signals the advent of a major poet who is strongly
influenced by the works of Edmund Spenser. Milton planned a
series of poems celebrating other events in the church calendar, but
the two fragments we have, "The Passion" and "Upon the Circumci-
sion," are both inferior and unfinished. However, they indicate that
Milton knew the metaphysical poetry of his day, for they are filled
with strong lines and labored conceits. From our perspective, Mil-
ton's poetic development seems satisfactory, even precocious; for,
by the time he was twenty-three, he had produced a number of
skillful minor poems in Latin and Italian, several competent elegies
(including a fine poem on Shakespeare), and a nativity ode that is
among the greatest in English. Yet the young Milton was driven by
ambition and felt that time was passing him by.

## II   *"How Soon Hath Time"*

The first of the three sonnets we shall consider in detail dem-
onstrates the iron control which helped Milton transmute pride into
magnanimity and ambition into patience.[2] Sonnet 7 ("How Soon
Hath Time") blends the structural conventions of Italian and En-
glish sonnets into a characteristically "Miltonic" form. The octave

sets a problem, the ninth line is a turn, and the sestet moves securely to a complete resolution. But within the eight-and-six division, the content divides into the English three-quatrains-and-a-couplet, even though the rhyme clearly signals the Italian form; for example, the sestet rhymes *a, b, c; b, a, c;* and yet the content is four-and-two:

> Yet be it less or more, or soon or slow,   *(a)*
>    It shall be still in strictest measure ev'n   *(b)*
>    To that same lot, however mean or high,   *(c)*
> Toward which Time leads me, and the will of Heav'n;   *(b)*
>
>    All is, if I have grace to use it so,   *(a)*
>    As ever in my great task-Master's eye.   *(c)*

The sonnet's imagery begins with an easy personification achieved by capitalizing an abstraction and by giving that abstraction animate attributes: "How soon hath *T*ime, the *subtle thief* of youth, / *Stol'n* on *his wing* my three and twentieth year" (my italics). But, rather than producing a little allegory, the imagery blends and shifts from subject to object: "My hasting days fly on with full career, / But my late spring no bud or blossom show'th." "Time" has the wings, but "My hasting days" do the flying, and the "full career" of a galloping horse is enclosed in the arrested development of a plant which has not flowered, even though the season is late. "Spring" is certainly a noun; but, in the context of "wing," "fly," "hasting," and "career," there is a suggestion that Milton is jumping too late.

The second quatrain, whose rhyme echoes the first, stops the action altogether as it considers the disparity between appearance and reality:

> Perhaps my semblance might deceive the truth,
>    That I to manhood am arriv'd so near,
>    And inward ripeness doth much less appear,
>    That some more timely-happy spirits endu'th.

Yet the imagery of the first quatrain is subtly maintained: "Time" is the "thief," but "my semblance" "deceives"; the absence of "bud or blossom" conceals an "inward ripeness."

Line 9, which turns the argument toward resolution, summarizes both the slow growth of ripeness and the rapid plunge of time: "Yet be it [growth] less or more, or [movement] soon or slow." Line 10 then makes of the two image patterns a paradox: "It shall be still in strictest measure ev'n"; for "still" means both "at rest" and "always," and "strictest measure" describes both an "evaluation" and a perfectly ordered "march." The paradox is "solved" by recognizing that stasis and movement, appearance and reality, are perfectly joined in Milton's foreknown "lot," and that "Time" is the perfect servant of the "will of Heav'n." The moral is drawn, in the final two lines, with the firm, richly allusive grace that is the mark of Milton's genius: "All is, if I have grace to use it so, / As ever in my great task-Master's eye." God is timeless: "All" the sequential flux is "ever" present, for growth and flight are designed by the "task-Master." Even the will of man ("if I have grace to use it so") comes within the divine dispensation, for "grace" comes from God.

Milton had decided against taking ordination, presumably because, like many Puritans, he found the tyranny of the church hierarchy intolerable;[3] but he stayed at Cambridge to study for a master's degree. Although the dating is not firm, he may have written, about 1631, the twin poems, "L'Allegro" and "Il Penseroso," which reflect the techniques of argumentation that were staple to the university. After taking his degree the following year (1632), Milton returned to his father's house to read and otherwise prepare himself for a career as a poet. The verse letter in which he announced to his father his choice indicates that he expected full tolerance and understanding, and his father gave it.

## III   *The Seeds of War*

In spite of the tranquility which this brief summary of Milton's early life suggests, affairs outside the Milton household were fast approaching a danger point.[4] James I, who had come from Scotland to rule England at the death of Queen Elizabeth (1603), spent his twenty-odd years as king dissipating the reverence for the throne that Elizabeth had spent her life fostering. When, in 1625, his son, Charles I, was crowned, both the religious and political situations were ominous. Charles could obtain no money from Parliament without severe compromises in what he firmly believed to be his God-given rights as king. And when he set about to impose a uniform church service on the splendidly fragmented and volatile Protestants of England, ministers were forced to surrender either their beliefs or their parishes; violent tracts were published; censorships were imposed. Although many of the most radical religious groups—including the founders of the Jamestown colony—had foreseen persecution and had left the country, enough radicals remained to insure conflict, if not revolution. Neither James nor Charles understood the rising tide of the middle class, neither could stomach the arrogance of Parliament, and both alienated an ever growing number of their citizens in religious matters. The conditions for war were brewing.

Milton, however, was steadfastly pursuing his preparations for a literary career; although two great works appeared during this period of political strife, neither of them reveals a concern with political turmoil. Milton's *Comus* (1634), a masque celebrating the installation of the Earl of Bridgewater as governor of Wales, was produced by Harry Lawes, one of the greatest English song writers. "Lycidas" (1637), written for a collection of Cambridge poems mourning the death by water of Edward King, is the greatest of English funeral elegies. The letters Milton wrote to Charles Diodati during the three years in residence at his father's country house suggest great tranquility of spirit, a growing mind, and developing skill in poetry. When, in 1638, Milton left Horton for the grand tour of Europe which was to complete his formal education, the world was all before him. But, while Milton was abroad, Diodati died, and Milton's Latin funeral elegy, *Epithaphium Damonis* (1640?) ("Damon's Epitaph"), records a personal grief much stronger than that evidenced in the formal mourning for Edward King.

When news of the impending English civil war reached Milton, he shortened his tour of Europe to return to England. There, in 1640, he set up a household and began to tutor his nephews, John and Edward Phillips. Meanwhile, Charles I had continued his disastrous religious and political maneuvers; he had married a French, Catholic princess; and he had sought, through his ministers, to maintain, if not increase, royal prerogatives. When Charles tried to impose the English Book of Common Prayer on the Scots, war broke out. Parliament was summoned, but it refused to grant war funds unless Charles agreed to political compromises. He dismissed Parliament; but, when the war went badly, he was forced to call it again. The two chief royal agents, Lord Strafford and Archbishop Laud, were impeached.

## IV  *Milton Joins the Conflict*

Milton entered the political controversy in 1641 with the first of a series of antiprelatical pamphlets in which he sided with those who opposed the king's notion of how a church should be organized.[5] Milton argued for the Puritan version of religious and political freedom, and from that point on the relationship between Milton's work and contemporary political events is strong. Even his first marriage (1642) embroiled him in controversy, for his wife, Mary Powell, was a young Cavalier lady who must have been totally out of her element in the studious and religious Milton household. She left Milton almost at once, and she returned to his house only after events had gone against the political faction to which her family owed allegiance. The less than perfect marriage prompted Milton to write three tracts in favor of divorce, and of course he was denounced as immoral.[6]

Meanwhile, an unsuccessful attempt to impeach five members of Parliament signaled the increase of political tension, and both sides made preparations for a civil war. Religious fervor rose to such a pitch in London that in 1642 the theaters were closed as places of corruption, sin, and decadence. On October 23, the battle of Edgehill signaled the beginning of armed revolution. Milton took no active part in the fighting, and Sonnet 8 ("When the Assault Was Intended to the City") suggests the Classical perspective from which he viewed both himself and the conflict. In this poem Milton compares himself to ancient poets whose artistry raised them above armed conflict. In 1644 he wrote *Areopagitica*, which is still a central document in arguments against censorship, and *Of Education*, a brief essay remarkable in its age for pedagogical understanding.

In 1645, Oliver Cromwell, who had created a formidable army through discipline and Puritan religious fervor, led the "New Model Army" to victory over the Cavaliers. His men went into battle singing hymns, secure in the belief that death was a passport to eternal salvation. Although the war split even the Milton family (Christopher Milton for a time supported the king), the business of life went on. Milton issued *Poems of Mr. John Milton. Both English and Latin,* his first collection; a daughter was born (Anne, 1646); Milton's father died (1647); and a second daughter (Mary) was born in 1648.

The ascendancy of the Roundheads increased Milton's involvement in politics, for the Puritan Parliament proved as tyrannical as the king. Milton responded to this tyranny with a satirical sonnet, "On the New Forcers of Conscience Under the Long Parliament," which concludes *"New Presbyter* is but *Old Priest* writ Large." Yet Milton had high hopes for the revolutionary government and in 1648 wrote Sonnet 15 ("On the Lord General Fairfax at the Siege of Colchester") which urged that the fruits of war not be wasted:

> For what can War, but endless war still breed,
> Till Truth and Right from Violence be freed,
> And Public Faith clear'd from the shameful brand
> Of Public Fraud. In vain doth Valor bleed
> While Avarice and Rapine share the land.

Despite his reservations concerning the failings of the new government, Milton remained an ardent republican; in 1649 he published "Of the Tenure of Kings and Magistrates" which argued that God's chosen rulers maintained their "divine right" only so long as they fulfilled God's purpose in their exercise of power.

England's new government faced severe problems both at home and abroad, for Europe's monarchs feared the spread of revolution. To combat the scathing attacks from the Continent, Parliament hired John Milton as latin secretary to the council of state (March, 1649); he was given a handsome salary and housed in chambers in Whitehall. For the next eleven years, Milton's work was primarily political. In 1651, he wrote *Pro Populo Anglicano Defensio,* a defense of the English people against the charge of regicide. The same year a son, John, was born; and Milton went totally blind. The specific cause of blindness seems to have been pressure on the optic nerve, and, although the blindness was absolute, Milton's eyes were not disfigured. He was given assistants in his political office, his salary was reduced, and the increased leisure allowed him to work on a personal theology *(De Doctrina Christiana)* and, perhaps, on *Paradise Lost.*

### V    *"When I Consider how my Light is Spent"*

In response to his loss of sight, Milton wrote his greatest sonnet. Sonnet 19 ("When I Consider how my Light is Spent") is a remarkable demonstration of the unity of the personal and the universal, which is characteristic of all Milton's poems. Its perfection of form is

stunning. All the traditional devices and divisions of form are pres-
ent, but they are so subdued to the content that we seem to be
overhearing a private meditation:

> When I consider how my light is spent,
>    Ere half my days, in this dark world and wide,
>    And that one Talent which is death to hide,
>    Lodg'd with me useless, though my Soul more bent
> To serve therewith my Maker, and present
>    My true account, lest he returning chide;
>    "Doth God exact day-labor, light denied,"
>    I fondly ask;

The rhyme signals two quatrains as the syntax forms one sentence;
the traditional end-stops flow on to succeeding lines, and there is
scarcely a pause at the end of the first quatrain. Milton had already
mastered the enjambing skill which was to produce the great blank
verse paragraphs of *Paradise Lost,* and yet the backbone of form
remains. The turn, which traditionally would come at the end of the
octave, begins in the middle of line 8, and "fondly" is juxtaposed
with "patience" as the two voices of the poem meet:

>                      But patience to prevent
> That murmur, soon replies, "God doth not need
>    Either man's work or his own gifts; who best
>    Bear his mild yoke, they serve him best; his State
> Is Kingly.

The only full stop within the poem comes in line 11, and the con-
cluding "couplet" occupies most of three lines. The moral, as in
Sonnet 7, is tersely drawn: "They also serve who only stand and
wait," but the rhyme of "State" and "wait" suggests that the last four
lines form a quatrain. The almost imperial skill with which Milton
bends sonnet forms to his own end will be evident as we examine his
major poems, for he also conquers elegy, masque, epic, and
tragedy.

The imagery of Sonnet 19 shows an equal mastery of religious and
poetic heritage; the first half of the poem casts Milton's personal
blindness in the familiar parable of the talents (Matthew 25) as
Milton utilizes the natural pun: "talent" as monetary unit and as
artistic gift. The pressure of time noted in Sonnet 7 yields to the

more immediate disability of blindness. Milton's sight, like money, is prematurely "spent," yet the "Talent" which he should spend in service to his "Maker" is uninvested, and Milton fears a divine reprimand. The "day-labor" without "light" parallels the impossible task of the Israelites' attempt to make bricks without straw, and God would seem to be, like Pharaoh, a sadistic tyrant.

The second half of the poem picks up the imagery of labor ("yoke") and of talent ("gifts") as it expands the dark, limited personal vision to the vast panorama of the universe: "Thousands at his bidding speed/And post o'er Land and Ocean." Patience articulates the same lesson presented in *Paradise Regained* and in *Samson Agonistes:* God does not need man or even the angels; the servant who awaits his lord's command is as surely a servant as he who carries a message. Christ in *Paradise Lost* and in *Paradise Regained* lives by that lesson; Adam, Samson, and Milton must strive mightily against proud impatience if they are to serve God.

In his service to the revolution, Milton had not long to wait; in 1654, the year after Cromwell's *coup d'etat,* Milton was called upon to produce a second defense *(Defensio Secunda)* of the English experiment in political freedom. The second defense contains a wealth of biographical material, for in it Milton defends himself against the personal attacks of the European scholar, Peter Du Moulin, who had claimed, among other things, that Milton's blindness was a direct punishment from God. The controversy, continued in 1655 with Milton's defense of himself *(Defensio pro Se),* is virulent. Perhaps Milton's own experiences and his observations of the debates in the Puritan councils of government provided the vivid detail for the devils' debate in book 2 of *Paradise Lost.*

Late in 1657, Cromwell died, leaving the Protectorate to his son, Richard, who had neither the will nor the ability of his father. The Rump Parliament was restored, and it began negotiations for the return from France of Charles II. On the eve of the Restoration, Milton published *The Ready and Easy Way to Establish a Free Commonwealth,* a most undiplomatic gesture. Thus, when Charles II came to the throne in 1660, Milton was dismissed from office, arrested, and released only after payment of fines. His actions contrast strongly with those of his talented assistant in the secretaryship; for Andrew Marvell, who had written in praise of Cromwell, had no trouble composing a paean in celebration of the king's return. Marvell may have been influential in reducing the severity of Milton's punishment.

## VI  *The Return to Poetry*

Although the Restoration took Milton's wealth and position and dashed the hopes he had maintained for an English commonwealth, his forced leisure allowed him to return to his calling as a poet. Both Mary Powell and his second wife, Katherine Woodcock, had died in childbirth, and in 1663 he again married. Elizabeth Minshull Milton ran the household in Bunhill Fields where the bulk of *Paradise Lost* was probably written. Because of his blindness, Milton employed both readers and amanuenses. Milton's own comments and the testimony of early biographers present a pleasant picture of his last years. Early each morning a man came to read scripture to Milton, and after breakfast he spent the morning dictating poetry and hearing it read back to him. He went for walks, played the organ, and talked with many visitors. But posterity has seized upon the fact that he forced his daughters to read to him in languages which they knew only phonetically as evidence of his insensitivity. Records also indicate that there was considerable friction between the third Mrs. Milton, who was completely devoted to her husband, and her stepdaughters.

Milton's last years were vexed with a gout that eventually killed him, but he is reported to have been cheerful, even while in pain. When he hurt, he sang hymns. In 1667, the ten-book version of *Paradise Lost* (revised to twelve books and reissued in 1673) was published. Although he got very little money, Milton's poem was well received. According to tradition, Thomas Ellwood, whom Milton tutored, is supposed to have asked what Milton had to say about "paradise found"; and Milton at once set to work writing *Paradise Regained*. Whatever the facts may be, Milton published his second epic, along with *Samson Agonistes*, in 1671. *Paradise Regained* suffered at once (as it still does) from comparison with *Paradise Lost*, but Milton is reported to have been impatient with such criticism.

Milton died in 1674 and was buried in St. Giles, Cripplegate, London. His life has been variously interpreted; for some, like Samuel Johnson, he was an "acrimonious republican"; for others, he was a saint. Ultimately, each reader must form his own image of Milton as he comes to terms with the poetry. Sonnets 7 and 19 show

Milton struggling with the demands of his art as he tempers artistic ambition to Christian patience, but there are many other facets to his character. Sonnet 18 ("On the Late Massacre in Piemont," 1655) shouts with the rage of an Old Testament prophet crying down destruction on his enemy:

> Avenge, O Lord, thy slaughter'd Saints, whose bones
>> Lie scatter'd on the Alpine mountains cold,
>> Ev'n them who kept thy truth so pure of old
>> When all our Fathers worship't Stocks and Stones,
> Forget not: in thy book record their groans
>> Who were thy Sheep and in their ancient Fold
>> Slain by the bloody *Piemontese* that roll'd
>> Mother with Infant down the Rocks. Their moans
> The Vales redoubl'd to the Hills, and they
>> To Heav'n. Their martyr'd blood and ashes sow
>> O'er all th'*Italian* fields where still doth sway
> The triple Tyrant: that from these may grow
>> A hundredfold, who having learnt thy way
>> Early may fly the *Babylonian* woe.

Here we see Milton's hatred of the papacy, his identification of Protestants as the new chosen people of God, and the lifelong synchronic vision which linked historical and contemporary events. In 1655 a Catholic army moved against the Protestant communities which for centuries had lived on Italy's northern border. Many Protestants who fled died in the snow of the mountain passes, others were butchered, and those who were captured were hanged. Cromwell took up the Protestant cause, Milton as latin secretary wrote letters of protest, and the victory Milton demands in the sonnet came about when the Vaudois defeated the Piedmontese army and regained their ancient rights.

In sharp contrast to the public, triumphant, vengeful voice of Sonnet 18, Sonnet 23 ("Methought I saw My Late Espoused Saint") shows us a Milton who is blind, lonely, and caught between the perfection of his inner vision and the terrible transience of human happiness. Although most discussions of the sonnet seek to determine which wife, Mary or Katherine, is the subject, strong but inconclusive cases can be made for both. Whichever wife occasioned the poem, the insight into Milton's interior life remains the same. As always, Milton sets his personal experience in Classical and Biblical contexts:

> Methought I saw my late espoused Saint
> > Brought to me like *Alcestis* from the grave,
> > Whom *Jove's* great Son to her glad Husband gave,
> > Rescu'd from death by force though pale and faint.

The allusion is to the story of King Admetus who in the hour of his
death was granted life on the condition that someone would will-
ingly die for him. Only his beloved wife, Alcestis, volunteered; and,
when Admetus discovered the price of life, he was filled with sor-
row. Admetus's old friend Heracles happened along, learned the
cause of the king's sorrow, and rescued Alcestis from Hades. Typol-
ogy easily equated Heracles ("*Jove's* great Son") with Christ and
Alcestis with the human soul, but Milton does not use the myth in
this manner; instead, he mixes it with another rescue from the
underworld. Orpheus, too, sorrowed at the death of his wife,
Eurydice; and, because of his great skill in music, Dis granted him
the power to lead his wife from Hades, on the condition that he not
look back to see that she followed him. When he reached the gate of
the underworld, Orpheus turned to see Eurydice, and she faded
back to the land of the dead. Milton describes his Alcestis-Eurydice
thus:

> Mine as whom washt from spot of child-bed taint,
> > Purification in the old Law did save,
> > And such, as yet once more I trust to have
> > Full sight of her in Heaven without restraint,
> Came vested all in white, pure as her mind:
> > Her face was veil'd, yet to my fancied sight,
> > Love, sweetness, goodness, in her person shin'd
> So clear, as in no face with more delight.

Since both of Milton's first two wives died in childbirth, and since
the Old Testament (Leviticus 22: 2–5) prescribed a period of
purification for the mother of a daughter, Milton fancies that his wife
has been returned to him under that old dispensation—even though
he realizes that only "in Heaven" can such a return be made "with-
out restraint."

The final two lines of the sonnet reassert the limited nature of
salvation from death, whether it be in the dim type of Heracles'
power, the pagan power of art, or in the Old Testament rite: "But O,
as to embrace me she inclin'd, I wak'd, she fled, and day brought

back my night." Of all Milton's great poems, only Sonnet 23 ends without affirming the possibility of triumph over sin and death. In the pathos of a blind man who sees clearly only in dreams, Milton acknowledges the very real power of darkness and so earns the right to set forth visions for those who dwell in darkness.

As we trace the perspectives from which Milton viewed the great metaphysical questions of existence and find the outlines of Christian vision emerging from the forms of ode, elegy, sonnet, masque, epic, and tragedy, we should remember that Milton is quite aware of the curses visited upon the sons of disobedient Adam, that he lived in the darkness of Comus's wood, that he despaired at the death of loved ones, that he found art long and time short, and that he shared our chaffing beneath the workings of an inscrutable providence. Despite the vastness of Milton's learning and the initial difficulty of his art, Milton's poems are enormously satisfying to a serious student, for everything we learn from a particular poem is of use in every other poem. When we come to the coda, *Samson Agonistes*, we will find that the melodies of the overture, "On the Morning of Christ's Nativity," have not been changed, only enriched by fifty years of strenuous grace.

CHAPTER 2

# Overture: "On the Morning of Christ's Nativity"

JOHN Milton chose to open the first collection of his poems (1645) with "On the Morning of Christ's Nativity," and according to Elegy 6, it was begun before daylight on Christmas morning, 1629. Earlier poems show artistic promise, but in the nativity ode we see for the first time a Milton who is in full possession of the poetic orchestration and the universal theme that characterize the great poems of his maturity.[1] The poem is even more remarkable if it is set beside others of the same kind, such as Robert Herrick's "An Ode on the Birth of Our Saviour" or Richard Crashaw's "In the Holy Nativity of Our Lord God."[2] Countless paintings and poems on the nativity form a rich background for Milton's poem, and Milton's admiration for Edmund Spenser (whom he called a better teacher than Aquinas) is reflected in the Spenserlike stanzaic form, the consciously archaic diction, and the allegorical tableaux.

## I  Typological Interpretation

The major thematic features of the nativity tradition are present in Milton's poem. To the miracle of human birth, a compound of pain and hope, the birth of Christ adds the astonishing mixture of man and God. Hundreds of artists had seized upon the paradox of a fragile baby, wholly dependent upon its mother, who was to be the savior of the world. The cast of characters is familiar: the gentle mother, the shepherds, the wisemen, the dumb animals, and the two heavenly manifestations of star and angels. But the choices Milton makes are not conventional.[3] The humble crèche scene and the human quality of the child are relegated to the beginning and the end of the poem. In between, Christ is Lord of the Universe,

28

and the poem's setting ranges from heaven to hell and from creation to the last judgment.

Milton's integration of time and space, his sense of the relationships between cosmos and history, is astonishing; and, since he evidences the same harmonious vision in each of the poems I discuss, we may profit by setting forth the typological mode of interpreting man's history. Put most simply, typology saw the life of Christ as the fulfillment of a pattern implicit in the history of the Hebrews. Christ, as the second Adam, restores man to his prelapsarian state. The mediator Joseph, the law-giver Moses, the holy remnant Noah, the one just man Lot, the hero Samson, the beloved David, and the wise Solomon all come together in the person of Christ. The pattern which Christ's predecessors set is not only the literal history of God's chosen people, but also a gradual revelation of the timeless mind of God. Thus, when Moses leads the Children of Israel from Egypt, he is a type of Christ who rescues man from sin. When David slays Goliath, he typifies Christ's defeat of Satan. Given the central idea, a modest amount of ingenuity, and a devout poetic license, there is scarcely a line or character in the Old Testament which cannot be related to the life of Christ.[4]

This typological method was not restricted to Biblical materials. Since God wrote two books, the Bible and the Book of Nature, the learned and devout could find in almost any event a prediction and revelation, however dim or misunderstood, of the great central event toward which mankind blundered. The similarity in myths and the repetitions of archetypal persons and events which in modern times led C. G. Jung to posit a collective unconscious mind was for the Christian humanist clear proof that all events figured in God's plan. The ten labors of Heracles, the visit of Orpheus to the underworld, the destruction of the Gorgon Medusa, and all the thousands of cosmogonic and sustaining myths of the pagan world were each thought to be distorted, dimmed, and perverted pieces of the great pattern whose teleos was Christ. The strength and the skill with which Milton unifies pagan and Christian patterns makes the nativity ode loom above the other members of its subgenre.

The birth of Christ marked a major shift in the mode of man's understanding. Before the nativity, the actor in history could not see the whole pattern. He could fill his role only by marching into the unpatterned (from his perspective) void of the future, sustained by faith in God's dimly understood promises. After the nativity, each man could see not only his own situation, but also something of the whole pattern. Thus, if we conceive of pre-Christian history as a horizontal line moving through time toward a yet unrevealed end whose form emerges slowly through history, we have made the first step. But Christian history is different; for, instead of speaking of Moses, Noah, and David as types of the antitype Christ (each of whom predicts unconsciously and incompletely the perfection of Jesus), we may speak of them as ectypes of the archetype Christ who in the past and throughout all time has set a pattern for man to imitate.

To express this distinction another way, the relationship between Christ and pre-Christian man is horizontal; for Christ lies in the unknown and unknowable future. For the Christian, the relationship between man and Christ is vertical; the risen Christ is a pattern above man, timeless, omnipresent, and knowable. The pre-Christian had to live and look forward to Christ; the Christian has to live up to Christ.

The linear conception of history is Hebrew; the archetypal conception, Greek. Milton and his fellow humanists saw the birth of Christ as unifying and ordering these two great modes of human thought. The Old Testament is no longer a straight line but an ascending spiral, and the Greek repetitions move inexorably toward a climax which exceeds all previous cycles. As the Christian patterns his life on that of Christ, he also moves forward through time toward the fulfillment of the last judgment.

From the combination of these two great systems, mutated through Milton's devout contemplation, comes "On the Morning of Christ's Nativity." The typological reading of the Bible and of pagan myth provides the stuff of the poem; the nexus between archetype and antitype supplies the method of organization, point of view, and moral lesson. The nativity ode may be represented by a cross; the horizontal member stands for progress through history from the creation to the nativity and from the nativity to the last judgment, and the vertical member represents the poem's celebration of Christ as a timeless archetype.

## II   Structure and Vision

The first four stanzas of the nativity ode are a proem which establishes the complex manipulation of time and point of view that allows Milton to celebrate both the historical birth of Christ and the omnipresent reality of the nativity. Characteristically, Milton sees Christ's birth rather than his crucifixion as the greatest of God's sacrifices. To suffer extreme pain for a day on the cross, in order to reassume deity, seems to Milton far easier than to surrender that deity to the thousand debilitations of "a darksome House of mortal Clay."

The proem begins with the historical "wedded Maid, and Virgin Mother," but in the third stanza a leap in time occurs. Either the birth of Christ is to be in 1629, or Milton and his muse are transported back to the historical moment in Bethlehem. English skies are filled with the same spangled host that kept watch at the nativity as Milton moves both the historical birth and himself to a meeting place outside of time. From that perspective, the wisemen have not yet reached the child; and, after placing his gift of a poem at the manger, the poet will join his own voice to the Angel Choir, timelessly rejoicing that Christ's birth has linked time and eternity.[5]

Milton begins "The Hymn" by constructing a myth from pagan materials. Primitive mother earth (Gaea) rejects her "Paramour," the sun. Chaucer's "younge sonne" who "Hath in the Ram his halve cours yronne" is perhaps the most famous predecessor of Milton's story, but whereas Chaucer's male sun and female earth are amoral symbols of spring, Milton's mother earth is a crone, caught at last by her master with an unworthy lover, deformed by her own licentiousness, shamed and begging forgiveness. The echo is not of Chaucer, but of Spenser: "Confounded, that her Maker's eyes / Should look so near upon her foul deformities" brings to mind Duessa, who in book 1 of the *Faerie Queene* must once each year assume her true but hideously deformed shape.[6]

Yet Milton, despite the strong echo, is not writing Spenserian allegory, for his female is both good and evil. By implication, Christ, the bridegroom, has caught his beloved *enflagrante*; and her outward deformity is the Platonic consequence of her willed infidelity. She also stands for Eve and her daughters; for original sin spread like a plague to deform and pervert the perfection of creation. Milton's little story has the explosive simplicity of myth.

Stanza 3, however, shifts from a mythic to an allegorical narrative. The gentleness of Christ is represented by the flat allegorical figure of Peace who comes with Olive and Dove, who waves a myrtle wand, and who spreads herself "through Sea and Land." The historical reference is to the *Pax Romana* which was interpreted to be nature's instinctive deference to Christ the creator. The imagery of this stanza constitutes a negative metaphor: although the syntax denies the din and blood of a chariot battle with sounding trumpets and clashing spears, the effect is to call forth cacophony in order to emphasize the literal silence asserted in stanza 5.

Silence and sound, darkness and light, constitute the major imagistic bases of the poem. By calling Christ the "Prince of light" (stanza 5), Milton introduces a potential of brilliance that emphasizes the peaceful dark of this first section. The Biblical echoes are to both Old and New Testament: birds were released by Noah as the flood ebbed; Christ stilled the storm upon Galilee. The brooding "Birds of Calm" suggest the Holy Spirit that visited Mary and approved the baptism of Christ. Perhaps the birds also suggest the creative spirit who in the beginning sat "with mighty wings outspread," "brooding on the vast abyss." The central point to note is that the images move backward and forward through time; and, by doing so, they both affirm the consistency of God's second book, the history of man in the world, and collapse linear evolution into timeless art.

Stanza 6 moves the focus from earth to the heavens. All of creation waits in silence with dimmed lights. That the planets should bend "one way their precious influence" incorporates both astrology and Plato's great year to Milton's occasion. The universe is lined up exactly as God created it. Only "Lucifer," who warns the stars of the sun's approach, is agitated. Literally, Lucifer (light-bearer) is the morning star; but, in recalling Satan's heavenly name and opposition to Christ, Milton hints at Fate's judgment that the birth of Christ will not complete mankind's struggle to regain the blissful seat.

The first major section of the poem (stanzas 1–7) ends by recalling the fructification myth of stanza 1. This time the paramour sun is shamed, and Milton revels in the sun-son pun. Christ is the light of the world, the husband of earth, the monarch of the planets, and the source of life. Milton was yet enough of an Elizabethan to respond strongly to the system of corresponding planes that made the entire universe a lesson in the coherence of God's creation.[7] Although the sun's "bright Throne" and "burning Axletree" are insufficient to bear the new son, they recall other facets of Christ as they judge the relative powers of pagan and Christian myth: Christ is the warrior adversary of Satan and the majestic judge at time's end.

The second major section of the poem (stanzas 8–15) begins by returning the scene to earth. The allegorical figures (Nature, Peace, and Lucifer) of the first section yield to the real shepherds who are abiding in the fields by night. The first unnegated sounds in the poem are their discussions of domestic affairs. When the music of heaven startles them, they mistake the signal of Christ's birth for the descent of Pan. But, since Pan means "all," their name for Christ is not inappropriate. Under the pre-Christian dispensation, they understand Christ in their own terms. Just as the pre-Christian might worship the devil under the name of Dagon or Ashtaroth, so too might he fumble after God under the name Pan or at an altar to the unknown god. Milton uses the happy collocation of two pastoral traditions: Classical Arcadia and the Hebraic shepherd Lord. The most intense and ingenious integration of the two comes in "Lycidas," but the rich possibilities of syncretic subordination also inform the nativity ode.

In the same fashion, stanza 9 unifies the pagan idea of sphere music with the Angel Choir. The universe which is God's lyre sounds; the angels respond; and all creation reverberates to "rapt" the shepherds into ecstasy. Such total harmony was the natural state until man sinned in Eden, and Nature (considered as a "second cause" through which God works his ways) perceives the breaking of the musical quarantine to be a signal that earth and heaven are in perfect accord; thus, her role as intermediary would seem finished. This false surmise is explored in the remainder of the second section (stanzas 8–15). The section culminates fortissimo in ecstatic optimism. The world's great age has come anew; Christ's kingdom is established upon earth; all shall be in all, forever and without end, Halleluia, Amen.

Almost unnoted, however, Milton slips in a subjunctive: "*if* such holy Song / Enwrap our fancy long"; and the "if" undercuts the ecstasy. Christ's birth announces, not a new "age of gold," but a further struggle in the battle between good and evil. As we shall see, Milton's vision looks forward to a paradise within, rather than to a restoration of the paradise without. Yet the subjunctive seems forgotten in stanza 15 as allegorical figures of Truth and Justice flank enthroned Mercy, and the gates of heaven swing open.

In both tone and image stanza 16 is the antithesis of the bright celebration which comes before. The sounds are no longer the harmony of creation but the anger of Jehovah on Mt. Sinai and the "trump of doom" that must "thunder through the deep." Clear angelic colors are obscured by red fire and smoldering clouds, the darkness of chained sleep lies ahead, and storms shake the earth from "the surface to the center." This third section (16 and 17) corrects the unduly optimistic second section, summarizes the new cycle, and predicts the end when our bliss will be full and perfect. But not yet. Although history must run its course, at least man will no longer be subject to all the nightmares which haunted him from the fall of Eden until the nativity:

> Th' old Dragon under ground,
> In straiter limits bound,
>     Not half so far casts his usurped sway,
> And wroth to see his Kingdom fail,
> Swinges the scaly Horror of his folded tail.

The poem's fourth section (stanzas 18–26) is a detailed account of the limitations placed upon evil by the advent of Christ. Certainly Milton appears to enjoy the sounding role of horrific gods in their death throes, but he also implies an identification between pagan gods and fallen angels. Each stanza in this section is a *tour de force* of sound and silence, light and shadow, beauty and terror. Taken together, they form an antimasque, a deformed dance that sets off the beauty of the rest of the poem.

Milton seems to banish the gods of Greece and Rome almost with regret, for they represent the highest climb of pagan insight. But when he turns, in stanza 22, to the Near Eastern gods, he relishes the destruction of lurid evil. Dagon, the "twice-batter'd god of *Palestine*," is left a stump. The beastial form of the false gods grows as Milton moves around the Eastern crescent of the Mediterranean, and culminates in the image of Osiris as a trampling, lowing bull pawing the earth. Stanza 25 links the new truth of Christ with the old truth of the Greeks.

At the birth of Heracles, Hera sent two huge serpents to kill the baby because she resented the philandering of her husband, Zeus, who had fathered the child. The powerful baby strangled a snake in each hand. Milton reads this tale typologically, and, in so doing, sets a pattern for integrating Classical lore with Christian truth. So read, the story is a distorted version of Christ's battle with Satan; the pagan story is not so much wrong as incomplete. Milton completes it by borrowing from another Greek myth. When the Titans assaulted

Olympus with the aid of a huge serpent, Typhon, they nearly overcame Zeus. But Typhon was thrown down into the bowels of the earth where he yet breathes resentful fire through Mt. Etna. Milton combines two "false" tales into one "true" story. Properly understood, Typhon is a mask of Satan, and Heracles is a type of Christ. In this way, the pagan myths can be saved without harming the truths of Christianity. This method may be called *syncretic subordination.* The incorporation of St. Nicholas, St. Philomela, and even the Christmas tree are less sophisticated examples.

The identification of the historical birth of Christ with the present moment of Milton's England is completed in stanza 26. The male sun is no longer Christ's rival but his viceroy, and each day the sun chases away the boogies of the English night. The diurnal repetition of the sun's exorcising function underlines Milton's assertion that the birth of Christ is both historical and timeless. In the final stanza, Milton returns to the traditional crèche scene as Mary lays "her Babe to rest." The fixed star is softened to a "Handmaid Lamp," but the still flash of divinity is veiled, not dimmed. "Bright-harness'd Angels" await their new lord's command.

The quiet power with which Milton closes the nativity ode was to become a hallmark of his great poems. After the battles of light and dark, of discord and harmony, of pagan and Christian myths; after the exhausting tragedy of *Paradise Lost,* the self-doubts of "Lycidas," the shouted death of Samson, and the stunning revelation of *Paradise Regained,* Milton returns the reader to the everyday world. The final chorus of *Samson Agonistes* says it best:

> His servants he with new acquist
> Of true experience from this great event
> With peace and consolation hath dismist,
> And calm of mind, all passion spent.

### CHAPTER 3

# Double Choice:
# "L'Allegro–Il Penseroso"

A familiar exercise for the college student in Milton's day was the stylized debate.[1] One week a student might be asked to argue for the superiority of day to night; the next week he might be assigned the opposite task. As in modern debate, the point was to train the student in the marshalling and presentation of evidence. Since the goal was style, not truth, the exercises must have produced a good deal of sophistry. Such debates were also firmly established in the lyric tradition. Milton could have found in Robert Burton's *Anatomy of Melancholy* (1621) "A Dialogue between Pleasure and Pain," and in Thomas Middleton's and John Fletcher's *Nice Valour* (printed in 1647) a song treating the merits of "vain delights" and "lovely melancholy." Andrew Marvell, Milton's younger contemporary, later wrote a dialogue between the "resolved soul" and "created pleasure." Milton himself, in the "Seventh Prolusion" (1632), solved such a debate between strenuous, serious poetry and gay, fanciful poetry in favor of the former.

Milton's twin poems, "L'Allegro" and "Il Penseroso" may have been written as early as 1629 or as late as 1632. They show a happy, contented man, looking forward to his growing poetic power. Their parallelism does suggest an exercise, yet they are consistent in almost every way with the judgments Milton makes after a life of toil, pain, and disappointment. John Milton is the most consistent of our great poets; for old age finds him, not changed, but more clearly sure of what he had sensed as a young man. His "mirth" is certainly not irresponsible ("L'Allegro"), nor is his "melancholy" pathological ("Il Penseroso").[2]

## I  *"L'Allegro"*

In "L'Allegro" (1631?), "loathed Melancholy," child of chaos and hell, is exorcised; and Euphrosyne, the goddess of mirth, is invited to be the companion of the persona. The poem then follows the imagined, generalized itinerary of a day in the life of the "mirthful" man. He rises at dawn, awakened by the lark, the cock, and the horns and hounds of a hunt. As he walks, not unseen, he observes the happy lives of English pastoral figures: the plowman, milkmaid, mower, and shepherd. Sometimes he visits a rural hamlet where a holiday festival is in progress. In the early evening, he listens to rustic tales of the supernatural, the bedtime stories of country folk.

An alternative day, spent in a city, is equally idealized. He watches tournaments and weddings, attends court masques and pageants; he spends his city evening at the theater, seeing comedies by Jonson and Shakespeare. The ultimate gift of mirth is tranquil music so beautiful that Orpheus rises from his bed of Elysian flowers to hear strains that would have completely freed Eurydice from death. The final couplet promises that, if Mirth can reify the poem's ideals, the poet will live with her.

## II  *"Il Penseroso"*

In "Il Penseroso" (1631?), the companion piece of "L'Allegro," "vain deluding joys," the offspring of folly, are banished in favor of "divinest Melancholy" who is invited to be the companion of the persona. The poem follows the imagined, generalized itinerary of a night in the life of the "melancholy" man who desires a peaceful, leisurely, and contemplative life in which he may enjoy study, meditation, and the arts.

He is called in the evening by the nightingale for a solitary walk in moonlight as he listens to the curfew. If the weather is unsuitable for outdoor activity, he finds a dim room and sits listening to hearth crickets and a bellman's chant. At midnight, he is high in a tower, studying the stars and the writings of Hermes Trismegistus and Plato. Sometimes he reads Greek tragedy or the few good tragedies of more recent poets. In his study, he seeks to probe secret and incomplete works: the tale of Orpheus, Chaucer's *Squire's Tale*, and perhaps Spenser's *Faerie Queene*.

At dawn, the melancholy man retreats deep into a dim forest, far from the paths of men, to sleep beside a murmuring brook. His dreams are "mysterious," and he is awakened by music played by the spirits of nature. He goes to church and joys in the dim light filtered through stained-glass windows. The music of organ and choir dissolves him into an ecstasy, and he has a vision of heaven.

In old age, he will find a hermit's cell where he will study the stars and herbs until he attains skill in prophecy. The concluding couplet promises that, if Melancholy will grant him the life he has just described, he will live with her.

### III    Two Poems in One

"L'Allegro" and "Il Penseroso" are more nearly a single poem than at first appears.[3] They are a gentle fusion of the rival claims of God and of the world. Milton did not feel that the silent, solitary life was always and intrinsically superior to the life of society, nor that there were not sober pagans and manic Christians. But the pattern of his poetry, from "Lycidas," to the Lady of Comus, to the Christ of Paradise Regained, indicates that Milton would quite likely have found the vision of heaven at the close of "Il Penseroso" superior to anything accomplished by mirth in "L'Allegro." Such a preference has nothing to do with black and white Puritans who smash organs. Rather, Milton's test of value is always the usefulness of a particular action in man's search for God.

The seeming separateness of the two poems is a strategy that enables the poet to give both play and study full and fair treatment before they are incorporated into a unified vision. Initially, the two poems appear to be neatly balanced: either mirth or melancholy is satisfactory. Man may sometimes have one, sometimes the other, or some men may choose study, some play. But the end of "Il Penseroso" provides a key that upsets the balance in favor of melancholy; and the reader can then go back to discover the limitations of mirth. The two poems are made up of parallels that are at the same time contrasts. Milton's organization is that of the neo-Platonic ladder that organizes Spenser's four hymns.[4] And, as with an extension ladder, the second poem overlaps the first and then reaches far higher; yet, without the solid base of "L'Allegro," "Il Penseroso" would fail. In poems so neatly parallel, the twenty-four extra lines of "Il Penseroso" should in themselves indicate the poet's judgment.

In the course of "L'Allegro," a diseased mind is healed. "Il Penseroso" teaches the healthy, amoral pagan the limitations of careless ease.

The use of music and sound in the two poems is typical of their relationship.[5] The Lydian airs which close "L'Allegro" encompass the morning lark, the cock, hounds and horns, a milkmaid's song, the rustic instruments of a rural festival, the joyous trumpets of a joust, wedding songs, and the light airs of Shakespeare's and Jonson's comedies. These sounds of life at its most pleasurable moments rival, perhaps even surpass, the song of Orpheus. He failed to bring Eurydice to life, but these sounds can free the soul of pain and so heal pathological deformity.

Parallel sounds fill "Il Penseroso." For the lark, there is the nightingale; for the cock, the curfew's sound; for the milkmaid's song, the bellman's chant. But, as the second poem progresses, the parallels become contrasts. Mirth's companions danced to the light fantastic; divinest Melancholy hears "the Muses in a ring / Aye round about *Jove's* Altar sing" (47–48). When Il Penseroso "unsphere[s] / The spirit of Plato" (88–89). the planets' unheard song contrasts with L'Allegro's joy in rustic pipes.

The most striking parallel-contrast is, however, the role that Orpheus plays in the two poems. In "L'Allegro," his song, as the supreme if futile achievement of the Classical world, concludes the poem. In "Il Penseroso," Orpheus is only one of many who might be raised through meditation. "L'Allegro" concludes with Orpheus's failure; "Il Penseroso" suggests that more divine music could have made "Hell grant what Love did seek" (108).[6]

Two kinds of music in "Il Penseroso" have no real complement in "L'Allegro." The "sweet music," "Sent by some spirit to mortals good" that awakens Il Penseroso from his mysterious dreams, indicates a benevolent animism in Nature that is absent in "L'Allegro." And the combination of "pealing Organ" and "full voic'd Choir" that dissolves Il Penseroso into Christian ecstasy is so qualitatively different from the "linked sweetness long drawn out" which ends "L'Allegro" that there can be no doubt of the poet's evaluation.

Milton is in perfect control of his poems. We note that, when the ugliness of loathed melancholy is banished, the stumbling, bombastic trimeters and pentameters give way to smooth tetrameter couplets. This prosodic trick is repeated in the opening of "Il Penseroso." The tower in "L'Allegro" holds a beautiful woman; the tower of "Il

Penseroso" supports a powerful mind. It is no wonder that the example of Milton's poems spawned a host of topographical imitations in neo-Classical literature.

A difference in degree of subjunctive mood may not seem very important, but everything is important in such carefully wrought poems. The superiority of Il Penseroso's life is subtly asserted by the relative security of the closing lines:

> These pleasures *Melancholy* give,
> And I with thee will choose to live.
>
> ("Il Penseroso")

> These delights if thou canst give,
> Mirth, with thee I mean to live.
>
> ("L'Allegro")

There is no doubt that Melancholy can give such pleasures; there is some question about Mirth's power. In context, the difference between the "mean to" that closes "L'Allegro" and the "will choose" of "Il Penseroso's" last line is indicative of the difference between Classical and Christian virtue. The delights of "L'Allegro" are real and valued; but, like the glories of Greece, cannot stand against the ecstasy of Christian contemplation. The juxtaposition of these two sets of values continues to form a major theme in Milton's poetry, but never again is the Classical given the advantage of such separate and balanced homage.

CHAPTER 4

# The Syncretic Path: Comus

W ITH the exception of Milton's verses on Shakespeare, *A Masque presented at Ludlow Castle, 1634* is Milton's first published work; *Comus*, as we call Milton's masque, was printed by Henry Lawes (1637) without Milton's name. Among Lawes's duties as tutor to the Earl of Bridgewater's children was court entertainment; and the masque—a compound of dance, song, and allegorical moralizing that was presented with elaborate costuming and stage machinery—was a popular form among the nobility.[1] *Comus* has few characters: The Lady (played by Bridgewater's youngest daughter, Alice, who was fifteen); The First Brother (played by the Earl's son John who was eleven); The Second Brother (played by another son, Thomas, who was nine); the water Nymph, Sabrina (who may have been played by an older sister); the Attendant Spirit, Thyrsis (played by Lawes); and Comus (actor conjectural). As the nature of the cast suggests, one function of Lawes was most likely that of prompter and director on stage.

The text of *Comus* gives a clear indication of the wide reading that Milton had been doing, now that he had left Cambridge and had retired to the leisure of his parents' home.[2] Scholars have discovered debts to earlier masques, to Spenser, to pastoral drama, to Plato, to Shakespeare, to neo-Latin literature, and to Greek drama. Yet the work is quite original; for, when Milton borrowed, he always transmuted his sources. In this case, he so expanded and modified the conventions of the masque that some critics have denied its right to Milton's title.[3] Milton did not call his masque *Comus;* and, although tradition has made the title convenient, there is some danger that it might lead the reader to view Comus as the central character. If we have to choose a character for the title, The Lady would be more accurate, for she is the center of the action.

The plot, as in most masques, is simple. Three noble children (The Lady, First Brother, and Second Brother) are journeying to their father's castle. They must pass through a dark wood where Comus, an evil magician, whose father is Bacchus and whose mother is Circe, has established the seat of his demonic revels. Any traveler who drinks of his potion is transformed into a monster with the head of an animal. When the brothers, at nightfall, leave their sister to seek aid, Comus disguises himself as a peasant and tricks the Lady into following him to his troup of deformed companions. She refuses to drink from his cup, but he magically imprisons her on his throne.

Meanwhile, the brothers meet the Attendant Spirit who has been sent from heaven to aid them through their dangerous test. He is disguised as the shepherd, Thyrsis, who has long served their father. Thyrsis gives the boys a magic root, haemony, to protect them from Comus's black magic, and the three attempt to rescue the Lady. Although they are able to chase Comus away, the Lady remains imprisoned on the magical seat; for, without a reversal of Comus's magic, she cannot rise from the chair. The Attendant Spirit calls Sabrina, a water nymph whose own history parallels the Lady's present plight; and Sabrina sings the Lady free. The three children proceed to their father's castle and partake in a celebration. The masque ends in a dance which mingles the dramatic characters with the audience.

## I  The Theme of Temptation

Often, the lesson of a masque seems to be primarily an excuse for elaborate amateur theater,[4] just as the academic debate was an excuse for ingenuity. But as Milton was able in "L'Allegro-Il Penseroso" to transform an exercise into a serious statement about the duties and dangers of Christian life, so too he seized upon the potential profundity of the masque's theme in order to present the earliest extended version of what was to become his mature ontology. The theme of temptation is central to Milton's poetry; and, although the Lady seems far less human than later protagonists, the substance of her trial is very like that which confronts Eve in *Paradise Lost*, Christ in *Paradise Regained*, and the blind Samson. In many ways, the character of Comus seems an early draft of Milton's Satan, and his attractiveness and his intelligence set the eternal Christian questions in a serious fashion: How is a human to distinguish between good and evil when they look so much alike? On what basis and with what aid is the Christian to know and follow God's will?

Rather than being a trivial exercise in which content yields to music and spectacle, *Comus* is a very sophisticated study of the problem of evil. As we read the masque, the serious nature of the conflict is clear; but, because we do not see the costumes and dances, or hear the music, or gasp at ingenious stage machinery, we are likely to forget that the spectacle of *Comus* bears much of the charm of a stage production of Shakespeare's *A Midsummer Night's Dream*. Milton's masque works on as many levels as the reader wishes to explore. Since the children are disguised as themselves, since they journey to a stage court which is also disguised as itself, and since Comus is a personification of the temptations which the real children must confront as they struggle through the real world, the reader should see their escapades as a mirror of his own battles with the world, the flesh, and the devil. If the weight of theological questions makes *Comus* somewhat atypical as a masque, that same weight makes it thoroughly typical of Milton's poetic practice. In both language and message, *Comus* is strongly related to the moral allegory and to the poetic techniques of Spenser's *Faerie Queene;*[5] yet, the mastery of Spenser's example is complete, and *Comus* is thoroughly Miltonic in forming conventional materials into fresh art.

## II *The Masks of* Comus

When, at the close of his first speech, the Attendant Spirit puts off his "sky robes spun out of *Iris'* Woof" and dons "the Weeds and likeness of a Swain," he establishes the mode of Milton's Ludlow masque. In *Comus* moral (and immoral) principles are simultaneously immanent and transcendent. This double quality is signaled by the *dramatis personae:* three of the characters (the Lady and her brothers) are human; the remaining three (Comus, the Attendant Spirit, and Sabrina) are metaphysical. But the wood in which physical and metaphysical intersect is not out of time, nor is it an arena where abstractions battle. Despite their quaint costumes, the travelers who have yielded to Comus's blandishments are not figures from fantasy, nor do they simply stand for fallen angels or men dancing to Satan's tune. The Lady's victory over Comus is not just a representation of the triumph of Reason over the Senses, nor is it merely a reenactment of Christ's rejection of Satan.

The weighty morality makes it unlikely that we would mistake *Comus* for *A Midsummer Night's Dream*, but since more is obviously meant than meets the eye or ear, the masque lends itself to zealous allegorical and typological interpretations which do less than justice to the richness of Milton's vision.[6] In attempting to sketch an interpretative mode for *Comus*, I have assumed that a full reading of Milton's masque reveals a shape consonant with that of his mature art; that youthful genius does not yield to confusion; and that no single "system" accounts for the poem.

Each character, act, and image in *Comus* partakes of a complex, coherent universe and thus resonates parallels in many realms. The reader should acknowledge, even seek out, the plurisignifications, but the complex parallels are *analogical* rather than *allegorical*. Of course any analogy may be read as an allegory, but in *Comus* the analogical reading is richer. Persons, events, and images are not only illustrations and examples, they are *instances*. If we assume that Milton's fictional world is intended as an image of the world God created, the fictional characters may be expected to understand their world as man is to understand God's universe. And this precept is reflexive: understanding the masque is a lesson in understanding the world. In both theory and practice, Milton spans the breach between the ideal and the real through *accommodation*.[7]

When God appears to Moses as a burning bush, He is a burning bush; but He is not only and always a burning bush. The discovery that God is Love does not invalidate the realization that God is Justice. Man is to understand God in the terms He chooses to reveal Himself and, at the same time, to realize that those terms are sufficient rather than absolute. In contrast, when Satan appears to Eve as a snake, he is only disguised as a snake. When he appears to Christ as an old man, his mask is false. Man is, thus, to accept with patience the masks of God, but he is to penetrate the manifestations of evil with all the impatience he can muster. As we shall see, the human characters in *Comus* search good and evil in precisely these ways.

To begin with the most obvious cases, when the Attendant Spirit becomes Thyrsis, he does not cease to be the Attendant Spirit, even though none of the characters recognizes his divine form. Likewise when Comus dresses as a rustic he does not cease to be Comus. Yet the two humble masks are qualitatively different. Comus pretends to be a rustic, and the Lady sees through him in short order because his reality does not fully inform his disguise. She does not need to see through Thyrsis because his being is completely penetrated by the Attendant Spirit. Although both evil and good "accommodate" themselves to man's perceptions, God's accommodations are real; Satan's accommodations are illusions. When the demonic assumes a mask, the purpose is to deceive; when the divine assumes a mask, the purpose is to instruct. As is always the case in Milton's poetry, demonic accommodations must be discredited before divine accommodations can be understood. Since, in *Comus*, audience and reader are integrated at the masque's close, our understanding of *Comus* should be guided by and grow out of the characters' understandings of their dramatic world.

The practical task of sorting divine masks from demonic masks is complicated by their mirror relationships. Since God is Form and Unity, whereas Satan is Form disintegrating toward Chaos, any demonic mask is bound to appear more holy than the face beneath. Evil's falsest disguise may seem very like God's most humble accommodation, for evil can exist at all only because it has license to copy the lineaments of the holy. Comus's cup resembles the Grail; his liquor, like Christ's blood, works a change in those who taste. The Lady's final speech penetrates Comus's protean masks and completely discredits his illusions:

> this Juggler
> Would think to charm my judgment, as mine eyes,
> Obtruding false rules prankt in reason's garb.
> I hate when vice can bolt her arguments,
> And virtue has no tongue to check her pride.
>
> (757–61)

The audience is thus given a tutelary instance of man's duty in the middle realm.

But this is to give the sum without the circumstance, and the dramatic action of *Comus* is designed to fill out the platitude and so make its lesson discursive as well as intuitive. The supramundane planes of accommodation are sketched by the Attendant Spirit before he becomes Thyrsis, and then cloaked. He comes from "the starry threshold of *Jove's* Court" where dwell the "enthron'd gods on Sainted seats" (1, 11). His task is to aid those who wish to seek

"that Golden Key / That opes the Palace of Eternity" (13–14), but the
divine wears a mythological mask from the onset. Both audience and
reader, guided by the Attendant Spirit, know the ultimate face to be
that of God, but none of the lesser characters hears the opening
speech. Fallen man's knowledge obscures the upper links of anal-
ogy; only at the end of the masque are the characters urged to climb
"Higher than the Sphery chime" (1021). Within the drama, the
Lady and her brothers are to accept the divine in the form that it
chooses.

Below the realm of God is a tripartite cosmos: the realms of "high
and nether *Jove*" and of Neptune. Neptune has given "this Isle" to
his "blue-hair'd deities" and placed a "noble Peer" (Bridgewater)
over "all this tract that fronts the falling Sun" (18–31). The accom-
modative chain is complete; within the masque, the Earl is the final
shadowing forth of God's rule. But that bright shadow falls upon a no
man's land, for Comus, son of Bacchus and Circe, has usurped the
"drear Wood." When the Attendant Spirit sketches Comus's
genealogy (46–58), and when Comus invokes the powers of ancient
night (128–42), we learn that dark is not simply the absence of light,
but an active, malign, perverted presence. As the lights of Bridge-
water's castle manifest the lowest rung of an accommodative series
that reaches to heaven, so Comus's darkness manifests the first
paving stone on the road that descends to hell.

The ambiguity of the cosmos as seen from the wood is signaled by
double mythological accommodation. The Attendant Spirit speaks of
both God and Satan as "Jove," and to balance the heavenly "*As-
syrian* Queen" (1002) there is Comus's "*Venus*" (124). One of the
struggles in the masque is to precipitate the moral referents of
Classical myth. For example, Comus asserts:

> Nay Lady, sit; if I but wave this wand,
> Your nerves are all chain'd up in Alabaster,
> And you a statue; or as *Daphne* was,
> Root-bound, that fled *Apollo*.
>
> (659–62)

His pursuit of the Lady does parallel Apollo's lust for Daphne, and
the threat is real ("this corporal rind / Thou has imanacl'd"). But
Comus does not see beyond his own demonic analogue to the full-
ness of Apollo's mythic significance. Apollo is, foremost, god of the
sun, and the "Sunclad power of Chastity" belongs to the Lady;

Comus's power is moon-clad license (116–33). By setting forth the analogy to Apollo, Comus unwittingly contrasts himself with Christ. The pattern is typical in that Comus always speaks as though the demonic analogue were absolute. He seems unaware that his verbal masks reveal him to be a reversed shadow of a divine shadowing forth.

Comus makes a similar error when he asserts that nature is analogically leagued with human license, and the Lady at once rights his distortions:

> the uncontrolled worth
> Of this pure cause would kindle my rapt spirits
> To such a flame of sacred vehemence,
> That dumb things would be mov'd to sympathize,
> And the brute Earth would lend her nerves, and shake,
> Till all thy magic structures rear'd so high,
> Were shatter'd into heaps o'er thy false head.
>
> (793–99)

As moonlight to sunlight, so is license to freedom; the brute earth seconds Comus's argument only in so far as it is the perverted reflection of its original form. The Lady's correction of Comus's central thesis terrifies him into acknowledging the prior claim of the divine to mythological accommodation (he is not yet willing to give up nature). Once, he tells us, Jove spoke "thunder and the chains of *Erebus* / To some of *Saturn's* crew" (804–5), and such power is in the Lady's voice. For a brief moment, Comus sees through the human manifestation before him to God's mythological accommodation and so discovers the divine analogy between his world and the realm of the gods that is the true version of his demonic use of myth.

Although it remains for Sabrina to demonstrate discursively the affinity of nature for the divine, the Lady has intuitively asserted that sympathy. But because her understanding has not yet been earned through action, Comus is able to continue the temptation. His final words to the Lady, "Be wise, and taste" (813), gather all his disguises: the philosopher, the gourmet, the physician, and the priest. Since each of them has been separately rejected, he cannot win, but "Be wise and taste" indicates the limit of the Lady's power. By inverting Satan's temptation of Eve to "taste and be wise," Comus casts the Lady as Eve's daughter, rather than as Christ's child. Because the Lady is Christ's child, her analogical parallels signal the timeless defeat of the principle that Comus manifests. But because she is also Eve's daughter, the best she can manage without metaphysical aid is a standoff. She remains in the wood, dependent upon human powers.

All three human characters, initially, depend upon their senses. "This way the noise was, if mine ear be true, / My best guide now" (170–71), says the Lady, and because her ear is not true, she interprets the sound of Comus's demonic revels as the ignorant celebrations of "unlettered Hinds" who "thank the gods amiss" (174–177). She is, however, dimly aware that malignity is present in the wood ("O thievish Night / Why shouldst thou, but for some felonious end"), and she is granted a vision of "Conscience," "Faith," "Hope," and "Chastity" to counter the "thousand fantasies" that Comus whispers. She draws the appropriate conclusion: "all things ill / Are but as slavish officers of vengeance" (217–18), and when her understanding is seconded analogically by nature ("a sable cloud / Turn[s] forth her silver lining on the night" [223–24]), the lesson of the masque might seem to be complete.

The Lady's first brief scene does, in fact, contain the entire masque in miniature. Comus in peasant garb is present as the "unletter'd Hinds"; the debate is adumbrated by the contest between the thousand fantasies and the holy abstractions; the Attendant Spirit is represented by the "hov'ring Angel girt with golden wings," and his final speech is anticipated by the Lady's song to Echo. If, as I shall argue, Sabrina instances nature, she is prefigured by the silver lining. But the Lady's song is not that of an angel, nor even that of Sabrina; its beauty is an accommodated expression of the potential harmony of earth and heaven, and the Lady yet seeks the earthly aid of her brothers. Neither she nor Comus understands the full import of their first encounter.

For a moment Comus stands stupidly good as he finds the Lady's music superior to that of his "mother Circe with the Sirens three" (253). But the "Divine enchanting ravishment" does not lead him toward God; rather, he wishes to make the Lady his "queen" and to attribute her divinity to "Pan or Silvan." Comus's limited understanding encourages him to proceed with the futile temptation, and the Lady's "mortal mixture of Earth's mould" places her partially within his power. Seeing a peasant, she assumes Comus to be a peasant. She then goes on to generalize from her misperception, praising his simple gentleness above the false gentility of the court.

Since the "peasant" is evil, and the gentility of her father's court, the height of earthly perfection, her first scene exemplifies the tenuous nature of human understanding. Despite her epiphany, the Lady cannot distinguish intuitively among shadows in the world's dark wood. Since she has not learned discursively, she accepts Comus as her guide.

### III   *The Accommodations of Divinity*

Three aspects of the aid necessary to correct the Lady's error and so move her from wood to court have occupied much of the criticism of *Comus*. Perhaps the many arguments as to the nature of the Lady's brothers, of the plant haemony, and of the nymph Sabrina may be synthesized if we remember that all three are accommodations and thus plurisignificative. Each plays a number of roles simultaneously, and the comparative directness of their dramatic roles masks complex functions in the interactions between masque and audience.

The brothers, like the Lady, are lost in Comus's wood, but their understanding of the league between the wood and evil is more precise than the Lady's. "Chaos," says the Elder Brother, "reigns here / In double night of darkness and of shades" (334–35). "Double night" is a key. That a "rush Candle" in some "clay habitation" can be their "*Tyrian* Cynosure" indicates their awareness of the coherence between earthly and astronomical light. In this, they are more advanced than their sister, but we are to remember that the relationships are parallels, not identities. A cottage light is not the north star, may even lead to a swamp; nor is the north star the light of God's throne. Even though the brothers realize that all light reflects its superior and illuminates its inferior, they cannot, as mortals, escape the wood.

The Second Brother, like the Lady, accepts sound as a guide when light fails, and light and sound parallel the complementary roles of the two boys. If we remember that the accommodative levels of perception are discrete, each made up of light to be seen and sound to be heard, and that within each level sound is inferior to light, the patterns of knowing within Comus's wood may be read coherently.

The sight of God would give a clearer indication of His being than does His voice, but God is too bright to be seen; thus, all lesser creatures know more of God by sound than by sight, and the same proportional relationships obtain within each accommodative level. When, at the close of book 11 of *Paradise Lost*, Adam's mortal substance can no longer endure the visions Michael sets before him, the lesson continues in narrative. And Adam learns more through his ears than through his eyes. Because sound is epistemologically inferior to light, man, paradoxically, may reach a higher accommodative level by hearing than by seeing. In sound the presence of God is more tempered to human capacity. Sabrina's instance of the divine is "inferior" to Thyrsis's haemony, just as nature is inferior to grace, but that very inferiority makes her "drops" efficacious for the Lady.

The First Brother's "light," philosophical truth, and the Second Brother's "sound," action, are earthly analogues of the sight and sound of God. But, on earth, philosophical truth can be perceived only through the process of speech. First Brother can "show" Second Brother only in words. Second Brother's response, "How charming is divine Philosophy" (476), acknowledges the superiority of doctrine to action; but First Brother assents to the lesser mode: "*Thyrsis* lead on apace, I'll follow thee" (658). This symbiosis represents the genius of Milton's masque. As the Lady's initial vision was too high to protect her from Comus, so the brother's action is too low. *Comus* is, among many other things, an essay on the difficulties a Christian has in knowing: if he looks only at his feet, he may walk into a tree; if he looks only at the stars, he may fall into a ditch.

The masque is an appropriate expression of a central, compound paradox: man is most himself when he is most unified with God; yet, the impatient reach for God leads to delay or failure. The corollary, that an individual is least himself when he is most separated from God, is not developed in *Comus* as it will be in the character of Satan. But the function of that corollary is present. The Lady is "free" to give up freedom by accepting Comus's cup, or his sophistry. The members of his rout have done so.

If we think of a scale, one side of which represents evil, the other side virtue, and if we also imagine that upon both sides are placed weights, far beyond the mass of man's individual will, so equally poised that a breath will shift the equilibrium, we have an image of free will in Milton's system. Yet free will is not dependent upon "Manicheism," for the finite series of evil exists within an infinite series of good. In *Comus* the Lady confronts such an unstable equilibrium as she sits imprisoned in Comus's chair. Neo-Platonically, that stasis may suggest the point at which reason balances the pull of the flesh so that the *mens*, the soul's memory of its abode in heaven, can reverse the downward movement. But such a reading passes too swiftly from the surface level. Dramatically, we have no indication that the Lady's soul moves at all. The soul-cycle satisfies the impulse to allegorize, but it is a vista which the dramatic world does not seem to incarnate.[8] The temptation is broken off, not by a memory of heaven, but by the intrusion of the brothers.

Taken together, the brothers are the best that man, unaided by the divine, can be. And, Thyrsis tells them, they are inadequate. To the First Brother's plan to drag Comus "by the curls to a foul death" (608), the Attendant Spirit replies: "He with his bare wand can unthread thy joints, / And crumble all they sinews" (613–14). Some further power, something beyond philosophy-in-action is needed. We have been given reason to expect that Thyrsis will be that power. But despite his pastoral mask, he is above the level of dramatic action; or, rather, only that portion of the Attendant Spirit's power which is incarnated in the pastoral figure affects the surface action.

Haemony, which Thyrsis provides the brothers to protect them from Comus's spells, is said to be the prize Thyrsis received for singing "a certain Shepherd Lad" to ecstasy. Its pastoral model is thus the carved bowl or weanling lamb, the traditional pastoral rewards for a pastoral song. But haemony is more than prize. Its leaves are "darkish" with "prickles"; only in another country does it bear a "bright golden flow'r" (629 ff.). Although the brothers, quite properly, accept it at face value, the reader is given an unmistakable invitation to allegorize. Thyrsis is an angel in disguise; his "country" is heaven. Christ too was a shepherd, his cross a root, his crown of prickles. He was the flower, sprung from Adam's dark root, who bloomed on the cross, and in that blossoming brought great medicine for the sin of man. Such one-to-one correspondences are tempting, but perhaps misleading. Haemony is many things.[9] A brief listing may suggest its inclusive complexity:

> Spiritual world—divine grace
> Neo-Platonic world—*mens*
> Mythic world—moly, white magic
> Pastoral world—art
> Natural world—medicinal herb.

Its demonic inversion is also multiform: Comus's cordial julep; Circe's cup; Bacchus's liquor; Eve's fruit. The list might be extended for both haemony and its inverted shadow, but the point is clear. Haemony is the dramatic instance of a power that occurs as a different mask in each of the possible realms of existence. As it joins the balm of nature with the blood of Christ within the form of art, it is the outreach of God-Christ to the wayfaring Christian.

Such allegorical readings lead us to expect that the assault force will succeed: Act, in accord with Philosophy, guided by Right Reason and shielded by Grace, will surely conquer the demonic illusion. It fails. In fact, the attack is redundant, for the brothers bring the Lady nothing that she does not already possess. The great debate between license and freedom is not a draw; Comus has been thoroughly beaten. As Jove to Saturn's crew, so is the Lady's argument to Comus's argument. If we read to final things, Jove's victory is a dim type of Christ's final victory over Satan. But we are not to rest in finalities, for the temptation of the Lady is broken off, not ended. Comus keeps his rod; the Lady remains "In stony fetters fixt and motionless" (819).

As mythic analogies may illuminate the significance of the masque, so perhaps the masque may illuminate myths. The Lady is in danger of a metamorphosis; such would be her pagan "salvation" from a lustful god. As stone, she would be as "safe" from Comus as was Daphne-as-tree safe from Apollo. Over and over, to thwart superhuman threats, pagan man was forced into subhuman form. Odysseus is a major exception: rope allowed him to hear the sirens without destruction; moly enabled him to drink Circe's potion without metamorphosis. Perhaps the myth of *Comus* revises the synchronic meaning of temptation, danger, metamorphosis, and escape manifest in Classical myth. Haemony does not free man from the world; it makes him sufficient to stand while leaving him free to fall. Comus's rod may be read as haemony's inversion in that it removes both sufficiency and freedom. The Lady's plight is that of fallen man; at best, evil may be avoided, but a miracle is needed to achieve good.

Sabrina, dramatically, is that miracle. But she is many other things as well. The Attendant Spirit's "adjuring verse" catalogues mythic water deities and reminds us that Comus's wood, like Bridgewater's court, is in Neptune's middle realm. Sabrina's brief song (890–901) places her firmly in nature's realm. She does not see through Thyrsis to the Attendant Spirit, nor does she (like both Comus and the Attendant Spirit) affect a mask. Thyrsis asks her to undo the work of a black magician, "unblest enchanter vile" (907). The drops she uses are from her "fountain pure," and they cancel Comus's spell, rather than baptising the Lady's sin. As genius of water, she plays Neptune to Comus's nether Jove and to Thyrsis's higher Jove. Mythologically, she is a divine version of Scylla and Charybdis. As Bridgewater's task is to instance divine political order upon earth, so Sabrina's is to animate the "brute Earth," and so release the purifying power shadowed forth in nature's echo of heaven.

The relationship between Sabrina and the Lady is close. Sabrina's history, if we substitute wood for water, parallels the Lady's present. When the Lady escapes Comus and returns to her father's protection, she echoes Sabrina's escape to the protection of Nereus. Were the Lady a virtuous pagan, she might be forced through the "quick immortal change" that transformed Sabrina, and the cost of such "salvation" is to remain root-bound: Sabrina "must haste ere morning hour / To wait in *Amphitrite's* bow'r" (920–21). Perhaps Sabrina is a pagan, mythic ectype and the Lady a Christian, human ectype of the same archetype. More simply put, Sabrina is a mythic analogue of the Lady. If Sabrina was played by the Lady Alice's older sister, even the occasion seconds their relationship.

The logic of an allegorical reading might tempt us to see Sabrina as some form of grace, as somehow a more efficacious haemony; yet her dramatic role is completely physical: she saves the Lady's body, not her soul. Furthermore, Milton's moral geography argues against Sabrina as a primary manifestation of the Holy Spirit. Unlike the Attendant Spirit who descends to the play, Sabrina rises. He is from a mythologized heaven; she, from a mythologized nature. He returns to heaven; she goes back to the sea. Her reward for saving the Lady is to continue as the genius of an earthly stream. But, although Sabrina is not promised the translation to the skies held out as a reward for Echo, when we learn that her banks may be crowned with "Groves of myrrh and cinnamon" (937), we may rightly see divine analogies to her role, particularly as the next line urges the Lady to leave the wood "while Heaven lends us grace." Despite several ambiguous vectors, an analogical reading makes Sabrina's station and function coherent. As the mask of nature, Sabrina has sufficient and appropriate power to purge the physical effects of evil upon a natural creature. As the Attendant Spirit is a "tool" of God, so Sabrina is a tool of Thyrsis. The goal of Milton's masque is not to transcend earth, but to emphasize the potentials of earth as a divine analogy. Sabrina, like the Earl who is shortly to join the masque, is an instance of the order and plenitude of God's immanence. That she, rather than the Attendant Spirit, frees the Lady asserts the sufficiency of the earthly manifestations of divine power. As it should, Milton's Ludlow Masque implicitly celebrates the ideal of a Christian court.

## IV  A Moral for the Audience

At some length, we have sought to fit the richly allusive strands of *Comus* into a coherent vision, and although the accommodative mode seems, for the most part, satisfactory, the Attendant Spirit provides a six-line interpretation for the reader who is tired of layers, levels, planes, chains, cycles, and masks:

> *Heav'n hath timely tri'd their youth,*
> *Their faith, their patience, and their truth,*
> *And sent them here through hard assays*
> *With a crown of deathless Praise,*
> *    To triumph in victorious dance*
> *O'er sensual Folly and Intemperance.*

(970–75)

It's all quite clear: the drama is a masque of temperance in which inexperienced children are tested. God is the examiner, and Comus, as the Lady suspected, is but a tool in the divine test. The children pass with high marks, and the masque ends as a loving and complacent father would wish.

Such a straightforward understanding is accurate, for it accommodates the lesson to the occasion and to the presumed audience. But the simple understanding is sufficient, not absolute. The children, as actors, have completed their task. But in his final speech, the Attendant Spirit sheds his mask, turns from the drama to the audience (which by joining the dance has become a part of the drama), and reintroduces metaphysical planes of understanding.[10] He will, he tells us, leave the court, pass through the realm of Neptune, reach the Western Isles, rise to the Elysian Fields of higher Jove where eternal summer and "jocund Spring" coexist.

"Far above" this mixture of Olympus, Eden, Hesperides, and Hades, "Celestial *Cupid*" possesses Psyche. This dizzying whirl up to the neo-Platonic image of completion represents the highest accommodative level of the masque, and the Attendant Spirit at once tunes his imagery to a simpler, pastoral level, for despite what he tells the audience (intuitive knowledge), they see him as Puck or Ariel:

> I can fly, or I can run
> Quickly to the green earth's end,
> Where the bow'd welkin slow doth bend,
> And from thence can soar as soon
> To the corners of the Moon.
>
> (1013–17)

Beyond this midsummer night's dream—that finds the corners of the moon to be the apogee of the spirit—is a higher orbit: "She can teach ye how to climb / Higher than the Sphery chime" (1020–21); and beyond all human soaring hovers a compassionate predator: "if Virtue feeble were, / Heav'n itself would *stoop* to her" (italics added).

Into the slight masque form, Milton packs as much of Christianity and humanism as his considerable syncretic power can manage, and, as we might expect, Christianity holds the upper hand. The Miltonic vision eventually required the larger canvas of an epic, but undoubtedly the Earl of Bridgewater got more than the occasional entertainment for which he had bargained.

CHAPTER 5

# Death the Gateway to Life: "Lycidas"

THE collection of verses made in 1637 to honor the death of
Edward King has as its Latin motto "If you reckon rightly
shipwreck is everywhere." The last poem of the collection is the
greatest of English funeral elegies, Milton's "Lycidas," and the
motto is a perfect summary of the problem Milton examines. The
occasion for the poem was the death, by shipwreck, of a young man
whose career parallels Milton's early life. Both Milton and King
were aspiring poets, both had stayed on at Cambridge for graduate
study, and both had been trained in preparation for Christian minis-
try. According to tradition, the twenty-five-year-old King knelt on
the deck of the sinking ship in prayer while other passengers scur-
ried about in vain to save themselves. There is no evidence that
Milton and King were bosom companions; but, since one tradition
suggests that they were rivals for a scholarship, they certainly knew
each other.

The real occasion for "Lycidas" was Milton's growing awareness of
his own mortality. A number of early poems are concerned with
death: "On the Death of a Fair Infant Dying of a Cough" (1628),
"The Passion" (1630), "On Shakespeare" (1632), "On the University
Carrier" (1631?), "An Epitaph on the Marchioness of Winchester"
(1631): but each of these earlier poems treats death as something
that happens to other people. Perhaps the death of Milton's mother
in April, 1637, made death seem real to the poet, or perhaps the
prospect of never using the poetic tools which he had spent the
previous five years polishing renewed his impatience with what he
considered to be a meager poetic accomplishment. Whatever the
case, the three years between *Comus* (1634) and "Lycidas" (1637)
mark a transition from an extraordinarily talented young poet to a
consummate artist.

56

Because the pastoral funeral elegy was a public form, Milton makes no effort to conceal his sources;[1] in fact, the echo quality which links the dead Edward King with illustrious ancients and the live Milton with great writers of the past is implicit in the genre. "Lycidas" is a perfectly polished and rhetorically stunning effort. Every detail is essential, every word is carefully chosen, and every image is both logical and yet fresh. The world of "Lycidas" is filled with water;[2] along with the poet, we float in a cursed ship; and shipwreck is everywhere. The modulations of tone, from despair to ecstasy to calm resolution, are built with musical precision; and the varieties of verse form are so thoroughly subdued to the whole that we almost seem to be overhearing the poet's meditation.

"Lycidas" may be divided into four major sections and an epilogue.[3] The four large units move from the world of pastoral to the Christian heaven, and within each unit are subsidiary organizations of almost formal dialectics. Each section emphasizes a different realm of existence, and each reaches a crisis which serves as the starting point for the next section. In retrospect, we can see that the conclusion is implicit in each movement; and, as we read, the pervasive and shifting patterns of imagery soften the battle of contending interests. The parts of "Lycidas" are as carefully ordered as the Platonic ladder reaching from man to God, but that ladder is painful to climb.

## I  The Pastoral World

Section 1 (lines 1–36) establishes a pastoral world which distances and gives form to whatever inchoate intensity of personal grief may have been associated with King's death. By setting the incomprehensibility of the event in traditional, public form, the "real" victim becomes "Lycidas," and the "real" Milton becomes a pastoral singer; thus the poem exorcises (rather than exercises) grief. But the first subject of "Lycidas" is not death; rather, it is the pressure of time upon the artist. Before we are told that Lycidas is dead, a mode of expression and a sense of time are established. The "Berries" to be plucked are lines of poetry; the clumsy picker is the persona; and the unripened fruit are the immature lines of poetry. The laurel, the myrtle, and the ivy from which the poem is to be gathered are each ambiguous announcements: laurel may symbolize victory or poetry; myrtle, death or love; and the "Ivy never sere" may represent either

Bacchus or the quality of poetry as eternal stay against the destruc-
tion of life by time and force. Thus the opening lines establish the
complex dialectical themes of the poem: fame, death, and eternity;
poetry, love, and sensuality.

Within the first section, there is a conflict of subject. Lines 1–7
focus upon the persona; lines 8–14, upon Lycidas; lines 15–22, upon
the persona. The two concerns are unified in the remainder of this
section (lines 23–36) by identifying both the persona and Lycidas as
pastoral swains who are as indistinguishable as two sheep. The mood
which closes this section is one of pleasant melancholy, almost that
of an old graduate who sits remembering the golden campus days.

Lines 12–14 introduce the complex, sustaining imagery of water
that in four aspects (death, birth, baptism, and feast) joins the four
worlds in which Milton seeks the reasons for death and so the pur-
pose of life: "He must not float upon his wat'ry bier / Unwept, and
welter to the parching wind, / Without the meed of some melodious
tear." Two of the poem's four worlds are present: the "real" water
that drowned Lycidas (King), and the tears (poems) of the pastoral
muses. Although Lycidas has drowned, he is fancied to be floating,
parched by the wind. Both water and dryness are, in the real world,
death since a bloated corpse is not restored to life by parching. The
tears (Milton's as well as the Muse's) are the first of several liquids
that seek to counteract the death-dealing sea. This first pastoral
liquid is to be a sort of cordial that revives, if not the body of
Lycidas, at least his fame.

Lines 15–22 turn again to the persona's problems. The muses are
of the "sacred well" that flows from beneath Jove's throne. In the
pastoral world, the muses are the nine patrons of arts and sciences;
but "sacred" establishes an overtone of Christianity (or at least re-
ligion) that will vibrate more strongly as the poem progresses. The
pressures of time force the persona to retract the apology for im-
maturity that opened the poem. He envisions his own burial urn
and hopes for the same kind of immortality in art that he is providing
for Lycidas. If one is remembered, all of life will not have been vain;
and art can assure remembrance.

The final verse paragraph of the first section (lines 23–36) tempts
an allegorical reading: high lawns are libraries; flocks are studies;
Satyrs and Fauns are unruly undergraduates; and "old *Damaetas*" is
Joseph Mede or some other favorite and kindly tutor.[4] Although this
level of interpretation is valid, it leaves the true subject of the poem

in favor of an imaginary occasion and raises the problem of sincerity in a destructive fashion. The biography behind the poem is interesting, but it only supports the poem's subject; the poem does not support biography. King and Milton were not shepherds; they had no sheep. The important friendship is metaphorical. Lycidas is dead today, the poet will die tomorrow, and who will outlive a century? By line 36 the poet has found Lycidas to be a mirror image of himself; thus, the recognition that "There but for the grace of God go I" moves the poem's focus from the dead King to the live Milton. When Milton weeps for Lycidas, he weeps for himself; as he weeps for himself, he weeps for all mankind; and "Lycidas" has become a public poem.

## II  *The Natural World*

The second major division of the poem (lines 37–102) shatters the illusion of a pastoral escape from death. As this section opens, plants mourn for Lycidas; his death is the occasion for grief in the pastoral world. But, in the next four lines (45–49), we learn that his death has destroyed the pastoral world, as into the thornless spring have come the canker and the taint-worm. The pastoral world was to have provided an escape from the fact of death; now, it too is dead. The melodious tears are not reviving cordials; themselves salt, they merely add to the destructive sea a few more drops.

Thus the pastoral path becomes a maze as the persona discovers that he has returned to the unacceptable starting point. He has so thoroughly identified himself with Lycidas, and some future "gentle Muse" with himself, that, at best, death will be immortalized, not himself. He turns from cataloguing the effects of Lycidas's death to search for the cause. By imagining that the tutelary spirits were negligent, rather than malevolent or impotent, he seeks an escape; for, if the failure to protect Lycidas is a slip, then the persona is not absolutely forced to see his own fate in the premature death of a fellow shepherd.

This tentative hope is quickly dismissed as the persona realizes, "Ay me, I fondly dream!" Even the greatest artist of the pastoral world, Orpheus, whose mother was a muse, could not escape death.[5] What hope, then, is there that lesser poets may escape "the rout that made the hideous roar" as Orpheus was dismembered? The persona discovers in the tale of Orpheus a reason for Lycidas's death. The barbarous power of nature is hostile to beauty and to life. Thus the persona confronts the implacable power of blackness and is tempted to despair.

Since death is inevitable, the persona wonders if the wise man would do well to spend his short life in pleasure, sporting "with *Amaryllis* in the shade, / Or with the tangles of *Neaera's* hair." Yet even as he considers *carpe deim*, he is unwilling to give up, for there is hope of fame, a "last infirmity of Noble mind"[6] that forces poets to live "laborious days." But even that active "infirmity" is futile, a false surmise, for the "blind *Fury* with th'abhorred shears" awaits every man, regardless of his desires or talents. As Milton joined Typhon and Heracles in the nativity ode in order to complete the imperfect pagan vision, he here joins two other Classical allusions. By confusing the blind and indifferent fates with the unrelenting, malevolent furies, he creates a causative force that is both indifferent to man's desires and hostile to life. *Carpe diem* is no solution, for even the sensualist may be cut off in mid-pleasure. It is as though the persona suddenly found "L'Allegro" and "Il Penseroso" equally vain.

Until this point in the poem, the speaker has been in control; he has been asking questions, supplying answers, following his own associative patterns, and making evaluations. Suddenly an alien voice intrudes, " 'But not the praise.' " Phoebus, god of sun and song, agrees that the fame of the pagan is only "glistering foil"; and in the pun, "broad rumor *lies*," he characterizes the fragility of human memory. However, the god has not come to second the poet's judgment but to correct a damning error. Once before, Apollo touched a human's ears, setting an ass's ears on King Midas for preferring Pan's music to that of Apollo, and the despair of the persona represents a similar error.

The good will be rewarded, but not on earth, for "all-judging *Jove*" grants meed in heaven, and he is neither indifferent nor malevolent. The persona finds this "consolation" unacceptable, for if all men get what they deserve, who shall escape hanging? "Die he or justice must." To escape "Old Testament" justice, the persona hastens back to the pastoral world, back to the ostensible subject, the death of Lycidas. The cloak of pagan half-truth is a more comfortable surmise than the naked justice of "an eye for an eye."

The flight from "justice" returns him to the same blind alley of pastoral consolation from which Phoebus had startled him; there he searches for the limited immortality of pagan metamorphosis. Folded into the blackness of Orpheus's horrible death is a bright hope. When Orpheus's head was thrown into the "swift *Hebrus*," it floated to the "*Lesbian* shore" and conferred great lyric skill upon the islanders. The most famous tale of saving metamorphosis is perhaps that of Daphne. When she fled lustful Apollo, she was changed into a laurel tree and so achieved a limited immortality by returning to life in a lesser form. The reference to "*Arethuse*" (line 85) suggests an even brighter hope. Arethuse, like Daphne, was pursued by a lustful god and escaped by turning into water; but her pursuer, unlike Apollo, also changed into water, and the two were at last united. Although the persona does not allegorize this tale, Milton and his "knowing" readers would have been aware that Alpheus and Arethuse were interpreted as the linking of justice and truth (Fulgentius, *Mitologiae*). What may seem, initially, to be just another tale of pagan lust contains a glimpse of Christian hope. Thus, the reeds of Mincius, proper pastoral instruments, are now shadowed by a truth beyond the Classical.

The persona appears not to notice the Christian implication, for he questions Neptune, god of the element that destroyed Lycidas, rather than God the Providential. And he gets the same answer that the nymphs gave: only the darkness of eclipse and the malevolence of an unspecified curse account for Lycidas's death. Milton's persona finds only the power of darkness to appall. With line 102, "That sunk so low that sacred head of thine," several movements of the poem are completed. The pastoral world is empty; the laws of nature are inscrutable; dead is dead.

From this point on, Milton's use of mythological allusions shifts: in the first half of the poem, the myths are pagan tinged with Christian. In the second half, they become increasingly a transparent code for Christian thought. Despite the despair of Camus, the anger of St. Peter, and the futility of burial flowers, the movement is gradually upward from despair toward Christian faith.

### III   *The Christian World*

The poem's third major section (lines 103–64) begins with the lament of the River Cam. Allegorically, Cam is Cambridge University where Milton and King studied the art of Apollo and the truth of Christ. Poetry, which began as a stay against mutability, is now a

means of service to God. In the second digression (lines 108–31), the
pastoral machinery is wholly Christian, and the songs are all ser-
mons. What had seemed merely an amoral turn from personal effort
is revealed to be bestial clamoring at the trough of sensuality. The
speaker is St. Peter, "The Pilot of the *Galilean* lake," who is to all
those who wander in the flood of life what a shepherd is to his sheep.

Here, then, is the third world of "Lycidas" in which the natural
world is filled with Christian imperatives. The pastoral singer for
fame has become the poet-priest, and so the loss of King is seen to
be not only the destruction of a poet but also the death of a priest.
St. Peter concludes the digression by indicating the impending
wrath of a just God. Whatever the specific reference we may choose
to find in "that two-handed engine,"[7] it is clear that selfish poets,
irresponsible shepherds, and corrupt clergymen are to be damned.
Phoebus's exhortation to do good so that one may receive meed in
heaven is reinforced by St. Peter's angry promise of punishment for
doing ill. A golden key will open heaven to the just, and an iron key
will lock sinners in hell. The prospect for man—who, like the ship
that drowned King, is "Built in th'eclipse" of original sin—is grim.

The dim hope promised by Alpheus as the successful lover of
Arethuse shrank from the terror of St. Peter, just as the pagan gods
of the nativity ode fled from Christ. Now hope returns as the "*Sici-
lian* Muse" calls upon the pastoral world to strew Lycidas's
"Laureate Hearse" with the flowers of beauty, sorrow, remem-
brance, love, and death. In culling flowers, the poet has again
turned, feebly, from the true vision to his "false surmise" of pastoral
comfort. Between the trauma of birth and the terror of judgment, he
seeks to "interpose a little ease"; but even the consolation of a
graceful funeral is impossible. Lycidas's body in the real world is
King's body, and that lies far beneath the "whelming tide" in the
"monstrous world." When set against real death, the pastoral is at
best a sedative.

Section 3 closes with a new, and higher, synthesis as the persona
seeks to forge an alliance between the malevolence of life and the
stern imperatives of God. Now he prays, not for justice, but pity.
Lines 163–64 ask that Michael (who is no longer seen as the wielder
of the two-handed sword but as a semimythological guardian)
"melt with ruth." Since Michael means "strength of God," and
since his traditional role is justice and punishment, the prayer is
thoroughly abject. Even if the dolphin had saved King, he would

still face the perilous flood of life in the human condition, cursed and eclipsed.

## IV   *The Blest Kingdom*

Despite the dim hints of grace we can find in the first three sections of the poem, the fourth section (lines 165–85) represents not a dialectical progression but a miracle.[8] The various tensions of the poem are resolved not by reason but by Christian ecstasy. Thus the climax of the poem reaches beyond the natural world, beyond the pastoral consolation, beyond the natural world impregnated with God's truth, into a fourth world:

> So *Lycidas*, sunk low, but mounted high,
> Through the dear might of him that walk'd the waves,
> Where other groves, and other streams along,
> With *Nectar* pure his oozy Locks he laves,
> And hears the unexpressive nuptial Song,
> In the blest Kingdoms meek of joy and love.

The imagery of this passage gathers in a single vision both the problems and the promises of the first three sections: the water which drowned King is conquered by the miracle of Christ's walking on the water; the groves and streams of Arcady are replaced by heavenly groves; the killing waters of nature are washed away in heavenly baptism; and Christ the bridegroom claims his church as the funeral becomes a wedding.[9] The justice of "all-judging *Jove*" and the punishment threatened by St. Peter are replaced by the mercy of Christ. The very destructiveness of the natural world falls within the divine plan and becomes the means of entry to the real pasture, the "blest Kingdoms meek of joy and love." Lines 178–81 celebrate the birth-marriage and complete the transformation of King-Lycidas through yet another liquid, for the waters of heaven replace not only the destructive sea, but also the melodious tears of art.

Yet the miracle is not alien to the natural world, for each day the sun sinks in the ocean and is not drowned but renewed. The diurnal cycle, which for the pagan affirmed the continuity of nature (but which excluded the individual) becomes, for the Christian, a promise of continuity not below the human level but above it. By linking Lycidas with the sun and the sun with Christ, Milton not only comforts those who mourn Lycidas's death, but also establishes a pattern for those who remain in the natural world.

There is yet a duty for shepherds, new pastures, and new songs. Like all of Milton's poems, "Lycidas" concludes with a concern for the wayfaring Christian. Lycidas himself is not completely dismissed from our world, for Milton inserts him into the mythic fabric of tradition. As an ectype of the archetype Christ, his life and his death form a pattern (based on The Pattern) for those left behind. Lycidas is now as real, or as unreal, as mythic and as traditional as Orpheus or Hippotades. With this poem, Milton has added to the store of myth. Astonishingly, "Lycidas" takes its life from a tradition that it revivifies.

Line 186 shifts attention abruptly from Lycidas, from sorrow, from ecstasy, and from salvation; for the speaker of the epilogue is not a participant in the elegy but an observer who is outside the experience of the poem. He judges the persona of the poem to be "uncouth" and *"Doric,"* if tender in his eager thoughts. The most straightforward way to read the final *ottava rima* is as Milton's farewell to the pastoral mode. In the hierarchy of genres, the pastoral was near the bottom and suited primarily for the apprentice. But Milton was not finished with the pastoral elegy; he returned to it three years later at the death of his great friend, Charles Diodati.[10] From our vantage we can see that the new pastures and fresh woods were further away than Milton supposed. God's poet was to become the Commonwealth's and the Protectorate's spokesman before he would have leisure to sing "Of man's first disobedience" in *Paradise Lost*.

CHAPTER 6

# *The Ways of God:* Paradise Lost

ALTHOUGH Milton gathered and edited his poems for publication in 1645, translated a number of psalms, and composed a handful of fine sonnets, the years between 1640 and 1660 were largely devoted to polemical prose.[1] Because Milton makes use of the standard convention, that only a good man can produce a true work, his assertion of personal excellence is frequent. But what seems transparently egotistical to the modern reader seemed far less so in Milton's day. Milton's arguing from authority, which often seems tedious to the modern reader, tells us a good deal about Milton's reading.[2] The effectiveness of John Milton in controversy is testified to by a grim fact: on the eve of the Restoration, a hangman was instructed to burn copies of Milton's tracts in public.

Politically, Milton became an ardent republican; theologically, he moved toward an ultimate Protestantism in which each man could be his own church; the only doctrine needed was the Bible; each Christian, under the guidance of the Spirit, might meet his God directly. Thematically, this combination resulted in a celebration of responsible free will.[3] Whatever the extenuating circumstance, man is responsible for himself and to his God. The nature of that joint freedom and responsibility is central to Milton's last three major poems, *Paradise Lost* (1667, 1674), *Paradise Regained* (1671), and *Samson Agonistes* (1671).

When Milton began *Paradise Lost,* he chose the most basic story of our civilization, cast his narrative in the most demanding genre man had developed, and set out to write the world's greatest poem. His understanding of "great" art can be summarized in a Renaissance platitude: art is to delight, to instruct, and to move the reader to virtuous action: it must be affective, didactic, and moral. Unless we demand all three objectives from *Paradise Lost,* we take the

65

poem less seriously than Milton intended it. To expect too much from *Paradise Lost* is almost impossible, but it is easy to expect the wrong things.

Since Milton was very conscious of his predecessors who used the epic form, we can expect to plunge *in medias res*, to see gods mingling in the affairs of men, to hear invocations of the muse, to trace the history of a people in the person of a hero, to meet epic simile after epic simile, and so on. An awareness of the echoes created by such epic machinery is desirable, but our simply spotting this or that convention is a game best deferred until the tenth reading of the poem. In essential ways, *Paradise Lost* is unlike *The Iliad, The Odyssey,* and *The Aneiad*; to read it only through its precedents is to miss both its artistic originality and its didactic purpose.[4]

Although we do Milton's poem an injustice if we do not examine it with the high seriousness usually reserved for philosophy or theology, *Paradise Lost* is neither; it is a work of art. The implications of this division, so natural to us, would likely have seemed arbitrary, or even wrongheaded, to Milton. For him, truth is beauty; and the perception of their unity is the proper way to mend the faults of humanity. Whether or not Milton achieved his grand design is a question to be answered by each reader—after he has faced the greatest poem in our language.[5]

In retelling the story of *Paradise Lost*, I have taken several liberties. The events are narrated in, roughly, chronological order, rather than in the order Milton presents them to us. Milton expected his audience to know the myth well enough to keep track of who-did-what-to-whom-and-when. More importantly, for an evaluation of his artistry, we need to know the chronology in order to see the effect Milton achieves by setting events as he does.[6] We must understand the base from which he moves in order to see the significance of parallels, contrasts, and highlights. To facilitate awareness of Milton's displacements of narrative chronology, I have included book and line references to *Paradise Lost* within my narrative summary: (5.600) means Book 5, Line 600. It is very difficult to hold the story of *Paradise Lost* in mind and at the same time to see it as a unified work of art. Finally, the style I have chosen for the narrative summary is meant to suggest a major displacement from our everyday world.

## I  *Resumé*

(5.600) On a day of eternity from amid the circling orders of worshipping angels, the Voice proclaimed a new order in heaven; henceforth, the Son of Deity would command the heavenly host as God's vice-regent. A warning followed the announcement: any who disobeyed his new commander would incur eternal wrath and be cast from heaven into utter darkness. At the pronouncement, the nine orders of angels raised a great chorus of praise, hymning the power and wisdom of the Omnipotent. All seemed pleased; but one at least, Lucifer, the greatest in power and glory of the angelic potentates, felt himself impaired. As soon as decently possible, he withdrew to meditate upon the implications of God's new dispensation.

At midnight, unable to sleep, he called for his great lieutenant (whose fallen name will be Beëlzebub); in ambiguous phrases, he cast the new order in doubt. Until that day he knew himself second only to God; now the Son stood in that place. At his order a host moved to his region in the north. One third of the angels marched with him, secure in the wisdom and strength of their bright commander. From his northern throne, Lucifer addressed them, asking if they were prepared to bend servile knee to this new yoke, urging their resistance to tyranny, and reminding them of their equality, of tradition, and of their destiny to rule, not to serve. There was wonder at Lucifer's bold words, and praise. But from the first rank of Seraphim stepped Abdiel, and he challenged the truth and wisdom of Lucifer. He asserted the omnipotence of God and argued that the angels were exalted by their new commander who linked them yet more closely with paternal deity.

Lucifer met Abdiel's arguments with scorn, called upon his angels to assert their prerogatives, hinted at armed resistance, and threatened Abdiel. Abdiel stood firm. Warning the gathered hosts of impending destruction, he walked out, accompanied by the jeers and boos of his former comrades. (6.1) All night he hurried toward the throne of God; and, as dawn broke, he entered God's encampment. The rebellion of Lucifer was already known, and the faithful angels welcomed Abdiel, rejoicing that one of Lucifer's host should refuse apostasy.

Across the heavenly plain, the ranks of Lucifer moved to chal-

lenge the power of God. Against them God sent half the remaining
angels. There was war in heaven. Secure in pride, Lucifer boasted
his strength, and to meet him stepped Abdiel. Returning the ritual
boasting of Satan point for point, Abdiel struck the rebel so that he
reeled backward ten paces and fell to one knee. At once the battle
began, and all that day angel fought with angel. The hosts of God
were impervious to the swords of their enemies. Cloven angelic
forms joined at once, and the obedient angels neither bled nor felt
pain. The rebels too were renewed after each blow, but from their
wounds flowed a staining liquid, and they knew pain. At the fall of
night, the hosts drew apart, and Lucifer called his chief captains to a
council. He boasted about their endurance; since they had with-
stood the hosts of God one day, why could they not do so forever?

Nisroch praised Lucifer's courage, but he noted the inequality of
the battle. The hosts of God fought in comfort; he had been hurt;
and an eternity of such unequal strife seemed to him futile. Some
new strategy or some new weapon was needed if the struggle were
to continue. Lucifer promised such a weapon, and the apostate
angels labored all night in digging the bowels of heaven. By dawn,
they had compounded gunpowder and formed cannon. Newly
armed, Lucifer's host marched confidently into the second day's
battle. The cannon were placed inside a hollow square of marching
angels; and, when God's host advanced, Lucifer's ranks opened to
reveal three tiers of artillery. The first rank fired, and the angels of
God were hurled back, unharmed yet overcome by the weight of
projectiles and the clumsiness of their own armor.

For a time, it seemed that Lucifer would prevail; but, gathering
themselves, God's obedient angels seized the tops of mountains,
shook them loose from their roots, and hurled them against the
rebel forces. Their cannon buried and useless, the contending force
hurled mountains in return; and, for a time, they fought under-
ground, so thick was flying soil. The night of the second day came
without clear advantage to either side; and, because God had
formed the angels equal, there seemed no end to the battle. At the
close of the second day, God spoke to His Son and gave him full
commission to throw the rebels out of heaven. Yet God found the
efforts of Michael's forces worthy of praise.

At the dawn of the third day, the Son of God rode forth in the
chariot of glory and power. The chariot seemed alive, composed of
four terrible cherubim, and from its circling wheels flew lightnings

too bright to view. Forth he drove and before him fled the rebel hosts, yearning for the mountains to cover them, throwing their weapons away and screaming until they were herded to the wall of heaven which opened wide to allow their passage. Over the precipice they streamed, putting on angelic speed to escape the terrible wrath of the Son of God. Down through chaos they fled, pursued by thunderbolts from the red right hand of God. Day and night they fell, fleeing, until before them rose the gates of hell. In they flew as to a refuge, so terrible seemed their pursuer; exhausted they dropped into a lake of fire; and the gates of hell were closed behind them.

(2.648–73; 2.746–809) To guard that gate, God set a monstrous pair, Death and Sin. Once in heaven, Lucifer had felt pain in his left temple. Full grown and beautiful, a female creature sprang from his head. She astounded Lucifer's followers, and they named her Sin. But soon all grew to love her, and Lucifer took her as his mistress. From that union was born a shapeless maw, hideously strong, who tore his mother's entrails, brandished his dart, and chased his mother lusting. From that rape were engendered yelling monsters who continually crept in and out of their dam's womb, gnawing and howling. To Sin was given the key to hell's gate; and her son Death was set as watchman. (1.44–53) The clang of the gate yielded to silence, and far within the dome of hell Lucifer's vast host lay in stupor; only the hiss of flame and eddy of liquid fire sounded through all the livid darkness. One third of the heavenly host was forever lost.

(6.880–92) Meanwhile, the Son of God returned triumphant to his Father, and the angels yet faithful hymned his victory, rejoicing in the strength of their new commander who by right of deed, as well as birth, held their full allegiance (6.880–92). Since the faithful angels spread themselves, filling all heaven, the apostasy of Lucifer left no gap in the ranks of God. (7.139–640) God the Father praised His Son, and set a new task: the creation of the universe. The Son went forth, and with him rode the power of the Father. Upon the roiling chaos of unformed atoms, Christ spread the power of the Word: "Silence, ye troubl'd waves, and thou Deep, peace," and discord ended. As the creative principle brooded on the vast abyss, light from darkness was separated, waters from dry land. The stars coalesced and began their eternal dance of praise, and the womb of matter teemed and gave birth to all living things. The sea surged

with life, and upon dry land awoke the microbe and the elephant.
Plants sprang forth in full bloom and in fruit, and the earth calved
the lion and the stag.

God saw that it was good, and blessed His creation. The Son had
worked the Will of the Father. Chaos was informed, and the new
creation was nearly completed. Then said the Eternal Father to His
Son:

> Let us make now Man in our image, Man
> In our similitude, and let them rule
> Over the Fish and Fowl of Sea and Air,
> Beast of the Field, and over all the Earth,
> And every creeping thing that creeps the ground.

Male and female He created humanity and gave the first commandment:

> Be fruitful, multiply, and fill the Earth,
> Subdue it, and throughout Dominion hold
> Over Fish of the Sea, and Fowl of the Air,
> And every living thing that moves on the Earth.

All things He gave beneath the power of Adam, save only one. In
the center of the Garden of Eden, He placed the Tree of Life, and
next to it stood a tree the fruit of which works the knowledge of
Good and Evil. The fruit of the second tree He forbade man, saying,

> In the day thou eat'st [of that fruit], thou di'st;
> Death is the penalty impos'd, beware,
> And govern well thy appetite, lest sin
> Surprise thee, and her black attendant Death.

The creation was complete, and the Son of God returned to heaven,
meeting there the praise of his Father and the loud hosannas of
worshipping angels.

(4.214–355) Upon the earth, in the garden God had prepared for
them, Adam and his consort Eve rejoiced in creation; they praised
each day their maker and tended in peace and comfort the plants of
the garden. Loving each other and themselves, content and joyful in
health and plenitude, they awaited the further manifestations of
God without longing or impatience.

(1.53–798) But deep in chaos, within the gates of hell and far out
in the fiery lake, there was movement; Great Satan (as Lucifer is

now called) raised his head and cast his eye over the ruins of his proud ambition. In despair, he wept, but he did so without repentance, for his pride so stirred that his punishment brought hate, not remorse. He called his lieutenant, Beëlzebub, mixing his words with scorn and sorrow. That great Cherub awoke, for the streams of Lethe were withheld from the fallen angels. Consciousness and gnawing desire filled the rebel pair, and shame at their defeat. Satan rose from the flood of fire like a great sea monster winged and found a standing place of solid fire. To his fallen followers he called, scorning their discomfiture, though he was inwardly wracked with sorrow and pity. They heard his voice and arose, chagrined that he should see them fallen, and their coming was like the hosts of history, and the swarming of stars, and the innumerable insects of a plague.

Through his tears spoke Satan, urging their loyalty and power. To each he assigned a task, and they, glad of occupation, hurried to obey his commands. Mammon led prospectors who discovered gold in the bowels of hell. Machines were built; and, under the guidance of the architect Mulciber, a great palace, all of gold and lighted with asphaltic lamps that glowed like stars, arose like an exhalation. Pandemonium it was named, and no sooner was it finished than Satan and Beëlzebub called a great council. Despite the width of its halls, the hosts of Satan filled it beyond capacity. At a word, they reduced their size to that of insects and, though innumerable, moved within.

(2.1–1055) Far inside, in their own huge dimensions, the chiefs of Satan's captains met to assess the present and to plan for the future. High in the center, on a throne more splendid than the imaginings of man, Satan exalted sat. He spoke words of comfort and scorn, urging that some plan be advanced to better their state or to discomfort their foe. The first to speak was Moloch, strongest of all the angels who fell. His desire was to have equaled God in force; that failed, he cared for nothing. War he advised, urging hell's hosts to rise against heaven, making of their punishments weapons, hell fire to hurl at heaven. But he ended in confusion, admitting the impossibility of success, and all his plan was for revenge, not victory.

The memory of recent pain filled the council, and the next to speak built skillfully upon that memory. Belial, the contriving hypocrite, named the flaws in Moloch's plan; and he urged that they not anger God, lest he abolish their beings. Belial's hope was that the never ending flow of days might change their fate, or that their substance might soon conform to its environment and hell grow pleasant. Recalling the fierce wrath of God, Belial urged their present comfort and held out for sloth, which he called patience.

Since Belial's plan found favor with many, Mammon built upon that favor. He saw no hope in Chance, no possibility that the power of chaos might capture causation from the hand of God; he scorned the thought that God might forgive; he was unwilling to be forgiven and to return to eons of forced bowings before the despot of heaven. His plan was to erect a rival kingdom in hell, for could not hell show as much pomp as heaven? Had they not plenty of gold? Could they not imitate God's light as He their darkness? His conclusion was to recommend hard work and adaptation. Though hell would not be heaven, it might be greatly improved.

The company applauded Mammon's proposal, and the issue seemed settled until Beëlzebub arose to recall the council to reality. God would hardly allow pleasure to the inhabitants of hell, nor would He suffer a rival kingdom. Although a direct attack on heaven was clearly out of the question, there was a possibility; for all had heard a rumor that God planned to create a new race. Perhaps it would be possible to attack God through the new creature man: either to drive man before the fire of hell, or to seduce him to the party of Satan. This plan was decided upon by Satan and Beëlzebub before the council, and it met with universal approval. There remained a problem, however, for none knew where or what the new creation was. Someone would have to venture upon a voyage of discovery; but when volunteers were called for, none answered; for all feared the known power of God and the unknown terrors of the deep. At last Satan spoke, taking upon himself the task of finding and perverting mankind, and assigning work for those who remained behind. Some should build, some explore, some exercise, and some keep watch. Others might sing; a few might wish to construct philosophy. The council closed with praise and worship of Satan, and each demon went to his assigned task.

Satan flew swiftly toward the gates of hell, eager to begin the great adventure; but, when he reached the gates, he discovered the hideous pair who were its wardens. Death rushed forward brandishing his dart, and Satan raised his arm in opposition. Between them stepped Sin, urging the father to spare his son, and the son, his father. When Sin had explained to Satan her identity and task, it took him but a moment to convince her that she should unlock the gate. From Satan's success, Sin expected voluptuous ease; and Death required food for his ever empty maw.

From the mouth of hell nothing but chaos was visible, and for a moment Satan hesitated. At last he spread his wings and sailed into the inchoate. Long he struggled, buffeted by contending formless forces, until at last he came to the throne of Chaos. In return for a promise to help Chaos regain the territory taken from him for the creation, Satan was shown the way to the universe. At last he won his way out of chaos and saw the Empyreal heaven and the golden chain which links the world to heaven.

(3.56–415) From the vantage of heaven, the Omnipotent saw not only the passage of Satan but the happiness upon the earth of Adam and Eve. God laughed at the puny foe who sought to sneak past Omniscience, yet he recognized that man would, in free will, listen to Satan's lies and eat of the forbidden fruit. Therefore he called for a volunteer in heaven to die so that man might not be utterly damned; but none answered. The Son spoke, urging that all man's sins be placed upon himself; and he agreed to die, for he had confidence in the redemptive power of the Father. God accepted Christ's offer, and He blessed His Son and all who would be His. When God ceased speaking, the angels sang praises of Father, Son, and creation, wondering in joy and love that Man should be so blessed. For though Satan, self-tempted, should find no forgiveness, man, seduced by the adversary, would receive a second chance.

(3.418–742) Meanwhile, Satan entered the newly created universe; and he passed the paradise of fools which in later times would be filled with those who sought heaven through other than the sacrifice of the Son. Looking upward, he saw the gates of heaven, bright with gold and precious stones, and from that gate the stairs whereon Jacob would see Angels ascending and descending. Satan turned and plunged through the soft, welcome air down to the golden sun. Changing his scarred gigantic form to that of a stripling angel, Satan landed upon the sun; and, with feigned meekness, he approached bright Uriel whose eyes are those of God to watch the created universe. Satan bowed low before the great Seraph and asked that he be shown God's new creation that he might worship the Omnipotent through contemplation of His works. Uriel, deceived, pointed down to the moon which neighbors earth and to the spot called Paradise. With thanks and speed, Satan flew to earth and landed on the top of Mt. Niphates.

(4.9–408) Satan's isolation and the beauty of the earth were for him a temptation. Now he missed the pleasures of heaven; now he remembered his present pain; now he foresaw his future torture. Three times his countenance changed from pale to red; and, high above, Uriel, who saw that change, recognized the mutability that beset none of those in heaven. When evening came, he sent a message to Gabriel, chief of the angelic guard of Paradise to warn him that some evil spirit had broken loose from hell. Meanwhile, Satan cast about for means to injure God, or failing that, to injure man, God's latest creation. Disguised as this or that inhabitant of earth, Satan approached Adam and Eve; and he was again tempted to good by their majesty and beauty. But, hardening his will, he resolved to share with them the gift of hell.

(4.411–538) Adam spoke to Eve, recounting the bliss of their life in Paradise and reminding her of the prohibition of the Tree of Knowledge. To Adam, Eve recounted the moment of her creation and the gentle lessons of love which had convinced her of Adam's superiority and her present bliss. All this conversation was torment for Satan, but he found in Adam's recounting of the prohibition of the Tree of Knowledge the germ of a plan: perhaps he might tempt them to disobey God's law. Turning from the blessed pair, he roamed through Eden, seeking tools for his new task.

(4.539–773) Meanwhile, night fell; and Gabriel, newly warned by Uriel, dispatched his night guard, sending two angels to the bower of Adam and Eve in search of the wandering devil. The parents of mankind, after praising God, retired to their private bower where came none of the creatures of the garden. They loved each other and turned to perfect sleep. (4.800–09) But Satan, in the form of a toad, squatted at Eve's ear and whispered to her a dream. (5.38–93) In that dream, a bright angelic form called to Eve; praising her beauty, he led her to the forbidden fruit; and it seemed to her that she ate and rose like an angel high above the bounds of earth.

(4.810–1015) At that moment, the two guardians arrived at the bower and, seeing a toad within, prodded it with a spear. At the touch, Satan, like gunpowder touched with fire, exploded into his giant form. The guardians challenged him; but he, disdaining to fight any but their chief, allowed himself to be led back to Gabriel. A mighty battle seemed at hand; but, high in the heavens, God hung his scales, measuring for Satan the result of flight or fight. The balance tipped in favor of flight; and Satan, obeying unwittingly, mounted and fled; and with him fled the shades of night.

(5.1–219) When morning came to the bower in Eden, Adam and Eve awoke to praise their creator and to tend the garden left in their care. But Eve was troubled; her dream had disturbed her sleep; and with tears she told Adam of the night's temptation. He, filled with love, comforted her, explaining that evil might come into the mind of God or man without stain, so long as it was unapproved by the thinker. Together they praised God and went to the pleasant task of pruning and tending the garden.

(5.224) God saw their trouble; and He, in pity and love, called Raphael, the affable angel, and ordered him to visit Adam and Eve. Raphael was to spend the afternoon on earth, answer the questions of mankind, and mix with his lessons additional warnings against eating the forbidden fruit. Down he flew to Earth and his coming was like a phoenix's flight. Adam and Eve had returned to their bower for their midday meal and for a pleasant rest before the afternoon's work. They greeted Raphael, and he joined their meal. (8.250) Many things they spoke of: he told them of the war in heaven and of the creation of the earth. Adam recounted the moment of his own creation. And in every answer to Adam's questions Raphael gently inserted the prohibition of the Tree of Knowledge, warning Adam of the adversary now loose upon earth, and finding in Adam's devotion to Eve's beauty a flaw in need of correction. Adam understood Raphael's speech, for his uncorrupted intellect was like in kind to the angelic; but he rejected the warning against worshipping Eve. With kind words and loving warning, Raphael bade Adam farewell. The angel returned to heaven, and Adam returned to his bower.

(9.53) Meanwhile, Satan had found fit tool for his temptation. Finding in the subtlest beast of the field an unwitting ally, he entered the form of the serpent as the serpent slept. In hope of what occasion might grant, he lay in wait. Again Adam and Eve greeted the new day with praises to God and with joy in their own well-being. But Eve suggested that this day they separate for their work; for, she argued, together they wasted too much time and their dinner came unearned. Adam, who answered by reminding her of the new danger loose in the garden, urged their mutual safety in league; but Eve felt his lack of trust in her obedience. And almost they quarreled. Finally, saying that her unwilling presence made her more absent than her absence, Adam agreed to the separation; and each left to work alone until noon.

Beyond hope, Satan saw Eve alone tending the unsupported flowers; and, weaving forward the beautiful body of the serpent, he approached. To Eve's astonishment, the serpent spoke; and his voice was full of worship for her beauty and his desire to serve her. When he claimed that he had eaten a marvelous fruit that raised his brute intelligence almost to human level, Eve asked about the fruit; and he led her with many windings to the center of the garden. When she understood that the tree of which he spoke was the Tree of Knowledge, she turned upon the serpent, chastising him for wasting her time. But he argued subtly; he feigned ignorance of the prohibition and urged upon her his own recent elevation by the magical power of the fruit. She was troubled by the complexity of his argument; she was unable to find flaws in his logic; her vanity was pleased by his rhetoric; and, since it was noon, her body seconded all other arguments.

(9.781) She ate of the fruit.

With the first bite, Eve lost all control of her appetite. She did not see the snake slip away, nor did she stop eating until she was gorged. Then, as though drunk, she turned and did obeisance to the tree, praising its intellectual fruit. For a time, she pondered whether to give the fruit to Adam; she doubted that he should share the advanced being she had achieved; but her fear of punishment from God and her despair at the thought of a second Eve, were she removed from the garden, made her decide to share the fruit with her husband. Plucking a branch of the fruit, she returned to the bower where Adam awaited. In his hand he held a chaplet of flowers made to celebrate their first reunion.

When Adam saw her coming, the flowers wilted and the chaplet dropped from his hand. He knew at once what she had done and brushed aside her explanation. But so strongly did he feel the call of his own flesh in Eve that he too ate of the fruit. Then, for the first time, he cast lusting eyes on Eve's nakedness. She returned the heat, and they went together to their bower to seal their sin with love sport. When they awoke, Adam, now sobered, chided Eve for eating of the fruit; and she returned the accusation, saying that he should not have let her go alone. They found leaves and sewed them together to hide their nakedness. In mutual blame, they contended; and there seemed no end to their quarrel.

(9.782) At the fall of Eve, the earth had trembled (10.1); and the guardian angels made haste to inform God of the sin and to beg forgiveness for their failure. God reassured them, for He blamed Adam and Eve who were "Sufficient to stand though free to fall." God then called His Son, charging him with the judging of the sinful pair. In accepting the task, the Son reminded the Father that whatever judgment he pronounced upon the humans would ultimately fall on him. The serpent was judged guilty by his flight, but the Son came to Earth and called Adam who had hidden himself among the thickest trees in Eden.

Adam came reluctantly forth and with him came Eve. When the Son asked if Adam had eaten of the fruit, Adam replied that Eve had given it to him. When the Son rejected the mitigation and turned to Eve, asking what she had done, she replied that the serpent had tricked her and that she had eaten. At once the Son pronounced the serpent's punishment: to crawl upon its belly and to have eternal enmity between the sons of Eve and itself. But in the promise of a bruising of the serpent's head by the Son of Man was hope for mankind.

(10.193) The Son pronounced Eve's punishment: in sorrow and pain should she bear children and her husband should rule over her. The punishment of Adam was to labor among thorns and thistles for his bread and to return at last to the dust of which he had been created. But, before leaving, the Son of God fashioned clothing for Adam and Eve from the skins of animals; for, from that day forth, the Earth knew seasons both hot and cold. He then returned to the Father as intercessor for mankind.

(10.229) Satan, now far from Earth on his swift journey to hell, found a marvelous thing. Sin and Death, sensing the sucess of their father, had begun a bridge, compounded of asphaltic slime, which stretched from the mouth of hell toward Earth. They passed him, pausing to praise his magnificent deeds, as they moved to Earth: she, to exercise her nature; he, to devour the results of Sin. Again disguising himself as a plebeian angel, Satan passed unnoticed through the ranks of demons and entered his high hall. He sat unseen upon his throne for a time and at last appeared to his fellows, star-bright in glory. The devils shouted in joy at the return of their lord, and he addressed them, detailing the trials he had been through and vaunting his success.

When he ceased speaking, there greeted his ears a universal hiss;

for his fellows fell on their bellies and changed into complicated monsters. Then Satan too felt a change come over him. His face drew out lean, his arms and legs twined round each other, and at last he fell upon his belly, a huge serpent, his voice reduced to a hiss from a forked tongue. Goaded by hunger and thirst, Satan and his followers rushed from the hall and seized the beautiful fruit which hung upon trees by the waters of hell. But each bite was bitter ashes; and, when they sought to slake their thirst, the water retreated from their mouths. Each year the transformation and the punishment are repeated.

(10.616) From on high, the Almighty looked down and saw Sin and Death approaching Earth. He pronounced them His hell dogs, fit to lick the drab and filth until such time as man's sin should be forgiven.(10.710) All creation was infected by Adam's sin. Beasts began to prey upon each other and to glare from the deeps at man. When Adam beheld the results of his sin, he sorrowed and repented that he had ever lived. (10.966) With Eve, he discussed not only celibacy so that mankind should cease but also suicide. But Eve begged his forgiveness; and, when he beheld her sorrow, he pitied her and forgave her. Thus, she taught him the way back to God, and the pair returned to the judgment seat. There they fell prostrate in contrition, confessed their sins, and begged forgiveness.

(11.1) Their prayers rose to heaven and were mixed with the incense of the Son's intercession. The Father granted the Son's request that man should not forever be lost, but He banished Adam and Eve from the garden lest they eat of the Tree of Life and think to live forever. On earth, Adam felt the acceptance of his prayers and rejoiced with Eve. But in the sky there appeared a blazing cloud: Michael, the power of God, had been sent to remove them from the garden. But he first instructed Adam as to the future history of mankind.

(11.370) Michael conducted Adam to the top of a hill, leaving Eve below, sleeping. He purged Adam's eyes of the film brought about by disobedience and showed him visions. The first was Cain killing Abel; the second, the miserable inmates of a lazar-house. Then a plain appeared upon which the sons of God consorted with the daughters of men; next, a land at war. Then again voluptuous peace until the heavens opened dropping a flood, and all were drowned save Noah and his three sons. Adam's terror was comforted by the vision of a rainbow, God's promise that he would not again flood the earth.

(12.8) Perceiving that Adam's sight was failing, Michael related
the history of man from the flood to the advent of Christ upon earth.
He closed by telling Adam that, in the end, the serpent, Satan,
should be dragged to eternal chaining, that Christ should judge both
the quick and the dead, and that a new Paradise, whether on earth
or in heaven, would be established—a place far happier than the
present Paradise.

(12.469) Adam scarcely knew whether to lament or to praise his
recent sin that seemed to be the root of so much final good; but he
worried lest the faithful, between the reascension of Christ to
heaven and the final judgment, should suffer terribly. For them,
Michael replied, the Lord would send a holy comforter, his spirit, as
a shield against the temptations of evil.

Michael and Adam descended to the plain, awakened Eve, and
made their way to the gate of the garden. Hand in hand, the parents
of mankind journeyed through Eden; and behind them gleamed the
fiery swords of the angels, now their forbidders as well as friends:

> The World was all before them, where to choose
> Thir place of rest, and Providence thir guide:
> They hand in hand with wand'ring steps and slow,
> Through *Eden* took thir solitary way.

## II  *Introduction*

The best introduction to *Paradise Lost* is Milton's own, for the
first twenty-six lines of the poem are packed with information that
establishes the mode, the scope, and the purpose of the epic:

> Of Man's First Disobedience, and the Fruit
> Of that Forbidden Tree, whose mortal taste
> Brought Death into the World, and all our woe,
> With loss of *Eden*. . . .

The subject, "Man's First Disobedience," is Eve and Adam's willful
eating of the fruit of the tree. The fruit is both literal and metaphori-
cal: "mortal," in the sense that it poisons humanity; and, by eating
it, Adam becomes a mortal—a term synonymous for us with human.
Milton promises to tell how that metamorphosis occurred. The
phrase "all our woe" includes the reader as victim of original sin.
When we consider the woe of man, ranging from the terrible visions

of Adam in books 11 and 12 to our own pogroms, our wars, and our
basic, incurable disease called "existence," Milton's three words
seem inadequate. But the understatement fits his perspective, for
Milton's vision is mythic and historical. Almost like his God, he sees
the history of man in each single moment; therefore, the endings are
implicit in beginnings: the creation is co-present with the
apocalypse.

The historical ending of *Paradise Lost* is the "loss of Eden"; Adam
and Eve will face a hostile and pregnant world. But the next two
lines, "till one greater Man / Restore us, and regain the blissful
Seat," deny the tragic ending. Christ, the "greater Man," will be the
fruit of another tree (the cross) whose taste will restore man's im-
mortality. Milton's perspective allows him to see Christ as a second
Adam. The "Seat" to be regained is both the "Paradise within" that
fallen Adam is promised and the ultimate healing of the separation
between God and man. These first five lines are an overview of
history, a suggestion of the magnificent cycle from Eden to
Gethsemane to heaven. Thus, *Paradise Lost* is a divine comedy.

"Sing Heav'nly Muse" turns to the immediate artistic problem.
By calling a muse, Milton invites comparison with other epics, par-
ticularly those of Homer and Virgil. But Milton's muse is not Classi-
cal; his inspiration is "Heav'nly" not only in the laudatory sense but
in a quite literal one. He identifies his muse in three aspects: (1) the
voice who dictated the law to Moses (That Shepherd) so that the
Jews (Chosen Seed) might move toward God. Moses' muse is ter-
rifying: "The Lord descended upon it [Mt. Sinai] in fire; and the
smoke of it went up like the smoke of a kiln, and the whole mountain
quaked greatly" (Exodus 19:18). (2) The muse is identified with
"*Sion* Hill" (Zion) which figures richly in Jewish and Christian lore
as a refuge associated with the City of David and the Temple of
Solomon. There the Apostles gathered at Pentecost; and, in es-
chatological lore, the Messiah is to appear on Zion at the end of
time. Milton's reference stretches, therefore, throughout the reli-
gious history of our civilization. (3) By naming his muse "the Oracle
of God," Milton establishes a comparison between it and that of
Classical literature. Delphi spoke in dark and destructive half-
truths; but Zion, in both the Psalms of David and the Revelations of
John, grants the full illumination of an omniscient God.

A similar comparison is suggested when Milton names "*Siloa's*
Brook." Mt. Parnassus had springs, the haunt of the Classical

muses; but, beside the waters of Siloa, Jesus healed a man born blind (John 9:7). Milton's own blindness makes the reference poignant, but the more important blindness is that inherited by all men from a disobedient Adam. Since the "Oracle of God" is Christ, Milton expects such aid to make his song soar above anything yet written. The Aonian Mount, which inspired pagan authors, is far inferior to Milton's inspiration.

A final aspect of the "Heav'nly Muse" encompasses both Zion and Sinai. "Thou O Spirit, that dost prefer / Before all Temples th' upright heart and pure" is the comforter whom Christ sent to earth when he returned to heaven. It dwells, not on some distant mountain nor in a city, a temple, or a stream, but in the hearts of men. This spirit is not a separate muse, for it "from the first / Wast present." Since it nested on the "vast Abyss," Milton calls upon that same creative energy which formed the universe.

In seeking such ultimate inspiration, Milton employs a series of metaphors. Line 7 speaks in terms of breath, "inspiration"; line 14, of flying, "soaring"; but perhaps the most interesting metaphor is that buried in the etymology of "instruct." To in-struct is to build within, to remake the temple of man which Adam's first disobedience destroyed. The same spirit that brooded the universe is asked to make Milton pregnant in artistry. When Milton prays for illumination, he recalls God's "let there be light." The concluding clause, "what is low raise and support," unifies several previous metaphors: the flight, the building, perhaps even the expansion of the lungs in breathing. In each physical metaphor lies a moral implication; for, as almost always, Milton's descriptions do double duty—they are both literal and symbolic. The universe of *Paradise Lost* is alive with moral imperatives.[7]

The invocation concludes: "That to the highth of this great Argument / I may assert Eternal Providence, / And justify the ways of God to men." The poem is to delight and instruct. The "argument" (theme, story) is the origin of evil and the path to salvation, an argument high enough to hold the reader's attention, but the purpose of the entertainment goes far beyond enjoyment. "Eternal Providence" is the outermost circle in a concentric series of causative powers. At the center of these causitive powers is man; his most immediate connection with events is chance; and beyond chance is luck (Fortuna). Encompassing luck is fate; and, in some larger sense, man is fated to lose or win. But ultimate causation is the will

of God, Eternal Providence. Chance has not even a ghost of an-
thropomorphism; Fortuna is a whore, whimsically favorable or de-
structive; the Fates are consistent, but there is only one eye for the
three weird sisters.

Only the Eternal has both the power and the concern for man that
is necessary if sense is to be made of the apparent inchoate. By
asserting eternal providence, Milton insists that the mighty maze is
not without a plan; and in line 26 he undertakes an awesome bur-
den. Not only does providence exist, but "just are the ways of God, /
And justifiable to Men." With God's aid, Milton intends to explain
the myths most crucial to man's knowledge and to make purposive,
infinite principles comprehensible to finite intelligence. The scope
and the ambition could not be larger. The first twenty-six lines are
the poem in miniature; like the overture of an opera, they contain
the melodies and motifs that inform its thematic tensions:

> Of Man's First Disobedience, and the Fruit
> Of that Forbidden Tree, whose mortal taste
> Brought Death into the World, and all our woe,
> With loss of *Eden*, till one greater Man
> Restore us, and regain the blissful Seat,
> Sing Heav'nly Muse, that on the secret top
> Of *Oreb*, or of *Sinai*, didst inspire
> That Shepherd, who first taught the chosen Seed,
> In the Beginning how the Heav'ns and Earth
> Rose out of *Chaos:* or if *Sion* Hill
> Delight thee more, and *Siloa's* Brook that flow'd
> Fast by the Oracle of God; I thence
> Invoke thy aid to my advent'rous Song,
> That with no middle flight intends to soar
> Above th' *Aonian* Mount, while it pursues
> Things unattempted yet in Prose or Rhyme.
> And chiefly Thou O Spirit, that dost prefer
> Before all Temples th' upright heart and pure,
> Instruct me, for Thou know'st; Thou from the first
> Wast present, and with mighty wings outspread
> Dove-like satst brooding on the vast Abyss
> And mad'st it pregnant: What in me is dark
> Illumine, what is low raise and support;
> That to the highth of this great Argument
> I may assert Eternal Providence,
> And justify the ways of God to men.

Line 28 returns to the opening statement of the invocation. Milton has commanded the muse to sing; he now directs that song with two questions:

> say first what cause
> Mov'd our Grand Parents in that happy State,
> Favor'd of Heav'n so highly, to fall off
> From thir Creator, and transgress his Will
> For one restraint, Lords of the World besides?

The first question, "Why did they do it?" implies both the illogic and the perversity of disobedience. The second question indicates that Adam alone could not have been so stupid; his act must have been someone else's fault: "Who first seduc'd them to that foul revolt?" "Seduc'd," a carefully chosen word, implies a swerving of will and a turning from Right Reason. Its physical connotations are to be developed in two aspects: first, Satan's conversations with Eve are a seduction in almost the Petrarchan sense, and the word "seduc'd" stirs nightmares of snakes copulating with women; but the second aspect is more unequivocal: Adam is not deceived, but "fondly overcome with female charm." In this question the basic conflict of the poem is established: reason and order versus passion and chaos. Milton does not, however, have a "Puritan" horror of the flesh; for his unfallen mankind is thoroughly and joyfully sensuous. The fall occurs not because the flesh gives pleasure but because sense usurps the place of reason and lures the will to act against man's best interest.[8]

Despite the announcement that the poem's theme is man's disobedience, Milton does not begin with man; for all cosmogonies push at least one step beyond the known in an effort to make the existence of evil and suffering comprehensible, and an extrahuman agent is usually at fault. In Genesis, the serpent is that agent, but we find no hint that the snake embodies the devil. Milton, following later tradition, pushes the evil causative principle one step further; for not only is the snake an animal and so beyond human analysis, it is possessed by Satan.

Although the story of the fall in Genesis 3 may have been in part an attempt to account for our aversion to snakes, Milton is concerned with far more metaphysical questions: "How is it possible for a perfect, benevolent, and omnipotent creator to produce a being so manifestly imperfect as man?" The paradox seems inescapable: if God is good, God is not God; if God is God, God is not good. Milton, at the very least, pushes the conundrum back one step. We may yet be puzzled as to how God could create an angel who could tempt himself; but, since a fallen, malevolent being exists prior to the creation of man, our concern need not be focused upon the genesis of evil but upon man's first confrontation with a given power of blackness. We are told almost nothing of Lucifer's fall until we are firmly grounded in Eden; pride, we are told, led Lucifer to envy, envy to revolt, and revolt to expulsion from heaven.

Unlike my summary of the story of *Paradise Lost*, the action of Milton's poem does not begin with Lucifer's revolt. If it did our initial interest would have focused upon the origin of evil in an angel presumably created perfect; but since Milton wishes to teach of mankind's disobedience, he does not set out to justify God's ways with demons. As the curtain rises (line 50), Satan is already literally and symbolically fallen: evil exists in opposition to good. If the poem is to sustain our interest, a plausible conflict must exist; and we must at least entertain the idea that Satan might succeed. Theologically, Manicheism will not do, but esthetically, it is necessary.

The solution to this paradox is ingenious. The *strategic* outcome of the conflict is a theological given, implicit in the nature of Milton's cosmos (Satan must lose). The *tactical* outcome of the conflict is a scriptural given (Satan must win). Thus, Milton's problem is to demonstrate that tactical victory is strategic defeat. To do this, he must assert the encompassing will of God while at the same time presenting angel, man, and devil in possession of free will within the dramatic *now* of the story. We may feel that the conundrum is disguised, rather than solved, for we may well wonder how an omnipotent God can grant power separate from Himself and yet remain omnipotent. If omnipotence is denied anything, it would seem to be less than omnipotent. Can God make a rock so heavy that He cannot pick it up? A possible answer lies in the existence of an infinite series which is contained in a greater infinite series: 1–3–5 . . . may go on forever and yet be contained in 1–2–3–4–5–6. . . . Like the philosopher devils of book 2, our reason in such a question is in "endless mazes wandering lost." But Milton's strategic and tactical division allows him to create a sense of dramatic suspense. His success is attested to by the surprising number of readers who align themselves with Satan.[9]

The first forty-nine lines of the poem assert eternal providence in unmistakable terms, but books 1 and 2 of *Paradise Lost* seem designed to make the reader forget that assertion. To the extent that we are led to sympathize with Satan, we convict ourselves of original sin. If we are guilty, our plight is fitting. God's ways with men are justified.[10]

### III  *Satan*

Against the overview of the opening of book 1 stands the character of Satan. If we consider him in the explicit theological framework of the poem, there appears to be no room for sympathy since Satan has made the bed in which he lies. Nevertheless, for generations sensitive readers have suspected·that Milton was of the devil's party. One reason for this sympathy is that Satan is a consummate poet. In fact, his only claim to existence lies in the tension and ambiguity inherent in poetic language. Plato (book 10 of the *Republic*) asserts, "hymns to the gods and praises of famous men are the only poetry which ought to be admitted into our State. For if you go beyond this and allow the honeyed muse to enter, either in epic or lyric verse, not law and the reason of mankind, which by common consent have ever been deemed best, but pleasure and pain will be the rulers in our State." Christ (*Paradise Regained*, book 4) asserts of Classical poetry:

> Remove their swelling Epithets thick laid
> As varnish on a Harlot's cheek, the rest,
> Thin sown with aught of profit or delight,
> Will far be found unworthy to compare
> With *Sion's* songs, to all true tastes excelling,
> Where God is prais'd aright, and Godlike men,
> The Holiest of Holies, and his Saints.
>
> (343–49)

Christ purifies Plato's strictures, but he and Plato agree that "other" poetry makes the worse cause appear the better one and prevents man from using "right reason." Still, our human response may be that pleasure and pain do rule and that the sweetness of the "honeyed muse" and the cosmetic effect of "swelling Epithets" are a comfort against the hideous oscillation of sensuous pleasure and pain. To the degree that we eliminate a rational causation, we find

Satan our fellow. Our reason may be more or less correct; it is
seldom "right" in Plato's sense.

Satan is the poet whom Plato banishes from the Republic, for he is
existential man, living in every moment by the conditions of that
moment. Satan's great speech might almost come from the mouth of
Plato's poet:

> What though the field be lost?
> All is not lost; the unconquerable Will,
> And study of revenge, immortal hate,
> And courage never to submit or yield:
> And what is else not to be overcome?
>
> (1.105–9)

The absurdity of his condition he takes as a fact; he submits himself
to the destructive element and with the exertions of his limbs at-
tempts to float. But Milton's universe is not Jean-Paul Sartre's, nor
Joseph Conrad's. Milton's God is nothing if not purposive; and, for
the Christian, freedom and independence lie in obedience, not in
self-assertive rebellion. In His will is our peace. Ultimately, Satan is
caught in a paradox: he exists only through self-assertion; but, for his
assertion to be true, there must be no God; and, if there is no God,
what is Satan doing in hell? The key to understanding Satan's
character is to realize, therefore, that *Paradise Lost* is a closed sys-
tem. Nothing and no-thing exist outside of God. Profoundly,
"Whatever is, is right."

But this ultimate understanding is strategic, and Satan lives in a
world of tactics. Once we see both the broad and narrow views, we
can no longer admire Satan; for, despite his bloody-but-unbowed
attitude, he is a fool. But we do continue to admire him, not just for
his bravura performance, but because fallen man is a creature of
tactics, not strategy. We see ourselves in Satan; rather than consider
ourselves devils, we consider him human.[11]

The essence of Satan's tactics is fragmentation. To justify his ways
to himself, to his followers, and to men, he must assert his indepen-
dence from God; and to gain such independence, he is forced to
fragment God and himself. His first challenge is to omnipotence:

> Who can in reason then or right assume
> Monarchy over such as live by right
> His equals, if in power and splendor less,

> In freedom equal? or can introduce
> Law and Edict on us, who without law
> Err not? much less for this to be our Lord,
> And look for adoration to th' abuse
> Of those Imperial Titles which assert
> Our being ordain'd to govern, not to serve?
>
> (5.794–802)

If we listen to Satan as he wishes to be heard, his speech asserts equality, freedom, and nobility of soul. He appears to demand a kind of heavenly democracy; hence, he sees the begetting of Christ, which disturbs "freedom," as the first step toward slavery. Such a challenge to omnipotence necessarily involves several other denials of constituent aspects of God; the most ironic denial is of omniscience. By removing his powers to the north, Satan implies that God is both localized and short in sight. If Satan can hide from God, God is neither omniscient nor omnipresent. Once God is stripped of power, knowledge, and ubiquity, Satan's rebellion is justifiable.

These denials are accomplished by operating in the cracks of language, upon those edges of meaning which shade off into their opposites. "Who can in reason then *or* right" makes of right reason two separate entities. The next line assumes that separation, and the meaning of *right* slides from "correct" to "privileged." The following line does the same thing to "equal"; for, "If in power and splendor less, / In freedom equal" grants the quantitative superiority of God's power without making it qualitatively different from Moloch's. Satan has, in moving his hosts to the north, implicitly recognized God's superiority. But at least we may agree that in freedom all the inhabitants of heaven are equal? "Equally free." The sophistry is marvelous; one misused term slides into another and that into a third. The whole complex maintains its unity, not through the primary meaning of words, but through their connotative similarities. Each term is granted, singly, to admit God's superiority, yet the focus of any single term implies its separateness from all the others. The motive for this slight of tongue is pride: "Our being ordain'd to govern, not to serve." If all are chiefs, where are the Indians? If an ordination took place, who, among equals, did the ordaining?

In book 5, Milton's readers are not required to penetrate Satan's sophistry alone; for Abdiel, the angel faithful to God, steps forward to reassemble fragmented language—to rejoin "right" and "reason." To Abdiel, Satan's speech is an "argument blasphémous, false and

proud" (809); and, in the next thirty-seven lines, he restores lan-
guage as a firm tool for knowing. Abdiel's speech destroys Satan
utterly, but that speech is not in book 1. Before we hear the "one
just man" refute Satan, we must deal with Satan's rhetoric with only
the undramatic narrative voice to aid us. Milton intrudes often to
correct our errors and point out the vast contradictions in Satan's
rhetoric. Yet, because we listen to the siren voice and because our
sensibilities accept what reason rejects, the reader is tempted be-
fore Eve meets Satan.

Satan's being depends upon this disjunction between connotation
and denotation; he is literally a creature of verbal reflections. God's
word creates; Satan's words miscreate. Although the perceptive
reader can validate this assertion at almost any point in *Paradise
Lost*, the most graphic illustration is a brief scene in book 10. When
Satan returns to hell, he speaks to the assembled host, addressing
them by their heavenly titles: "Thrones, Dominations, Princedoms,
Virtues, Powers" (460). They respond to this miscreative naming by
becoming "complicated monsters, head and tail, / Scorpion and Asp,
and *Amphisbaena* dire" (523–24). Satan's words are "creative" in
hell, for in his upside-down language Thrones and Dominations are
Scorpions and Asps. And, as his language asserts its miscreative
power, it reflects back upon him. The shout of praise is "A dismal
universal hiss." The demons naming is also effective; Satan loses his
"Star-bright" shape and becomes a "monstrous Serpent."[12]

Throughout *Paradise Lost* the power of language is not denied but
asserted. All the "swelling Epithets" are stripped away, the varnish
is wiped from the "Harlot's cheek," and appearance is reunited with
reality. Poetic language shares in the poem's central paradox: sepa-
rate beings exist only within the ultimate unity of God. Satan's
metaphors are after all only similes; the unity of sacred metaphor is a
function of deity. That all of Satan's basic assertions come true,
ironically, attests to God's ultimate allness. Tactically, Satan is free
to choose his own path; and his choice may be short or long, painful
or pleasant, creative or destructive. But, strategically, the path will
end where God wills; for all roads lead to the exit provided by the
creator. Independence in Milton's system is chaos. Satan's chosen
role is a thankless one. Such a vision does little for man's vanity. At
best, our accomplishments are those of a clever rat in a maze with
one exit. But the distance between the wisdom of God and the
wisdom of man is at least as great as that between the wisdom of man

and the wisdom of a rat. God is omnipresent in time as well as space. Endings are beginnings. There is play in the tactical rope, but God holds the end.

For Satan, and for many modern readers, the lesson of *Paradise Lost* is unacceptable. Satan sees his free will only in terms of self-assertion; therefore, he cannot understand that a decision to obey is equally an exercise of freedom. That the freedom of obedience must be endlessly repeated whereas a single disobedient act is decisive, is savage, too demanding for frail mankind. God provides Christ so that man may fail and yet live. Only the hard-of-heart who continually refuse grace are beyond salvation. The central lesson of *Paradise Lost* has an almost Orwellian ring: obedience is freedom; independence is slavery. Outside the confines of Milton's epic, man is at liberty to prefer any causative system that he desires, or even to assert the absence of causation. Whether man is thus better served or satisfied is moot. Certainly, Milton's great argument is humbling, if not humiliating; but such is his goal.

## IV   *The Debate in Hell*

Falling and separation are the major images of evil in Milton's epic; and, fittingly, Satan's "progress" from the brightest angel who is the one closest to God's high throne, to a serpent groveling on the deep throne of hell sets the limits of evil. His physical separation and his fall, manifested by the deterioration of his form, correspond precisely to his moral fall. The geography of *Paradise Lost* is moral: high is good, low is evil; unity is good, separation is evil. Falling and separation produce darkness; ascension and unity generate light. The interplay of these basic images informs and emphasizes the coherence of Milton's vision. Between the extremes of hell and heaven, the patterns hold; but, at their extremes, opposites meet. God is "dark with excessive bright," and hell is "darkness visible." Milton is not suggesting that far enough west is east, that evil enough is good; rather, Satan, hell, and evil are reflections and parodies of God, heaven, and good.

Since God is all in all, anti-God can be only a distorted, mirror image of God. The highest point in hell is deepest below God's throne; the closest union in hell is the most isolated from good. Satan is at least partially aware of the hellish condition:

> where there is then no good
> For which to strive, no strife can grow up there
> From Faction; for none sure will claim in Hell
> Precedence, none, whose portion is so small
> Of present pain, that with ambitious mind
> Will covet more.
>
> (2. 30–35)

As always, we find a good deal of intelligence and awareness in Satan's speech; but, when we note that he gives the pronouncement from "High on a Throne of Royal State," the irony is great: his actions and words do not accord. He, in fact, "aspires / Beyond thus high" (2. 7–8) even while asserting the stupidity of downward aspiration. So taken is he with the tactical moment that he conceals strategic implications even from himself: "where there is then no good / For which to strive, no strife can grow up. . . ." The numbing political rhetoric which equates disparates by seeming to identify *strive* and *strife* mocks language as an instrument of truth. The pattern yet appears today: "Nothing to fear but fear itself"; "Not what your country can do for you but what you can do for your country." When the crisis of *Paradise Lost* comes, Satan will say to Eve, "Your fear itself of Death removes the fear" (9. 702).

Evil's second image, separation, is tied closely to the patterns of falling. God is ultimate height; any movement from Him, in any direction, is down. Conversely, since Satan is ultimate depth, movement toward his "bad eminence" is separation. When God "separates" the Son from Himself, the separation accomplishes a closer unity between creator and creation. When Satan unites sexually with Sin, the "union" produces additional separation when she gives birth to Death. That separation is followed by another sexual union between Sin and Death which entails the separation of Sin birthing the hell hounds, but that separation is reversed as they creep back into her deformed womb to gnaw upon their miscreator. This hideous feeding is the ultimate image of sexually perverse unity: a unity that is total separation from The Unity, God.

The measure of both falling and separation is time, and the time into which Satan's separation and fall have thrust him is signaled by mutability. As Milton demonstrates in early poems, one pagan consolation for death is the fact that the stuff of being returns to the soil to feed new, if lesser, life. Even that small comfort is denied Satan. His temporal framework allows no regeneration, only a descending chain of metamorphoses leading to a disgusting pool of excrescence. But, as *Paradise Lost* opens, the devils have still a compelling grandeur: for each of the speakers is the father of a type that has spoken in every council from the cave to the United Nations. Milton had doubtless heard them all in Cromwell's government, for he holds them up as the great originals of political man.[13] From the ectypes in literature, history, and life, Milton reads back to his archetypes; and each of the speakers is a fragment of Satan and so an aspect of hell. *Paradise Lost* is, therefore, the supreme mirror for magistrates.

Each devil is like one of the proverbial blindmen investigating an elephant. The first speaker in the debate is the embodiment of Satan's basic challenge to God: Moloch is blind, brute force: "His trust was with th' Eternal to be deem'd / Equal in strength" (2. 46–47). For Moloch, God is force; and having lost in the first ramming of heads, he advises running again against the wall. If his head does not split, he may perhaps cause some vibration in the stone; if his skull fractures, the wall may be stained with his very small brain, "Which if not Victory is yet Revenge" (2. 105). Moloch is the mindless pattern we have met in the jingle, "Better dead than Red." He is pure visceral response, Satan's adrenal gland. But the strength of God can no longer be doubted. Moloch's threats are impressive to "less than Gods"; God has laughed at force and has flicked Moloch away.

The challenge of Moloch to omnipotence carries with it a denial of omnipresence and omniscience; and Moloch's failure suggests that all three attributes of God are real. Belial, the second speaker, lover of vice and lewdness, is quite willing to restore God. His refutation of Moloch, which ultimately boils down to a sniveling, "Better Red than dead," is clothed in gorgeous language; for, as a poet, Belial is second only to Satan:

> Or could we break our way
> By force, and at our heels all Hell should rise
> With blackest Insurrection, to confound
> Heav'n's purest Light . . .
> . . . . . . . . . . . . . . . . . . . .
> for who would lose,
> Though full of pain, this intellectual being,
> Those thoughts that wander through Eternity,

> To perish rather, swallow'd up and lost
> In the wide womb of uncreated night . . .
> . . . . . . . . . . . . . . . . . . . . . . . . . . . . . . . . . . .
>                                 or from above
> Should intermitted vengeance arm again
> His red right hand to plague us?

(2. 134–74)

The poetry is the more powerful in that Belial almost speaks truth. He restores to God every attribute save ultimate causation, and upon that single denial any demonic effort must now be grounded: "what hope the never-ending flight / Of future days may bring, what chance, what change / Worth waiting . . ." (2. 221–23). By separating God and Fate, Belial holds out the pattern of Prometheus. It is true that the company is in a bad way at the moment, but perhaps the world's great age may sometime begin anew. The tyrant Zeus will be cast down, and the long-sufferers will be freed. Against Belial's last hope, the flat words that God speaks are fatal, "And what I will is Fate."

The wished separation between God and Fate is Belial's strategic fantasy; but, in more immediate terms, he hopes for changes in the tactical situation. Perhaps the pains of hell will diminish; perhaps angelic forms can become enured to pain; perhaps the angels will mutate and hell become familiar. In this hope, the irony of free will is clear: Belial desires to become a demon whose natural element is fiery pain. Satan has chosen to separate himself from God; and, since separation is fall, he has chosen his fall. He will choose the form of plebeian angel when he approaches Uriel; he will choose the form of carrion crow and the motion of a thief when he enters the garden; and, finally, he will choose to take the form of serpent. The meshings of assertive will and ultimate ordination are frightening, and Milton means them to be so. Rough hew them how we will, God guides our ends: "All is as ever in the great task master's eye." Belial counsels acceptance of God's will, but his acceptance is informed by fear and sloth, not by love. He recognizes that, for the moment, God and Fate appear to be one. The war makes him hesitate to burn his fingers again, but it has taught him nothing of the true nature of heavenly fire.

The next speaker, Mammon, likes Moloch's advice no better than did Belial; but, since Mammon is a thoroughgoing materialist, the conjectures about Fate, Free Will, and Destiny strike him as ludi-

crous: "him to unthrone we then / May hope, when everlasting Fate
shall yield / To fickle Chance, and *Chaos* judge the strife"
(2. 231–33). Even though he does not reject the thought that God and
Fate may be separate, he is not really interested. Suppose God
should allow them to return to heaven, what then? Such forgiveness
is to Mammon that of the master who agrees to put the collar back
on a runaway slave. God would still be envied; obedience would still
be servile; and who would wish to spend eternity "in worship paid /
To whom we hate?" He advocates letting God have heaven; for, if
hell is dark, so is God's throne. Moreover, gold and jewels are in
hell, and "What can Heav'n show more?" For Mammon, the only
reality is appearance. Perhaps, he suggests, Belial is partially right;
angelic substance may conform to the hellish environment and so
end pain. Mammon concludes by asserting their place in time:

> how in safety best we may
> Compose our present evils, with regard
> Of what we are and where, dismissing quite
> All thoughts of War.
>
> (2. 280–83)

The hosts of hell are pleased, for their desire is to build an empire
"In emulation opposite to Heav'n" (2. 298). Their hope is to produce
a mirror image in which right is left, up is down, and to discover in
that reversal that pain has become pleasure.

Had Mammon's counsel prevailed, Milton's story would have a
very different ending. Ages of earth history could have been
skipped, for Mammon's proposal is just the situation that will obtain
after the second coming of Christ. But there is slack in the temporal
rope so that the devils are "free" to increase their own damnation
and to test the will of man. Neither Satan nor Beëlzebub is willing to
rest. So long as there is slack, so long will they race to its limit,
though they strangle themselves in the event. Ironically, in order to
divert attention from Mammon's plan, Beëlzebub acknowledges all
those aspects of God against which they have rebelled:

> For he, be sure,
> In highth or depth, still first and last will Reign
> Sole King, and of his Kingdom lose no part
> By our revolt. . . .
>
> (2. 323–26)

The rebels and the debate are at an impasse. Moloch is wrong: their power cannot disturb God. Belial is wrong; fate will never replace God as causative principle. Mammon is wrong; God will not permit hell to rival heaven. Satan has already been reduced to "ever plotting how the Conqueror least / May reap his conquest" (2.338–39). The self-mockery is unintentional but complex; for, since the "debate" in hell has been settled by Satan and Beëlzebub before the council began, appearance and reality have been totally sundered. Glorious armed rebellion against their peers is now reduced to guerilla activity against puny man at the "utmost border" of God's kingdom.

The motive for Satan's enmity to man is to pester God; to

> interrupt his joy
> In our Confusion, and our Joy upraise
> In his disturbance; when his darling Sons
> Hurl'd headlong to partake with us, shall curse
> Thir frail Original, and faded bliss,
> Faded so soon.
>
> (2. 371–76)

Satan casts man as but a pawn in a game far higher than Eden, and thus Satan's success, so drastic from the human point of view, is in cosmic terms but a skirmish. And a tactical victory for Satan nevertheless fits into the larger strategic defeat: "But thir spite still serves / His glory to augment" (2. 385–86).

In spite of all the glorious rhetoric, the debate has come full circle in that the war which Moloch proposed is still the goal, for the only possible plan is to attempt a return to reality; and, since the only reality is God's light, there remains but the choice of who is to place a bell around the cosmic cat's throat. Satan, of course, volunteers; and his heroism is a parody of Christ's sacrifice. The contradictions in Satan's actions will be pointed out, much to Satan's embarrassment, by the guardians of Eden. The best the demons can achieve is "God-like imitated State" (2. 511), but Milton reminds us that fallen man is even less admirable: "Devil with Devil damn'd / Firm concord holds," only men are incapable of honor.

Earth, before the fall, is patterned after heaven; as Beëlzebub hopes, it is a tempered version of the precincts of felicity. Satan's plan is to reverse the image so that it will be the shadow of hell, and he succeeds to a remarkable extent. The tasks set for fallen angels to perform in Satan's absence constitute a catalogue of man's highest deeds. The first Olympic games are in hell; the great tournaments of chivalry are patterned upon demonic play; even the softer arts find their originals in hell—singers, philosophers, poets; and the heroic explorations of far seas and distant continents that ignited the Renaissance imagination are anticipated by Satan's minions. In this description of hell, Milton asserts the same unswerving, grim truth that Christ articulates in *Paradise Regained:* the world, as a goal, is vanity.

With Satan's departure from hell, the lowest of Milton's three stages is nearly completed. The hellish archetype for man and earth is clear:

> A Universe of death, which God by curse
> Created evil, for evil only good,
> Where all life dies, death lives, and Nature breeds,
> Perverse, all monstrous, all prodigious things,
> Abominable, inutterable, and worse
> Than Fables yet have feign'd. . . .
>
> (2. 622–27)

The key word is "perverse"; the reality of hell is a "turning the wrong way" of heaven. Pandemonium is a mad child's model of God's palace; Satan is self-mocked—he is a twisted miniature, not of God, but of the great angel Lucifer. Should man choose to follow Satan's pattern, the first mockery will be of human nature.

## V  Sin and Death

Each of the speakers in the debate has a double aspect; for, although they each achieve some individuality, they are also particular facets of the adversary, Satan.[14] As such, they become almost allegorical figures: Moloch is Hate; Belial, Sloth; Mammon, Greed. In doublings of this kind, Milton finds a technique for presenting the cosmic paradoxes that plague the plot of *Paradise Lost.* The original pattern for such double unity is, as with each aspect of existence, heavenly. The Father and Son are at once individual and unified; and God is both the many and the one, both transcendent and immanent, both everywhere and nowhere. He is the still point whose circumference is infinity. Books 1 and 2 show the mirrored, perverse echo of that divine pattern. As God is made up of all virtues, Satan is composed of contending fragments of evil. Those fragmented aspects of the devil were represented in Medieval art (and in Spenser) by the seven deadly sins: wrath, pride, lust, envy, sloth, avarice, and gluttony. The concluding episode of book 2 compresses those many evils into three personalities: Satan, Sin, and Death. Respectively, they represent cause, act, and effect; and their chaotic family tree is an obvious perversion of God's own begetting of the Son. Presumably, the Son is produced by a mystical separation of deity, a separation that yet constitutes an undivided whole. The begetting Sin is the hellish version; and, when Adam begets Eve, the three levels of being, suited to the three levels of the stage, are ready for action.

Each pair of doubles, God-Son, Satan-Sin, and Adam-Eve, produces offspring: Holy Ghost, Death, and Cain-Abel. The heavenly birth is perfect; the hellish birth, perverse; and the earthly birth, ambiguous. Both Holy Ghost and Death are absolutes; Cain and Abel are potentials. In their diverse ends is set the pattern for mankind: part good, part evil; part faithful, part disobedient; part murderer and part victim. In a third "trinity," God, Mary, and Christ, the possibility of eternity will be restored in time. Adam and Eve, created in the image of Father and Son, chose to pattern themselves on Satan and Sin. Christ as second Adam will be born of Mary, second Eve; the reversed image will be renewed. The Christian era is not to be a return to the Edenic; instead, it is a progress toward a second blissful seat.

The earthly version of diverse unity makes possible the drama of books 9 and 10. Adam is a man complete, but he is also the "masculine" aspects of mankind: courage, strength, and reason. Eve is a complete human and also the "feminine" qualities: beauty, sensuousness, and fancy. But since we are yet far from book 9, the point to note is that, for each movement in hell, the lowest stage, parallel ones exist in heaven and upon earth, the other two stages. Moloch is a fierce captain and the personification of Satan's rage. Sin is Satan's daughter-mistress and his act of disobedience. Christ is the Son and the creative aspect of monotheos. And Eve is both the mother of Adam's children and untutored fancy.

The first trinity—Satan, Sin, and Death—shown to the reader is the demonic one. As a person, Sin has never seen Pandemonium; as a characteristic, she dominates the entire structure. So far as we have been told, no death has occurred in hell; yet Death sits within hell's gate. Both Satan and the reader are too busy to trouble much about these paradoxes. When Satan first sees Sin and Death, he fails to recognize his daughter or to acknowledge his son. To Sin, he says he has never yet seen "Sight more detestable than him and thee" (2. 745). The reader shares his reaction as he recognizes the dim, primordial monsters as obscenities locked from the light of civilization. Satan and the reader have a considerable problem. If Satan recognizes his offspring and so acknowledges Sin and Death as parts of his own being, the last pretense of respectability must be dropped. If he refuses the kinship, he will remain locked in hell. If Satan and Death should fight, as they nearly do, the battle would be between primary aspects of Satan's own being. Whoever won would, in winning, destroy himself.

Satan is, therefore, quite literally damned if he does and damned if he doesn't. Until a being knows himself, he knows nothing; but, in recognizing Sin and Death, Satan admits to his own perverse deformity. Satan has no leisure for such metaphysical speculation because he is bound by the tactical demands of a temporal creature: he wishes to get out of hell, and to accomplish that he would admit anything. When this "detestable" pair becomes "Dear Daughter" and "fair Son" (2. 817–18), the agility of Satan's mind is a measure of its shallowness; for although he has just protested complete ignorance of the pair, he now asserts that they are the reason for his effort: "I come no enemy, but to set free / From out this dark and dismal house of pain, / Both him and thee . . ." (2. 822–24). Satan, of course, thinks that he is lying; but the irony is that, in strategic terms, he tells the truth. Since they are thirds of his being, he, in striving to free himself, seeks their freedom. When Satan leaps into chaos, he thinks that he has left Sin, Death, and hell behind. Only later does he realize that he himself is hell: Satan as cause contains both act (Sin) and result (Death) in his every fiber.

Sin knows more than does her father, for she is quite literally Satan's act. God has told her to keep hell locked; but since Sin is disobedience, her granting of the passage to Satan follows from her very nature. The speech in which she affirms her allegiance to her creator, father, and husband is a compound of psalm and prayer, of liturgy and confessional:

> Thou art my Father, thou my Author, thou
> My being gav'st me; whom should I obey

> But thee, whom follow? thou wilt bring me soon
> To that new world of light and bliss, among
> The Gods who live at ease, where I shall Reign
> At thy right hand voluptuous, as beseems
> Thy daughter and thy darling, without end.
>
> (2. 864–70)

Her key opens the gate of hell upon chaos: "The Womb of nature
and perhaps her Grave" (2. 911). On the narrative level, we cannot
but admire Satan's courage in venturing into the unknown; but,
symbolically, he is again the fool. He leaves hell, the perversion of
form, for chaos, the absence of form. It is significant that he falls in
the vacuum of space; his natural motion is down, not up (2. 933 ff.).
He is saved by chance, the most mindless of the cogged wheels of
causation.[15]

Satan's encounter with Chaos and Night repeats the meeting with
Sin and Death, but he has developed considerable skill in impro-
vising. He at once proposes a partnership with Chaos: "Yours be th'
advantage all, mine the revenge" (2. 987); but Satan again blinks the
implications of a situation. Chaos objects to the existence of hell as
much as to that of earth; to Chaos, all form is hateful, including
Satan's. In allying himself with Chaos, Satan makes a pact that will
lead him through downward mutations until he becomes a thirsting
serpent upon hell's throne. As for his promise to Chaos, it is at once
violated; for the "broad and beat'n way" with which Sin and Death
link hell and earth stretches over Chaos. And yet, as always, there is
an irony. Satan will unwittingly do his best to remove form from
matter; he has begun that destruction upon himself.

When, at the close of book 2, Satan, "Accurst, and in a cursed
hour," speeds toward earth, Milton has completed his nether stage.
We read no more about literal, physical hell until book 10, and then
little that is new is added. In book 4, Satan discovers the psychologi-
cal dimensions of hell; but, essentially, when he reaches the uni-
verse, one of man's alternatives is complete, one pattern for earth:
one system of glory, honor, love, economics, politics, and
philosophy. The pattern is strong, and Milton has given Satan good
lines. If the Devil were a man; if God were another man; if the
bounds of the possible in action and in knowledge were those prob-
abilities and relativities which circumscribe our own lives; if reality
were limited by sensory preception—if all this were true, then, like
our archetype Adam, we might say: "full of doubt I stand, / Whether

I should repent me now of sin" (12. 473–74). Satan is a magnificent Romantic Hero; and, were his context ours, we might well side with him.

But—none of the "ifs" holds. The world of Satan's actions is a world of absolutes. Milton's cosmos is closed. God is both God and good. God can make an infinitely heavy rock and lift it with ease. What grandeur exists in hell, what power "To suffer, as to do" (2. 199), is but the partially dimmed, partly ruined creation of God, self-damaged. Satan is not Tennyson's Ulysses reaching for the Pillars of Hercules; he is much closer to the motiveless malignancy of Shakespeare's Iago. It is a measure of Milton's confidence in the powers of the heavenly muse to say, and of the fit audience to understand, that he shows us Satan, not like the hideous giant of Dante's *Inferno*, but as a compound of heroically futile humanity.[16]

## VI   God

Much that we know of Milton's God and of heaven we learn as we see the perversions of hell. From distortions and inversions we intuit the original pattern. But, since God and Satan are different orders of being and since the central fact about God is that He is beyond comprehension, Milton takes us directly to heaven. The progress from the lowest to the highest of the three stages is skillfully accomplished, but not without great effort. We have journeyed with Satan, up through chaos, to the place where three paths meet. Behind him is hell, above extends "Empyreal Heav'n," and "fast by hanging in a golden Chain / This pendant world." Milton too has flown out of hell, with some relief:

> Thee I revisit now with bolder wing,
> Escap't the *Stygian* Pool, though long detain'd
> In that obscure sojurn, while in my flight
> Through utter and through middle darkness borne.
>
> (3. 13–16)

We note that Milton's effort parallels Satan's and that the identity of author and character is startlingly close. The invocation to light not only renews the vigor of poetic inspiration so vastly expended in books 1 and 2 but also serves to recover Milton's own identity. The sense of relief in "thee I revisit safe" reads as if the limits of Satan's vision had almost become Milton's own, and the personal digression

(3. 22–55) is a reassertion of Milton's humanity. As he severs himself from Satan's strength, there is a moment of self-pity. The adversary has returned to light; primal, uncorrupted Eden lies before him: "Day, or the sweet approach of Ev'n or Morn, / Or sight of vernal bloom, or Summer's Rose, / Or flocks, or herds, or human face divine" (3. 42–44). All these, God's "Book of knowledge fair," Satan will see; but John Milton is blind. The identity of symbol and meaning which makes of light an icon of God must for him be forever separate. The essence of mythic vision is that moral qualities inhere in physical objects. As fallen men, we see a tree as only a tree; the physical remains, but the moral is lost. For Milton, the opposite has happened; he senses the moral, but its physical manifestation is beyond his reach. Like Tiresias and Phineus, he sees only with the third eye. If he cannot now visit the realm of physical light which will comfort and torment Satan, Milton can pray for Celestial light to "Shine inward, and the mind through all her powers/ Irradiate, there plant eyes" (3. 52–53). The second way of knowing God, through sight of His creations, is impossible for the poet.

Milton masters his own disability and makes of it an emblem for mankind, for his physical blindness becomes metaphorically the blindness heired from Adam. And yet light is the best, if not the only, metaphor for God:

> Hail holy Light, offspring of Heav'n first-born,
> Or of th' Eternal Coeternal beam
> May I express thee unblam'd? since God is Light,
> And never but in unapproached Light
> Dwelt from Eternity, dwelt then in thee,
> Bright effluence of bright essence increate.
>
> (3. 1–6)

"Holy Light," inspiration, bears the same relationship to God that physical light has to its source. Light cannot exist without flame, nor flame without light, but the two are not identical. In this metaphor, Milton finds a satisfactory description of the relationship between God-the-immutable and God-the-creator, and thus between God the Father and God the Son.

The culmination of the metaphor, "Bright effluence of bright essence increate," is itself dazzling. At first reading, the words "effluence," "essence," "increate" blur intellectually, almost as though we had come upon sudden light in total darkness. At a second reading, the meanings can be deciphered: from an uncreated (hence eternal) flame flows brightness, unconsumed with that by which it is nourished. Milton's image suggests a standard myth: the pitcher that is always full; the loaf that renews itself; the purse with infinite golden coins; the loaves and fishes. But, since the idea is compacted almost beyond recognition, we cannot see if we look at it directly; only by turning to one side, shading our eyes, can its meaning be realized. Milton helps us do so by picking up the idea of "flow" from "effluence":

> Or hear'st thou rather pure Ethereal stream,
> Whose Fountain who shall tell? before the Sun,
> Before the Heavens thou wert, and at the voice
> Of God, as with a Mantle didst invest
> The rising world of waters dark and deep,
> Won from the void and formless infinite.
>
> (3. 7–12)

Light and water are to herdsmen, to farmers, and to dwellers in a dry land the most essential, the most longed for, the happiest events of all. But is is not light and water; it is light as water; for it was light that invested the rising world. The two symbols are mingled as Milton gives thanks for his escape from the "Stygian Pool" and from "utter" and "middle darkness."

But, for a Puritan of any kind, God is not satisfactorily described as light and water; He is a voice, the omnific word. And so, from ultimate light and height, from a perspective so removed from the earthly creature that past, present, and future are simultaneously visible, God speaks.[17] Whatever the reader may have expected Milton's God to sound like, whether thunder or harmony, he is scarcely prepared for what he gets. God is jeering at Satan. All that pain, cerebration, deceit, and bravery in the first two books of the poem are, to God, a joke.

To the extent that God is like His creation, the laugh seems monstrous. But of course that is just the point: God the Father is strikingly unlike His creatures. His very being violates all the rules of psychology and physics. For God, there is absolutely no drama, for drama depends upon change, and change upon time. God is both atemporal and immutable; hence, He must be radically alien to human understanding; and, from our perspective, God is a monster.

Romantic critics, from William Blake to William Empson, having discovered this obvious point, have cried out against Milton and his God; for the Romantic is bound to prefer a god he has created to one who has created him.

Milton does little to soften the shock, and there is scarcely a simile in God's speech. As nearly as possible, the divine voice is stripped of both ornament and connotation. As we have seen, Satan operates in the connotative cracks of language and so speaks as a poet; but God strikes the keys of meaning as squarely as possible with so writhing a medium as English. The result is as unwelcome to our poetic sensibilities as was His laughter to our self-respect. God's argument moves swiftly forward, but upon flat feet; fault, free will, independence of act and foreknowledge, the dangers of freedom, and the distinction between angelic and human disobedience. His speech is all summary—the circumstance, the detail, the drama, the sensuous bridge to understanding are left out. Such poetic devices are present in the language of Christ, of Raphael, and of Milton, but not in the Father's speech.

And yet the conclusion of God's first speech is tender: "Mercy first and last shall brightest shine" (3. 134). It is important to note that mercy is a ray coming from God, not God Himself. The ways of God are justifiable to men, not God Himself. The primary way is, of course, Christ, the light of the world, who links man and God: "Most glorious, in him all his Father shone / Substantially express'd" (3. 139–40). As "substance," Christ can take part in the drama, though the suspense is not great. He pleads with his Father almost as if the issue were in doubt, or as if he were in ignorance of it. But, since the heavenly "debate" lacks tension, we are likely to find Satan's consultations a good deal more exciting.

God's handling of the stumbling block of Calvinist theology is remarkable. There are the elect: "Some I have chosen of peculiar grace/ Elect above the rest; so is my will" (3. 183–84). Some are predestined for heaven, but everyone else has the chance to choose heaven:

> The rest shall hear me call, and oft be warn'd
> Thir sinful state, and to appease betimes
> Th' incensed Deity while offer'd grace
> Invites; for I will clear thir senses dark.

(3. 185–88)

God promises grace to all who will accept it: "Light after light well us'd they shall attain,/ And to the end persisting, safe arrive" (3. 196–97). Only the hard-of-heart, "They who neglect and scorn," are excluded from salvation: "none but such from mercy I exclude" (3. 202).

Since these twenty lines are the theological center of *Paradise Lost*, let us see what God's words say in the plainest sense possible. Some men will be saved by "peculiar grace," for God exercises his right to be arbitrary. To say that He should not do so, or that such a selection is inconsistent, is to deny the prerogatives of omnipotence—the decision is not subject to review or appeal. Here, then, is one half of the dreaded predestination in the baldest possible terms; but what of the other half? As some souls are predestined for heaven, are others predestined for hell? The answer is a clear NO. Syntactically, "the rest," which includes all except those chosen of peculiar grace, are to have their senses cleared so that they can perceive those things necessary for salvation. Within all men will be placed God's "Umpire *Conscience*," so that they may judge correctly the honest data presented by their cleared senses and comprehended by their softened hearts. Thus, the saved are composed of two groups: the arbitrarily elect and as many of the rest as choose within the realm of grace to seek God.

Some are damned, but their damnation is not willed by God. Possessing conscience and sufficient information, they choose sin. Once they have chosen sin, God augments the decision. The hard are hardened; the blind are blinded more. In eating the fruit, Adam incurred for all mankind both blindness and hardness of heart; but God, through Christ, offers to repair that loss. Those who refuse Christ re-enact Adam's disobedience and so increase (and make individual) their inherited share of Adam's guilt. Ontogeny repeats phylogeny; the ectype repeats the pattern of the archetype.

And yet nothing of man's damnation is foreordained: "Foreknowledge had no influence on their fault" (3. 118); "free they must remain, / Till they enthrall thesmelves" (3. 124–25). The basic theology seems clear enough. God, at least, is satisfied and turns his attention to the means of softening hearts and of clearing vision in fallen mankind. And he also turns to the final conundrum expressed with terrible succinctness in "Die hee [man] or Justice must" (3. 210). Christ will play a dual role; he is to judge mankind and to suffer the punishment of his own pronouncement. The wages of sin

must be paid so that at last "wrath shall be no more / Thenceforth,
but in [God's] presence Joy entire" (3. 264–65).

The process of choosing a hero to battle encroaching destruction
is the original pattern unwittingly mocked in the council of Pan-
demonium, and there are several important differences between
God's original and Satan's copy. Christ goes in love; Satan goes in
hate. Christ knows what he is about to sacrifice; Satan goes in ignor-
ance. Satan's journey is an escape from the physical torment of hell;
Christ deserts utter beatitude. Such is the distinction between the
divine pattern and its demonic shadow. The hymn which closes the
visit to heaven (3. 372–415) is itself timeless, for it summarizes
the ineffable nature of God, the elevation of the Son, the creation
of the universe, the war in heaven, and the end of strife between
mercy and justice. To the eternal choir, Milton adds his own voice:

> O unexampl'd love,
> Love nowhere to be found less than Divine!
> Hail Son of God, Savior of Men, thy Name
> Shall be the copious matter of my Song
> Henceforth, and never shall my Harp thy praise
> Forget, nor from thy Father's praise disjoin.
>
> (3. 410–15)

And so farewell to heaven.

## VII  *Earth*

Just as Milton escaped with difficulty the limitations of hellish
vision at the end of book 2, so now he carries with him to earth
something of God's atemporal vision. As Satan approaches the
created universe, he passes a region to be known as the Paradise of
Fools. Milton sees from this dramatic moment far into the future
when those who seek God wrongly will be swirled into that limbo.
Such vision, which sees both the history and the future of an object,
place, or person in its present dramatic moment, is the gift of the
heavenly muse. Since the reality of war in heaven is beyond human
comprehension, books 5 and 6 demonstrate the gulf between human
understanding and divine action. The reader is likely to be disap-
pointed in Milton's presentation of God and of heaven, for he would
prefer to find in heaven the same sense of particularity and
specificity that gives hell a three-dimensional existence. But, by

definition, that cannot be done: any heaven which human intelligence can comprehend is no heaven at all. However reluctantly, we must accept the paradox and proceed; for the central action of the poem is mundane: God's ways with mankind, not God Himself.

The earth that Milton has to present, the middle stage, differs in important ways from the earth we know.[18] It is without sin, sickness, pain—without all those elements which for modern man have served increasingly as parameters in the definition of existence. Even time differs, for we measure time by decay, whether of a spring's tension or the radioactivity of carbon or the death of a star. Unfallen earth is without decay; and, logically, the esthetic problem Milton faces is insoluble. His "failure" with heaven is not fatal to the poem; but, since a similar failure with earth would be, he must present a believable Eden. If the poem is to succeed, Adam, Eve, and earth must have a sensuous reality which a fallen reader can perceive only through time. Milton's solution is ingenious, successful, and illogical.

To present immaculate Eden to fallen man, Milton makes use of a complex system of points of view.[19] The primary "lens" is that of the inspired bard who incorporates the Classical vision into his Christian vision. In familiar fashion, this incorporation permits an intricate system of typological relationships that add temporal complexity to Biblical myth. We see in every event the long chain which leads through time to eternity, but the familiar equations also allow us to see in Satan's actions the future history of a fallen world.

The major voice of the epic is frequently interrupted by a persona based firmly in seventeenth-century England: line 193 of book 4 is a characteristic example. After presenting Satan's entrance to Eden in images consonant with Biblical and bardic omniscience, Milton asserts: "So since into his Church lewd Hirelings climb." The speaker is a polemicist who is in command of the rich vituperation of the pamphlet wars. The surprising anachronism defines the relationship between myth and history, for Satan's actions are the more real in that they are repeated (validated) by Milton's contemporaries.

Within the bardic voice, uninflected by the contemporary persona, exists a dramatic point of view. In the dialogues of Adam and Eve and in the soliloquies of Satan, we forget both narrator and commentator. The epic voice is reduced to a nearly transparent equivalent of "he said"—"To whom thus *Eve* repli'd" (4. 440)—or to stage directions: "So spake our general Mother, and with eyes / Of

conjugal attraction unreprov'd . . ." (4. 492–93). Clear distinctions
in narrative voice are difficult, perhaps unnecessary. "So spake the
Fiend, and with necessity, / The Tyrant's plea, excus'd his devilish
deeds" (4. 393–94) is both stage direction and historical comment as
well as evaluation. In practice, Milton's points of view are like con-
centric circles: the dramatic is at the center; the bardic encompasses
all. *Paradise Lost* can thus shade at will from drama to lecture as
Milton increases and decreases the reader's awareness of a strong
narrative presence.

Despite the advantage that Milton gains from the interaction of
these three perspectives, a major esthetic problem remains to be
solved. Book 4 must present a garden sufficiently attractive to fal-
len man to make the reader regret its loss; but that garden must
also be beyond fallen man's comprehension. Somehow Eden must
be a place of variety and action—balanced between a climb toward
static perfection and a fall to the chaos of sin. Either extreme is, for
fallen man, a kind of paralysis; either, artistically, would be disas-
trous. In summary, Milton must present an unfallen garden to the
fallen reader, forecast the fall, and yet maintain a sinless dramatic
present.

Surprisingly, Satan allows Milton to validate the unfallen garden,
for he is in Paradise but not of it. His vision allows two gardens to be
present at the same time: the blissful bower and the bower of bliss.
Satan's responses to the perfect bower make it, in his eyes, a place of
degenerate perversion. As he settles on the Tree of Life, meditating
death and ignoring the virtue of "that life-giving Plant," Milton
comments:

> So little knows
> Any, but God alone, to value right
> The good before him, but perverts best things
> To worst abuse.
>
> (4. 201–4)

As the archetype of fallen man, Satan is both a forecast of fallen
human potential and a representative of the reader.

A close examination of the opening lines of book 4 demonstrates
Milton's manipulation of bard, self, drama, and shadow—the com-
plex manipulation of time is a primary characteristic of Milton's
reach for mythic, almost Godlike vision:

> O for that warning voice, which he who saw
> Th' *Apoclypse*, heard cry in Heav'n aloud,
> Then when the Dragon, put to second rout,
> Came furious down to be reveng'd on men,
> *Woe to the inhabitants on Earth*! that now,
> While time was, our first Parents had been warn'd
> The coming of thir secret foe, and scap'd
> Haply so scap'd his mortal snare; for now
> *Satan*, now first inflam'd with rage, came down,
> The Tempter ere th' Accuser of man-kind,
> To wreck on innocent frail man his loss
> Of that first Battle, and his flight to Hell.

(4. 1–12)

The urgent repetitions of "now" are set against the temporal complexity of "While time was." The bardic voice is here quite omniscient. To see both past and future, Milton simply looks at a different point in the continuum of time spread before him. John cried the warning in Revelation. Satan fought the original battle in heaven.

But in the dramatic now, stands Satan. Since he is, for once, removed from the necessity of role playing, he sees heaven and earth with a clarity that tortures him worse than the physical fires of hell. Past, present, and future—heaven, earth, and hell—rush in upon him. The psychomachia is more to modern taste than even the hell-bound rage against fading light, for book 4 shows us Satan as the existential hero: not the bold rebel swathed in romantic robes but an angel with broken wings, hands grasping the cage of his own ego. Satan's consciousness in book 4 is uncomfortably like our own, and we catch with Satan our first view of Eden. Like a persistent guide, his reactions color and shade all that we see. Against Satan's shadow is ranged Uriel who balances light against dark so that Adam may yet have free will. But for the reader, the sun has set; and the bright harnessed angels are distant stars of secondary efficacy. Satan's presence, his shadow upon our perceptions, constitutes almost a fourth point of view. Unlike the omniscient bard, Satan's inspiration is "darkness visible"; unlike the historical Milton, Satan is present in the drama; unlike Adam and Eve, he is fallen. As the great pattern of fallen man, Satan makes every sinner a participant in the epic.

The garden is described in terms suggestive of a womb whose

"hairy sides" deny access to strangers and so protect Adam and Eve, but a rapist is at hand. Inside the garden the wolf dwells in peaceable kingdom, but its potential violence is asserted as Satan leaps the wall. Even upon the fount "Rolling on Orient Pearl and sands of Gold" (4. 238) falls the temporal shadow: "Thus *was* this place." The innocence of the dramatic present includes Satan, and, thus, for the reader, that innocence is already lost.

Lines 257–63 are a striking case of foreshadowing through hindsight and the presence of Satan:

> Another side, umbrageous Grots and Caves
> Of cool recess, o'er which the mantling Vine
> Lays forth her purple Grape, and gently creeps
> Luxuriant; meanwhile murmuring waters fall
> Down the slope hills, disperst, or in a Lake.
> That to the fringed Bank with Myrtle crown'd,
> Her crystal mirror holds. . . .

For the worldy wise reader, Eve's lake is the mirror of Narcissus which held her until the gentle force of voice and hand drew her to Adam. Eve, herself the "mantling Vine" of Adam, is to lay forth "her purple Grape" to Satan; for, lulled by the murmuring of his voice, she returns to the "Crystal mirror" of her vanity and, crowned with Aphrodite's myrtle, yields. Although Milton might have drawn the details for this passage from a hundred conventional gardens or from his own primal dreams, they are particularly like a purified version of Spenser's Bower of Bliss (*Faerie Queene*, 2. 12. 60–62). When we remember that the special place of Adam and Eve is called the "blissful Bower," the ironic juxtaposition is attractive.

This description of Eve's lake is followed by a series of negative similes which, in denying the perversion of the present garden, bring future perversion clearly to mind. Paradise is more beautiful than the field whereon Proserpina was raped; it is more beautiful than the grove where lustful Apollo hunted Daphne; it is more secure than the sanctuary of infant Bacchus; it is safer from sedition than the paradisiacal prison atop Mount Amara. The similes represent the passion and violation made possible because of Satan's future success. Taken together, they forecast the sullied future of earthly gardens: rape, frustration, sensuality, sedition, and distrust. The Bower of Bliss will supplant the blissful Bower. Satan sees in the unfallen beauty of Eden torment and occasion for future evil;

guided by his presence, our hindsight sees the same. Eve's "wanton ringlets" and her "mysterious parts" are to Satan pornographic, for they inflame his fierce lust that is as hot as hell flames. The reactions of Satan to innocence insist that a descent to bestiality is possible. The fall has been motivated, made to seem almost inevitable, without Milton's having placed sin within either Adam or Eve. The dramatic ironies which forecast Satan's victory are projections of Satan and the reader. Guided by our own knowledge of good and evil, we respond concupiscently to details that are quite innocent.

### VIII   *Adam and Eve*

Satan's sin-jaundiced eye, Milton's typological allusions to pagan gardens, and the reader's own projected incapacities assert that Eden cannot last because it is tied passively to its masters. As "mortal" archetypes, they surely will fall; but, unlike the passive garden, Adam and Eve have free will. It is easy to think that because they have free will, they must disobey to prove it; yet, obedience is as free as rebellion. In the event itself, the fall results from the same willful and perverse misunderstanding of the relationship between obedience and command that had caused Satan to feel impaired when Christ became his announced commander. Because the hells in books 1 and 2 have shown us the inevitable result of disordering God's hierarchy, we recognize that Eve can easily make a hell of earth. The faithfulness of Abdiel, in book 5, demonstrates that obedience is possible in the face of a temptation that is greater, perhaps, than Eve's. The subservience of Christ to the Father, the Creator's love for His creatures, and the unrelenting rooting out of the disobedient from heaven set the bounds for Adam's complex role. He must obey his superiors and command his inferiors; he must know which is which. To do so, he must realize his worth without pride and accept his insufficiencies without shame. To act with unflinching love for beings both above and below his station is Adam's central task.

Adam is both like and unlike Lucifer. Lucifer was never primate of heaven; in a sense, Adam is god of earth. Until his sin, Lucifer had no opportunity to dote upon a fragment of himself; Adam has a fit consort, closer than sister or daughter:

> Two of far nobler shape erect and tall,
> Godlike erect, with native Honor clad

> In naked Majesty seem'd Lords of all,
> And worthy seem'd, for in thir looks Divine
> The image of thir glorious Maker shone.

> (4. 288–92)

Reciprocal obedience and command are innate. Adam and Eve are

> Not equal, as thir sex not equal seem'd;
> For contemplation hee and valor form'd,
> For softness shee and sweet attractive Grace,
> Hee for God only, shee for God in him.

> (4. 296–99)

Inevitably, Milton seems today a male chauvinist. Eve's very crea-
tion and form are inferior to Adam's. She is fancy; Adam, reason;
Eve is body; Adam, mind. In Platonic terms, she is all that pulls the
soul earthward; he is that which aspires to heaven. But these
dichotomies, so easy for us, are not present in the garden. There,
contemplation is not antithetical to softness, nor valor to grace. Eve
and Adam are as complementary as flower and fruit: "So hand in
hand they pass'd" (4. 321). For Milton, the war between flesh and
spirit is not a divine creation. The conflict is the result of, not the
cause of, the fall. The mode of the garden is myth, not psychological
realism.

In myth, a perfect congruity exists between the individual who
represents a function and that which is represented; but, in realism,
the bearer and the function are often at odds. If we read the charac-
terizations of Adam and Eve realistically, the charges of liberated
women against *Paradise Lost* are powerful. But such a reading mis-
construes the poem's mode, and is, at the same time, inevitable, for
one result of the fall is our loss of mythic perception. As heirs of
Adam, we sever appearance and reality, character and function,
tenor and vehicle. But a third mode, one inferior in power to both
myth and realism, can serve as a bridge between the two; for, in
allegory, the disunity of character and function is set aside without
being denied. We read as if there were no conflict between concre-
tion and universal.[20] Thus, momentarily, we satisfy our instincts for
unity without violating our empirical censor. Milton has a difficult
problem. Only myth can reify Eden, but myth is precisely the mode
of perception beyond fallen man's ability. A realistic reading is in-
evitable, yet such a reading makes a vicious monster of God, a petty

tyrant of Adam, and an idiot of Eve. Allegory is possible, but it has
neither the power of realism nor the magic of myth. Perhaps the
complicated mode of *Paradise Lost* incorporates all three ways of
knowing. By seeing the first humans as simultaneously realistic and
allegorical, we may get a glimpse of their mythic reality.

Realistically, Adam and Eve are each complete human beings;
allegorically, they are complementary halves of the human total. As
a person, Eve is sufficient to stand against Satan or anything else
(she is also free to fall). But, as the personification of the feminine
principle (sense, fancy, passion), her fall, should she separate from
Adam as masculine principle (reason), is inevitable. To separate
passion and reason and to allow passion governance constitutes
original sin. *Logically,* Milton cannot have Eve be both partial and
complete, but in books 8 and 9, *affectively,* Milton manages the
paradox. As Adam becomes uxoriousness and Eve becomes vanity,
we see the fall present in the unfallen characters.

Adam's first speech to Eve, "Sole partner and sole part of all these
joys, / Dearer thyself than all" (4. 411–12), is literally without flaw.
Since she is the only other human being, and since humans are
prime upon earth, he is merely stating an obvious, God-given situa-
tion. Dearer than all, however, is ominous. If "all" looks down the
chain of being, Adam is safe; but if "all" includes God, Adam is
terribly vulnerable. His love for Eve can disorder the chain, disturb
hierarchy, and pervert the relationship between obedience and
command. Again an allegorical reading is helpful; as reason, Adam
must order passion. The head must command the heart even as it
draws nourishment from its servant.

Eve's first speech establishes her potential flaw somewhat more
blatantly, for vanity is more natural to the feminine principle than
subservience is to the masculine. In fact, Eve's vanity is not even
dangerous so long as Adam fills his proper role. When they wed, she
willingly acknowledges that role by asserting the perfect hierarchy
of masculine and feminine: Adam is her "Guide and Head." Her
glory is her secondary relationship to Adam; for, as Adam is to God,
so is Eve to Adam. In Adam's will is Eve's peace. But, just as the
garden must grow beyond its daily bounds in order for gardeners to
have useful work, so must Eve exfoliate so that Adam's position of
command and tutelage may be purposive. The charming vignette in
which Eve recalls her creation illustrates this dynamic. As sense,
she prefers her reflected image to the reality of Adam, who is "less

fair, / Less winning soft, less amiably mild" (4. 478–79). Eve's re-
sponse is unabashedly narcissistic and yet wholly innocent. Al-
legorically, self-centeredness is her only possible response if she is
to be true to her senses. But since feminine sense must be tutored
by masculine reason, she at once obeys the voice of God and is
taught "How beauty is excell'd by manly grace / And wisdom, which
alone is truly fair" (4. 490–91).

The magnificient hymn of love which Eve presents to her hus-
band (4. 641–56) places Adam at the center of her existence. Eve's
love song is a circle that begins and ends with sweet, but there is a
tiny oversight in the catalogue of beauty which is ominous. Line 644
reads, "His orient Beams, on herb, tree, fruit, and flow'r"; and line
652, its echo, reads, "On this delightful land, nor herb, fruit,
flow'r." It is too much to say that Eve knows she can find a tree that
is sweet without Adam, and yet . . . Although the total effect of the
love song is complete tranquility, a moving static circle around
Adam, Eve at once wanders from her center by asking "wherefore
all night long shine these [stars], for whom / This glorious sight,
when sleep hath shut all eyes?" (4. 657–58). Adam trims this exfolia-
tion at once: Adam and Eve are not the goal of the universe, for the
chain of being has God at the top: Eve is to center upon Adam
(reason, the guide of sense) as Adam is to center upon God (deity,
the guide of reason). Adam knows the lesson; but, as Eve's lover, he
becomes the pupil rather than the teacher.

The glory and damnation of humanity is written in the tenuous
symbiosis between the potential contrarieties of Adam and Eve—of
heart and head, sense and reason, flesh and spirit, servant and
master, feminine and masculine. If Adam adopts Eve's mode, his
upward reach to heaven will break, and mankind's climb to God will
become a slide to hell. Their dynamic interaction—the possibility of
deserting husband for self, the possibility of yielding benign com-
mand of wife for passionate subservience—makes the fall possible.
The forbidden fruit can thus be understood as a material emblem of
the forbidden potentials of their many-sided love. Although it is
easy to feel that the fall is *inevitable* because Milton makes it seem
*possible*, we can make no greater error in reading *Paradise Lost*.

## IX  Eve's Dream

As Eve's tutor, as passion's reason, Adam can explain questions
which occur naturally to Eve. But, since the dream inspired by

Satan is extraterrestrial, it is beyond Adam's understanding. As Satan shadowed our view of the garden, he now shadows Adam's garden, Eve. In sleep, Adam explains, reason retires and fancy holds sway. Thus Eve, who is realistically farther from God than Adam is, is made doubly vulnerable: her literal reason and her allegorical reason are both asleep.[21]

The dream, in its tight economy, recalls and anticipates Eve's life from creation to fall. As when she first awakened, a voice calls her to consciousness, whereupon she mistakes an illusory form for reality: at creation, her shadow for her self; in the dream, Satan's voice for Adam's. At creation, she was led to her proper tree, Adam; in her dream, she is led to the forbidden tree. The voice of the winged one anticipates the serpent's arguments: the fruit gives wisdom; the forbidder's motives are suspect; the fruit will lead to swift, upward mutation. Finally, the balance in dream and reality is tipped by Eve's hunger. The dream ends with a flight to the clouds; the real fruit lifts Eve upon the wings of alcohol.

If, like Adam, we consider the dream to have its origins in Eve's unconscious mind, to be a breaking through the censor of repressions, three basic psychological interpretations are possible.[22] With Alfred Adler, we can read the dream as a rebellion against the dominance of Adam: Eve's soaring above the earth indicates her desire for power. Or, if, with Sigmund Freud, we consider the libido to be sexual, Eve's dream represents her desire for intercourse with an angel. But C. G. Jung's theory of syzygy best fits the context of Eve's dream, and he would read her dream in somewhat the following manner: Eve as feminine principle has buried within her a male archetype, the animus. Once she has overcome the shadow of her own ego (which she accomplishes when she leaves her reflection in the pool to follow Adam), the next threat to the development of her self is the imago of her father; and her "father" is quite literally Adam. If the ego is captured by the imago of father, it can never come to terms with its own latent masculinity, and Eve must remain narcissistic. To "cure" this psychic disorder, she should establish a real relationship with her husband to replace the fantasy relationship with her own projection. Her animus should meet Adam's anima, and the conflict should call forth the benevolent, spiritual dimensions of anima and animus. For Jung, a marriage of spirits should occur as logos unifies with eros.

As intriguing as this pseudo-Jungian explanation of the

psychological dimension of Eve's dream may seem, it must not be pushed too far. For Jung, anima and animus projections are chthonic (a disease of the self), not demonic. In *Paradise Lost*, Eve's animus is distorted by Satan. The action of the dream is neither wish fulfillment (for sex or power), nor is it the working of an ego toward the discovery of self. In the first case, Eve would already be fallen; in the second, she would have been created with the psyche of a child. But neither is the case: the dream comes from outside, not only outside Eve's psyche, but from outside the created universe. Once the fruit is eaten, the heir of original sin will dream as Adler, Freud, and Jung have conjectured; but dreams in the unfallen garden cannot be so interpreted. Here is yet another dimension of Milton's myth, for in the dream, in the quarrel between Adam and Eve, and in the fall, we can find the cosmogony of the human unconscious. When they eat the fruit, Adam and Eve grant squatters' rights in the human psyche to darkness and old night as well as to Satan, Sin, and Death.

## X  *The Education of Adam*

In the materials for *Paradise Lost*, Milton found two basic and antithetical interpretations of the fall: was the eating of the fruit the reduction of a demigod accompanied by a diminution of power and insight, or was it rather the over-abrupt rise of a childlike noble savage? In the latter case, the fall would be an addition; for man, the tragic knower, emerges from the passive cocoon of ignorant bliss into the destructive grandeur of adulthood. Such a pattern is re-capitulated in every birth; for each individual is thrust from the dark warmth of the womb into the cold light of independent existence. Such a reading is attractive from a number of perspectives because, most traditionally, it supports some version of *felix culpa:* without the fall, Christ could not have come to earth; mankind would never have become his bride; and the perfect union of human and divine would have remained an unrealized possibility in the imagination of God.[23] In more contemporary terms, such a reading of the fall shows existential man as the bloody-but-unbowed captain of his soul or, less trivially, as the squire of Bergman's *The Seventh Seal* who affirms the glory of ego in the moment of death. Classically, such a reading allows us to have Oedipus will his own banishment and so remain free even as he bows to the halter of necessity. In some measure, to read the fall as the end of childhood elevates the human form divine at the expense of a transcendent God.

Unfallen man-as-child does occur in *Paradise Lost*. When Raphael tells Adam to mind his own business instead of disputing Ptolemaic and Copernican astronomy, "to know to know no more," he suggests either that Adam's bliss is that of a fetus that is protected by the womb of the garden or that Eden is a backyard, safe from dogs and traffic, that is provided by the careful heavenly father until such time as the children's development prepares them for the great world of divine society. All such limitations of man's actions and thoughts in the garden, however, are accompanied by a promise that someday man will be equal to his curiosity. Adam is nurtured by limitations, not confined by them. The great statement of the growth which awaits obedient Adam is Raphael's tree analogy in book 5:

> So from the root
> Springs lighter the green stalk, from thence the leaves
> More aery, last the bright consummate flow'r
> Spirits odorous breathes: flow'rs and thir fruit
> Man's nourishment, by gradual scale sublim'd
> To vital spirits aspire, to animal,
> To intellectual, give both life and sense,
> Fancy and understanding, whence the Soul
> Reason receives, and reason is her being,
> Discursive, or Intuitive; discourse
> Is oftest yours, the latter most is ours,
> Differing but in degree, of kind the same.
>
> (479–90)

Here Milton has pushed the questions implicit in hexameral writings (the lore surrounding the six days of creation) in an interesting direction. At issue is not how man came to be as he is, nor even how he was before the fall; instead, the issue is what he would have become had he been obedient. The whole of creation, from angel to mineral, is subsumed in the metaphor; for all things serve their immediate superior in the hierarchy and find glory and upward mutability in that service. Mutual interdependence is the key: as root to stalk, as leaf to flower, as bloom to scent, so is Adam to Eve. For it is she who is Adam's flower: he acts upon her, and they both act upon the garden. In this downward exercise of benevolent power, they rise in service to God. Raphael's presentation of God's

plan for obedient humanity reveals no trace of restraint or confine-
ment, no diminution by law, no taint of *felix culpa*. Through hu-
manity's kinship and symbiosis with all creation, Adam and Eve may
grow to spirits: "time may come when men / With Angels may
participate" (5. 493–94).

God's creation has not been completed in six days, and the middle
stage of earth is shown to be temporary. The garden is not just a trial
by the fires of temptation; it is a kindly nursery and playground
where the beloved last born can grow and mature, can find their
own path to glory through the exercise of granted potential, can be
tutored and trained by their inalienable free will. Thus the central
lesson of Raphael's visit is not "Thou shalt not" but "Thou shalt."
The reminders of the prohibition are the lowest form of the lesson.
Man may fear God and obey lest he be thrust to hell; but the proper
service of God is in love, not terror. The details of Adam's lesson are
many, but the central issues are clear: (1) serve God in love, and all
things will be added; (2) man has not reached his potential; (3)
disobedience begets death.

The core of the lesson is Adam's understanding of loving obedi-
ence and benevolent command. Although the dialogue with
Raphael moves throughout the universe, it comes to rest on the
proper relationship between Adam and Eve: how is man to serve
and command his own rib? How can he cherish without worship-
ping, how can he love without doting, how can he be magnanimous
without pride, and how can Adam know himself without forgetting
God? If we look at the war in heaven as an answer to these and like
questions, we discover that Raphael does not emphasize defeat,
revolt, and damnation; rather, he celebrates obedience, right
reason, and love.

From a narrative point of view, the role of faithful Abdiel is too
large; he is only one among innumerable angels; certainly he does
not compare in power and majesty with Lucifer, for he is not even of
the inner council. The purpose of his large role is pedagogical, not
dramatic. By first presenting the right conduct of a creature of God
and by then setting forth the results of wrong conduct, Raphael's
narrative asserts the priority of love over fear. The war in heaven
presents Adam and the reader with two great patterns: obedience
through the love of Abdiel and revolt through the pride of Satan.
The narration of the war does not end with the gates of hell closing
upon the rebel forces but with the song of the obedient angels who

welcome the Messiah as he returns to the "right hand of bliss." That
the welcome should parallel Christ's entry to Jerusalem, "Shaded
with branching Palm" (6. 885), is more than a forecast of future
events in Christian history; it sets the context of the whole lesson:
love, humility, and obedience are the path to glory.

In sketching God's plan for upward mutability, Raphael has
fulfilled half of his mission; in informing Adam of the possible causes
and results of disobedience, he accomplishes the other half. Since
Adam has intuitive reason, he can learn in other ways than by
experience. When Raphael finishes the story of Lucifer's revolt,
Adam is no longer ignorant of evil; and the lesson completes man-
kind's possession of free will. Adam is now an adult, and he likes the
feeling. His first question is cosmogonic; and, prefacing the answer
with a brief lesson on temperance in knowledge, Raphael indulges
Adam's curiosity.

Genesis presents two quite distinct versions of creation. The first
version (Genesis 1 and the first three verses of Genesis 2) is a grand,
spare, almost aloof account. The creation is accomplished by pro-
nouncement: "Let there be . . . and there was." The creative force is
not anthropomorphic; there is no suggestion of God's hand mixing
mud figures. The only commandments for the newly created hu-
mans are positive: they are to multiply the race and to hold domin-
ion over the earth. This "priestly version," as it is called, forbids
nothing to man. The "Jahwist" version of creation (Genesis 2:4–25)
presents a very different view of man and God. Eve is created not
simply by "Male and female created he them" (Genesis 1:27), but by
the hand of God that opens the flesh of Adam to extract a rib. In the
Jahwist version, Adam and Eve are set in Eden to garden; and Adam
participates in creation by naming all living things. In this version,
we find the negative command: "But of the tree of knowledge of
good and evil, thou shalt not eat of it: for in the day that thou eatest
thereof thou shalt surely die" (Genesis 2:17).

Raphael's narration of the creation is a skillful blend of these two
Biblical versions.[24] He maintains the sense of an infinite God who
creates the universe with a word; but, when the earth calves and a
"Tawny Lion" paws to free its hindquarters from the womb of earth,
the viewpoint is earthy. The dual nature of the Creator is particu-
larly on Milton's sixth day: Man is formed from "Dust of the
ground." God into man's "Nostrils breath'd / The breath of Life."
But the "male he created" is Adam; and Eve is the "Female for

Race." The mode of the creation is that of Genesis 1; but Adam, who recounts the anthropomorphic details of Genesis 2, tells in his version what it is like to be created. As a result, Milton absorbs human perspective into Adam as narrator. In telling Raphael of his pleasure in Eve, Adam unwittingly brings the lesson back to its principal theme: obedience and command. For the first time, Adam demonstrates that he has not taken the previous lectures to heart. To him,

> so absolute she [Eve] seems
> And in herself complete, so well to know
> Her own, that what she wills to do or say,
> Seems wisest, virtuousest, discreetest, best;
> All higher knowledge in her presence falls
> Degraded, Wisdom in discourse with her
> Loses discount'nanc't, and like folly shows.
>
> (8. 547–53)

Adam's speech is ominous because the head is willingly doting upon the heart. Raphael, who is so distressed that he almost seems to act out of character as the "affable angel," contracts his brow and speaks sternly: "In loving thou dost well, in passion not" (8. 588). To this point, Adam—eager to learn, inventive, and receptive to correction—has been the perfect student; but he now becomes recalcitrant. He is only "half abash't" by the reprimand, and he begins to quibble. Since he has been commanded to "love," why should he not love Eve? Do not the angels love each other? And do they not find means to express their love in sexuality?

The *tu quoque* is too much for Raphael; his momentary sternness melts in a blush.[25] He admits that angels love each other, but he also notices that it is time for him to leave. Remember, he tells Adam, "first of all" love God, whom to love is to obey, and take heed "lest Passion sway / Thy Judgment to do aught, which else free Will / Would not admit" (8. 635–37).

Raphael's lesson ends on a dangerous note, for his last words are an assertion of Adam's present free will: "to stand or fall / Free in thine own Arbitrement it lies." Determinism is rejected. Adam understands the lesson, but he is unwilling to apply it to his own situation. The angel flies from the thick shade "up to Heav'n"; Adam returns to the bower where Eve waits. Although man is as yet unfallen, the directions are symbolic: Adam goes to his rib; Raphael goes to God.

### XI  *The Quarrel of Adam and Eve*

As Milton begins book 9, he pauses to consider the books which have preceded it. As an omniscient bard, he knows the sad event of Adam's failure to understand Raphael; but, as a postlapsarian human, he feels heavily the limitations which the fall has fixed upon all mortals. The notes of his song must now be changed to "tragic," for the disobedience which occasioned "all our woe" is at hand. As he again thinks of his predecessors in epic, he is still confident that Homer, Virgil, and even Spenser have misunderstood the "better fortitude." As a result, Milton asserts that true heroism is spiritual, not physical; and he considers Eve's loss to Satan to be a far greater tragedy than Hector's fall to Achilles. Moreover, Christ's victory over Satan in the wilderness is more heroic than his victory over Lucifer in heaven. The greatest poets have consistently misjudged the nature of heroism, and the root of their error is about to be uncovered. Almost in despair, Milton invokes the "Celestial Patroness"; for, like Samson, he now doubts his own capacities to serve as God's instrument. He is old and blind; the world, too, is senile; and the climate of England is depressing. With obvious personal effort, Milton conquers the melancholy of his subject and person. Even though his eyes are gone, and his world lost, he can still hear the muse as she brings him each night the poetry of God and man.

Sun has set upon Eden; and, with the departure of Uriel to the precincts of light, Satan returns. For a week he has hidden in the shadow of earth; now he brings hell to Eden. As a scarcely animate mist, he flows into the garden, finds the sleeping serpent (as earlier he found Eve asleep), and enters his final metamorphosis; and the form that he now willingly assumes for his tactical goal will be his true shape until the end of time. He has learned nothing since last we saw him, for the garden is again torture and temptation for him:

> the more I see
> Pleasures about me, so much more I feel
> Torment within me . . . all good to me becomes
> Bane, and in Heav'n much worse would be my state.
>
> (9. 119–23)

His grand scheme to regain heaven has come to a petty exercise in spite. The worst pain would be to be in heaven and not belong there. Satan's pride, as always, pulls him back from stasis and allows

him to go on with his futility. We are less likely to sympathize with
Satan than in earlier scenes for his rhetoric grows stale. Like a
drunkard, he rationalizes his precious infirmity:

> O foul descent! that I who erst contended
> With Gods to sit the highest, am now constrain'd
> Into a Beast, and mixt with bestial slime,
> This essence to incarnate and imbrute,
> That to the highth of Deity aspir'd.
>
> (9. 163–67)

The paradox that exists is bare: Satan is "constrain'd," a power
greater than he exists; if he chooses the form of serpent, then he has
only himself to blame. Even this degeneration is a parody of Christ,
who willingly forsook the "Courts of everlasting Day" for "a dark-
some House of mortal Clay." Since the tactical success of evil consti-
tutes its strategic downfall, Satan, after the temptation of Eve, is
only a malign shadow of a once great archangel.

At dawn, Adam and Eve rise to sing, for the last time, their
innocent praise of God. The season is yet "prime for sweetest Scents
and Airs" (9. 200), but a new test confronts Adam. The misguided
zeal of Eve as efficiency expert is to be the next step in Adam's
education, for she has sprouted a new dimension for her husband to
prune. Adam's failure to understand Eve's dream has left a vulnera-
ble spot in the garden's defenses, but Raphael's visit should have
mended the crack. Adam, theoretically, is prepared for anything
that Eve (or Satan) can devise; but, since Eve means for him "all,"
he deserts in the moment of crisis his role as mentor.

The complexity of daughter-wife-self, of the possible separation of
Adam's fancy into allegorical Eve, parallels another complexity; for,
since Adam is father-husband-self to his wife, he is the allegorical,
external form of her interior reason. C. G. Jung's theory of anima-
ànimus is useful in examining the psychological complexity of the
first domestic quarrel (about working together or separately) in
Eden. The anima is not woman, but the female aspect that is buried
in every man. The animus is the male aspect that is buried in the
dominant femininity of every woman. From lines 205 to 384,
Adam's anima battles his masculinity for supremacy, and Eve's
animus conquers her allegorical personification as femininity.
Throughout the quarrel, they switch roles. Eve, as a lower link in
the chain of being, has some justification for trying to ascend to the

next higher stage; she is supposed to grow, but Adam has no excuse for descending to Eve's level. Eve's conversation has the singleness of purpose characteristic of the animus-possessed woman, and Adam has the petulance and indecisiveness of the anima-haunted man. Eve deserts eros for a logos imago; in Adam, logos and eros battle for supremacy.

In her first speech (9. 205–25), Eve suggests a division of labor; for, as we have observed, she says that they waste time working together and that "Supper comes unearn'd" (9. 225). Her attempt at reason has led to a trap, perfectly understandable, but nevertheless her attempt is an error in Eden; for, rather than their serving God as He has commanded, she wishes to improve their service. In facing her free will, she forgets that "God doth not need / Either man's work or his own gifts" (Sonnet 19, 9–10) and the corollary of Sonnet 7, that "All is . . . As ever in my great task-Master's eye" (13–14). Again that simple, central principle of Milton's vision is the key: any accomplishment, however magnificent, that becomes its own end leads away from a proper relationship with God. Eve's planning is quite rational; her animus is in control.

Adam's response begins exactly as it should, for he opposes right reason to her false rationality. First, he praises her for her good will, "for nothing lovelier can be found . . . than to study household good" (9. 232–33); but she is guilty of an excess that demonstrates both the inferiority of her station and a proper aspiration. Adam's proper role is to guide her growth so that the mutation will reach upward, straight toward God in its climb through Adam. He explains that their labor is not valuable of itself, that God will grant children if more trimming is needed, and that labor is not a punishment but an emblem of their acquiescence to God's plan. Adam and Eve must serve God patiently. Furthermore, the very qualities she sees as distractions can be a metaphorical garden; for the nourishment of loving intercourse and the paths of mutual solace are as vital to man's growth toward God as any lanes they might clear or any fruit they might grow in Eden.

But, before we can breathe relief at Adam's proper husbanding of Eve, a strange thing happens. Adam's masculine reason yields to a feminine sensuousness as his anima steps forth to deny the mode, if not the truth, of his rationality: "But if much converse perhaps / Thee satiate, to short absence I could yield" (9. 247–48). This statement is very nearly a petulant "If you are *tired* of me" that is de-

signed by Adam to elicit Eve's response that "nothing without thee
is sweet." Adam is playing an anima game. As he asserts the sym-
biosis of male and female, he casts the lesson not as a benevolent
command but as a plea. The insecurity of his tone invites develop-
ment of Eve's animus, and she almost scornfully tells him that she
knows those arguments; she has heard Raphael's warnings. To her
emerging masculinity, Adam's would-be protectiveness seems mis-
trust: "But that thou shouldst my firmness . . . doubt . . . I expected
not to hear" (9. 279–81). And she then reasons:

> His fraud is then thy fear, which plain infers
> Thy equal fear that my firm Faith and Love
> Can by his fraud be shak'n or seduc't;
> Thoughts, which how found they harbor in thy breast,
> *Adam,* misthought of her to thee so dear?
>
> (9. 285–89)

The familiar "you don't trust me" is presented in the guise of a
carefully reasoned argument. Adam is unable to manage the dis-
junction of form and content, for sensuous rationality, sophistical
rhetoric, is a new experience, and he turns the argument upon
himself. He needs her support (role reversal) to inspire him to
heroic deeds.

Milton characterizes Adam's speech: "So spake domestic *Adam* in
his care / And Matrimonial Love" (9. 318–19). Eve's reason had
demanded a governor, Adam has failed to fill that need, and so her
misunderstanding grows. The pattern of her thought is familiar:
Satan thought himself impaired by the bounds of heaven, and Eve
feels the same about Eden. If, indeed, she and Adam are in danger
and must constantly be alert, then *"Eden* were no *Eden* thus ex-
pos'd" (9. 341). Her rhetoric echoes Satan's pronouncements to his
followers and anticipates the mode of his temptation of Eve. Adam
is, for the moment, shocked out of his effeminancy; and Eve is no
longer "Daughter of God and Man"; now, she is "O Woman." In this
naming he finds new strength and he tells Eve exactly what he
should be telling himself: "Wouldst thou approve thy constancy,
approve / First thy obedience; th' other who can know, / Not seeing
thee attempted, who attest?" (9. 367–69). All their problems should
be cleared, for the answer (despite the implied limitation of God's
omniscience) is perfect for the occasion; but Adam at once deserts
the very advice he has just given Eve. Forgetting his role as protec-

tor and mentor, he raises her to his own level: "Go; for thy stay, not free, absents thee more" (9. 372). Adam understands that the walls of the garden are a benevolent nursery, not a prison; but he cannot quite understand that, as the walls are to Adam, so is Adam to Eve. His last words, "God towards thee hath done his part, do thine" (9. 375), are heavily ironic, for Adam has not done his part toward Eve. To obey God, she must obey Adam; for Adam to serve God, he must command Eve. At their severing, Eve is born from the allegorical to the literal world, and she goes forth as Everywoman, leaving behind the symbiotic ladder whereby she was to have ascended toward God.[26]

As she walks away, Milton joins his love to that of Adam, but her association with all mythological virgins (a "Wood-Nymph," a "Dryad," and Diana) incorporates a dark note: when Milton compares Eve to "Proserpina," we know about Dis. The dim pagan vision of reality has in it a prediction of the outcome of Eve's gardening; for Satan, like Dis, will carry Eve to the underworld, thereby causing Christ (like Ceres) all that pain and mankind "all our woe." The typological equations are very like those with which Satan shadowed the garden in book 4. Eve's promise of prompt return at noon to prepare Adam's lunch is pathetic. She will indeed bring him a dinner: a feast of death. And he, dutiful husband, will eat what is set before him.

## XII  *The Fall of Eve*

Although the encounter between Satan and Eve is the thematic and dramatic center of *Paradise Lost* in that it gathers images, fulfills anticipations, and turns the action, Satan's snake-borne approach to Eve is as overstated and trite as the climax of a melodrama. The unsuspecting victim, who goes about her trivial tasks as the unseen violator creeps nearer and nearer, is the central figure in a tableau of sensuously fragrant vulnerability. Eve is a country virgin; Satan is cast as the jaded cosmopolitan. He finds new game, and he even seems to slaver a bit in anticipation of spoiling the very innocence that gives him pleasure.

The imagery associated with Eve names her the primate of the garden's feminine aspects: the "fairest unsupported Flow'r" binds up other flowers with the myrtle of Aphrodite. Satan's initial lust is transformed into Petrarchan terms as her "Heav'nly form / Angelic"

(9. 457–58) reminds him not only of the purity which he hopes to ruin on earth but also of the beauty which he has lost in heaven. But his discomfiture is only momentary. Whatever nobility may exist in the "starved lover's" worship of an unattainable lady is at once extinguished as he turns both his lust and his awe to the needs of the occasion. He decides that he will only pretend to be love-sick in order to accomplish her ruin. Milton earlier expressed his scorn of Courtly Love, for the "Serenate, which the starv'd Lover sings / To his proud fair, best quitted with disdain" (4. 769–70), for he regarded it as a parody of wedded love. But Satan has not even the slim claim of the smitten lover; he twirls his mustache like a stage villain.

Milton interrupts the drama to characterize the serpent's appearance; and, as always, the physical description has moral and typological dimensions. The first equation is between Satan-serpent's beauty and that of the snakes into which "*Hermione* and *Cadmus*" were transformed. Again there is an "error" in the myth: Hermione, daughter of Menelaus and Helen, married Neoptolemus after the Trojan War; later, Orestes killed her husband and carried her off. The story of Harmonia and Cadmus is that of the beautiful, cursed treasure. As a wedding present Cadmus gave Harmonia a beautiful necklace whose history is a bloody trail of misfortune, lust, and murder. By mixing the two tales, Milton recalls two curses— that on the house of Atreus and that upon the necklace—but both tales may be regarded as versions of original, inherited sin.

The final comparison of Satan-serpent is to serpents who seduced women: Alexander the Great and Scipio Africanus, the primates of Greece and Rome, claimed deity because their mothers cohabited with Zeus-Jupiter in the form of a serpent. Although Milton may be obliquely commenting on the source of all earthly glory, the reference to Jupiter as a seducing snake suggests, more particularly, the dark tradition which reads the fall of mankind as Eve's copulation with the devil in serpent form. Milton does not cast the fall in such lurid terms; but, in cabalistic fashion, a surface story which is apparently orthodox and decorous conceals a more basic account of the fall.

The next simile (9. 510–15) for the serpent compares the tempter's approach to that of a ship seeking to enter the mouth of a river. In the context of the preceding comparisons, a Freudian dimension to the nautical simile is certainly available; but even if we reject so primal a reading, we have no doubt that Satan-serpent enmeshes Eve sensuously. With many a "wanton wreath," he seeks to "lure her Eye"; he bows his crest, fawns, and licks the ground at her feet. Milton labels Satan's first speech to Eve a "Proem," the introductory lines for a sonnet sequence, and Satan's diction and tone are Petrarchan: "sovran Mistress," "sole Wonder," "Heav'n of mildness," "disdain," "awful brow," "Celestial beauty." The serpent describes himself as "insatiate," as ravished by her beauty, and as a beast unfit to appreciate properly her charms. The entire speech is an expansion of the stock metaphor of Courtly Love, for Satan casts Eve as a goddess.[27]

Satan's approach is seductive because it builds upon Eve's desire to climb the ladder of being. She feels herself equal to Adam, perhaps superior, since Adam worships her; but Satan offers a more heady vista. She should be "A Goddess among Gods, ador'd and serv'd / By Angels numberless" (9. 547–48). The temptation is for Eve to skip rungs in the divine ladder and to be, first, above Adam; then, above "Gods"; then, like God Himself, to be served by the hosts of angels. Because of the natural vanity of Eve, Satan finds a means of introducing far greater temptations. His reasoning certainly seems logical: Eve is fairest; fair implies good; good indicates superiority; superiority means power. Therefore, because Satan's Eve is a "goddess," she is woefully out of place in the backwater of Eden. His argument is the more convincing to Eve in that it is a "logical" extension of Eve's argument with Adam.

Eve's new reasoning powers are not sufficient to recognize the temptation; instead, as she wonders about the serpent's ability to speak, she unwittingly suggests the next stage of Satan's attack. Milton tells us that Satan's words made way "Into the Heart of *Eve*"; she is "Not unamaz'd." Milton chooses this characterization with great care: the serpent is himself a maze; his path to the tree will be maze-like; the best of the demons in hell are in "endless mazes wandering lost"; a maze is where one keeps the Minotaur, the archetypal result of bestiality. Eve's balance between reason and confusion is at a knife edge, for Satan has appealed to her weakest characteristic, curiosity. Mankind has been told to "know to know no more," but Eve cannot resist the temptation to inquire into the seeming miracle of a speaking serpent.

Satan's response to her curiosity links three temptations: "Empress of this fair World" (power), "resplendent *Eve*" (vanity), and "to tell thee all" (knowledge). Furthermore, Satan, in characterizing himself as formerly interested only in food or sex, casts the complex of temptations in the form most likely to tempt the feminine Eve; for, since the food is to lead to greater discernment and apprehension, he also tempts her masculine animus. When the serpent describes the fruit, the terms are sensual, even sexual; "savory odor," "Teats" dripping with milk, "sharp desire," "alluring fruit." Adam has been characterized as the tree around which Eve as a vine should wind herself. Satan says he wound himself about the trunk that would require the "utmost reach" of Adam or Eve; and, in sating his appetite, he found "Strange alteration" in his reason and inward powers: his ability to speak is claimed as the expansion of his native intellect. He joins all of the temptations by saying that all his advance merely has taught him more fully to appreciate the divine beauty of Eve; heretofore, she has been the unappreciated "Sovran of Creatures."

Satan has, however, almost overdone his praise, for Eve sees the fulsome quality of the flattery: "Serpent, thy overpraising leaves in doubt / The virtue of that Fruit" (9. 615–16). By "virtue," Eve means power; but the ironic pun does not occur to her. Her answer is patterned on Raphael's speeches and upon Adam's, for she recapitulates the promise of upward mutability, if mankind is found obedient. Yet she will go and see. To reach the fruit of the forbidden tree, Eve must return to the place of her birth; for the tree stands beyond Aphrodite's "Myrtles, on a Flat, / Fast by a Fountain." The small thicket of "Myrrh and Balm" contains, typologically, the traditional gift of bitter perfume brought by the magus at the birth of Christ and the ointment for his crucified body. If Eve accepts Satan's conduct, her path sets mankind on the road to Calvary.

When Eve says to Satan, "Lead then," she deserts Adam, her proper head and guide. The path of the serpent which "made intricate seem straight" is a physical anticipation of the mental process whereby Eve will convince herself that the quickest road to heaven is that which leads to death. For the light of reason, she has substituted a "wand'ring Fire," the *ignis fatuus*, the comet, the flashing gunpowder, darkness visible. But she has not as yet sinned, for she rejects the tree: "Fruitless to mee, though Fruit be here to excess." The pun on fruit is conscious; Eve has slipped into Satan's rhetorical game, but the pun on excess constitutes a dramatic irony. The reader knows that her desire is based upon excessive appetite for flattery, for knowledge, for power, and for food; but Eve does not. She is "yet sinless" (9. 659), but Satan's game is afoot. He takes his cue from Eve's speech: "Reason is our Law" (9. 654). Allegorically, Eve's reason is Adam, willfully left behind: but, as a complete human, she has reason of her own. Satan's strategy is to substitute rationality for right reason and so form Eve in his own image.

First, he emphasizes the unreasonableness of the prohibition; if Adam and Eve are "Lords declar'd of all in Earth," how is it possible that something of earth is forbidden them? Are they forbidden to eat of all the trees in the garden? Eve quotes God's prohibition, but with a significant addition: "of this *fair* Tree . . . Ye shall not eat" (9. 661). Satan has grounds for reasonable doubt, and he rises to the task like a Classical orator. His argument is sophistical, legalistic, and untrue; for the snake has not eaten the fruit. Upon that false first premise, he builds a glorious rhetorical argument which climbs to the central paradox of theology. How can evil exist if God is both benevolent and omnipotent:

> God therefore cannot hurt ye, and be just;
> Not just, not God; not fear'd then, nor obey'd:
> Your fear itself of Death removes the fear.
>
> (9. 700–702)

God is unfair; He is jealous lest His creatures should be His equals; and He knows that, if Adam and Eve eat the fruit, they will "be as Gods" (9. 708). Eve should consider Raphael's promise of exactly that eventuality if man be found obedient, but she does not; rather, she seizes the opportunity to achieve godhood on her own. Earth has produced the fruit, not God: moreover, how can Eve's actions injure an omnipotent God? "What can your knowledge hurt him, or this Tree / Impart against his will if all be his" (9. 727–28). Upon this argument better men than Eve have foundered, and Satan adds to it the temptation of physical appetite and flattery: Eve has need "of this fair Fruit"; she must "reach" and "freely taste." For the perceptive reader, the irony is heavy since her reach is that of the over-reacher and since her "free" taste will enslave mankind. Her belly seconds all Satan's arguments; it is noon, and she is hungry.

But, since Eve's action is to be the perversion of reason, not its absence, the action pauses so that she can make Satan's arguments her own. She begins with his false premise, she believes the snake ate the fruit, and she swiftly moves to her version of Satan's theological paradox:

> For good unknown, sure is not had, or had
> And yet unknown, is as not had at all.

(9. 756–57)

She pauses, pleased at her own cleverness, and then ties the knot of the argument:

> what forbids he but to know,
> Forbids us good, forbids us to be wise?
> Such prohibitions bind not.

(9. 758–60)

Although she has disposed of a benevolent and fair God, there remains the possibility of malevolent omnipotence: suppose God kills her despite the unreasonableness of the prohibition? But, since He has not killed the serpent, death is perhaps reserved for man alone. This problem she cannot answer and so retreats into sophistry.[28] Since she has not eaten of the fruit of knowledge, she cannot know that it is wrong to eat of it. How can she be guilty "Under this ignorance of Good and Evil, / Of God or Death, of Law or Penalty?" (9. 774–75).

Conveniently, she has forgotten that her obedience was to be motivated by love, not fear. She summarizes all facets of Satan's temptation and localizes them in the fruit: "Cure of all," "Fruit Divine," "Fair to the Eye," "inviting to the Taste," "Of virtue to make wise." The fruit has become an icon: it is representative of a dimension beyond itself and is also that which is represented. When she resolves to "feed at once both Body and Mind" (9. 779), she is, ironically, correct. The poison of the fruit is both spiritual and physical. Her reason, following Satan's, has created nothing new, for she simply perverts the God-given.

The fall of Eve is accomplished in four words: "she pluck'd, she eat" (9. 781). In dramatic terms, nothing could be simpler; but the symbolic dimensions of "pluck" and "eat" are multiplied by the larger context. It is Eve, as flower, who is plucked, and with her all humanity. Ravening death and foul digestion, the banquet with Raphael, the Platonic lecture on digestive ascension, the myriad references to food, appetite, nourishment, poison, and temperance add an astonishing richness to Eve's first bite. Milton's preparation for the fall has been so thorough, the build-up so great, that the reader is unprepared. The understatement is itself appalling. We have come 7,501 lines for these four words.

In the hexameral tradition, Milton found two major readings of the fall.[29] The first version is straightforward Old Testament. She was forbidden to eat poison, she ate it; but Satan's question remains: How was it that God placed poison in the unfallen garden? Perhaps, as a second tradition suggests, it was the disobedience, rather than the fruit itself, that poisoned Eve. If the fruit is a more or less arbitrary symbol of obedience, the tree is moral rather than magical. Still, in either case, God has placed the possibility of death in the garden. Milton follows the legalistic suggestion of Genesis 2:17, but he is clearly aware of a third, less literal, interpretation of God's prohibition whose long roots go back to the Aristotelian mean: "Nothing in excess." Perhaps the excess of an act, rather than the act itself, is evil.

Such a reading is attractive for a number of reasons. First, sin-as-excess accords with Milton's moral stance: nothing of itself is good or evil, for the motive of the actor, the use to which an act is put, defines the moral dimension. Such is the implication in the sonnets "How Soon Hath Time" and "When I Consider how my Light is Spent"; both "Lycidas" and *Comus* define sin in terms of motive. Second, the Aristotelian interpretation removes the fangs from the notion that good creates evil. Morality becomes a continuum, stretching from absolute black to perfect white. The starkness of the Old Testament interpretation simply does not match the mixed nature of morality that Milton articulated so passionately in *Areopagitica*. Of Milton's heroes, only the Christ of *Paradise Regained* imposes total moral absolutes; and his conduct has been an embarrassment to generations of "humanist" critics.

It might also be argued that the fall as excess, rather than as act, accentuates man's free will and elevates him toward deity. But continuums, degrees, situational ethics have no place in myth; for a major function of myth is to precipitate the grays of morality into absolute black and white. Philosophy and ethics take note of the variegations of experience. Myth, it may seem, falsifies experiential reality. On the other hand, philosophy and ethics obscure the binary imperatives upon which existence is based. One sees the forest; the other, the trees.

Milton's solution is to read the fall both ways. When it comes to the point, the fall is Old Testament: it is an absolutely forbidden act, not the excess of an act otherwise blameless; and it would have made no difference had Eve taken only one small nibble of the fruit. Furthermore, the act itself, rather than the thought of the act, constitutes the fall. In prelapsarian Eden, "Evil into the mind of God or Man / May come and go, so unapprov'd, and leave" no trace of sin (5. 117–18); but, once the act has been committed, the rules change. Excess, which, though blameless, might lead to sin, becomes the result, the act, and the cause of additional sins. Were the only purpose of *Paradise Lost* to teach of the fall, Milton could have rendered the act in purely mythic, absolute terms. But the poem is directed to fallen man; hence, the fall contains a lesson couched in experiential terms. Everyman lives in a world of degree, of shaded good and evil; he needs to know of temperance as well as abstinence.

Theologically, the combinations of contrary theses are puzzling; esthetically, they work well enough. At moments of crisis, when man meets an archetypal decision, the absolute, mythic bivalence operates. But, in day-to-day experience, temperance can guide his decisions among the multivalent faces of experiential relativity. Ultimate morality is a matter of black or white; daily morality is frequently made up of shades of gray. *Paradise Lost* is for Everyman, not simply for Adam.

## XIII   *Temperance*

For all of Adam's sons (except the very special case of Christ), the luxury of absolute mythic choice is rarely presented. To live in the world is to partake of it, and all the world is in some degree corrupted by the fall. Hence, to Milton's audience, each of the voices of *Paradise Lost* counsels temperance. The lessons are given in exactly the terms that Satan employed to seduce Eve: vanity, power, knowledge, and food. The ordering of narrative makes the first lesson a negative: Satan's intemperance and his pride cost him heaven. His desire "to have equall'd the most High" (1. 40) is more transparent than Eve's or Adam's: he wanted power. The futility of that naked aspiration is revealed in the bluster of Moloch, and the application of the lesson to man is spelled out by Raphael: the devils are guilty of "too high aspiring" (6. 889). Although the acts of Adam and

Eve are more complexly motivated, the bald sin of overreaching is the root of man's disobedience. God forsees that man, in "Affecting God-head" (3. 206), will disobey.

The masks of overreaching are various. For Adam, the chief means to inordinate power is knowledge. The temperate use of literal power is, in a mythic universe, straightforward: obey the given superior; command the given inferior. But, when power becomes knowledge, classification of superior and inferior is difficult. The desire to increase one's knowledge is not sin but virtue. When Satan sneaks past Uriel (3. 636 ff.), he does so by pretending a desire to know more of God's creation; and Uriel approves:

> thy desire which tends to know
> The works of God, thereby to glorify
> The great Work-Master, leads to no excess
> That reaches blame, but rather merits praise
> The more it seems excess.
>
> (3. 694–98)

Adam and Eve are not to remain static, for Raphael's urging of digestive ascension (5. 405–30) makes it clear that, like a plant's fluids, Adam ought to rise ever higher to increased levels of being. Knowledge is good, but not good in and for itself. The key line in Uriel's approval of excess is "thereby to glorify / The great Work-Master." Such is not Faust's purpose, or Satan's, or Eve's. Satan's version of Uriel's pronouncement is, of course, twisted. He asserts that to really serve God, Eve should disobey Him; for a creator who can produce a creature capable of rebelling is greater than a creator who produces dutiful robots. God says as much:

> Not free, what proof could they have giv'n sincere
> Of true allegiance, constant Faith or Love,
> Where only what they needs must do, appear'd,
> Not what they would?
>
> (3. 103–6)

When Satan argues that the ability to disobey, necessary for free will, carries with it the obligation to disobey, Eve cannot manage the argument. The emblem in *Paradise Lost* of man's overreaching is the curiosity which both Adam and Eve frequently exhibit about the stars. Just as any talk of separation between Adam and Eve signals a crisis in the drama, so too do the questions about the stars signal danger. The stars are, for several reasons, exemplary of man's desire for inordinate knowledge and power. Spatially, they are farthest from the center of the created universe, Eden. Man cannot look at the stars and at his own path at the same time; for, if he looks only upward, he may fall in a ditch. To Milton, the contemporary debates spawned by Copernicus, Brahe, and Galileo seem the earthly equivalent of the demon's futile mapping of hell. The astrological calculations which still fascinate man were a means by which he sought to outwit providence by probing the secrets of causation.[30] In fact, astrology was a rival pagan force so potent that the church spent a good deal of effort attempting to extirpate it. The very names of the planets, the constellations, and the zodiacal houses preserved the ancient nightmare myths of cosmogony and causation. If all man was or could be was bound up in the conjunction of stars, free will was obviated as surely as by the most rockbound Calvinist. Milton, as Christian, had to reject the pagan; and, as humanist, he rebelled against the reduction of man to the unwitting conflux of implacable, alien powers. The threat of astrology was not simply a bugbear to be dismissed in broad daylight; for, despite Pico della Mirandola's brave assertions of man's freedom from compulsion, tradition held that astrologers had predicted the exact hour of Pico's death. Man could not simply dismiss astrology as superstition, but it was possible to incorporate astrology into the Christian vision. Sometimes the tutelary deity of each planet was associated with a demon, a fallen angel. In this way the power could be acknowledged, but kept separate from and subordinate to God.

A more comfortable solution for the Christian astrologer was to replace Apollo with Uriel; or, by analogy, each of the zodiacal houses might be equated with one of the twelve disciples. The effort is to acknowledge the power of heavenly bodies, assign them as second causes, and so keep ultimate causation in God's hand. Milton, if we take Uriel as an example, chose to equate tutelary spirits with angels. Yet the darker side is also present; the Classical gods are equated with fallen angels (1.508–20); and Milton places a fallen angel in each pagan oracle. However the complicated equation is worked out, man's search of the stars could be seen as an impious attempt to probe causation, to know more of the ways of God with men than He chose to reveal.[31] Raphael explains:

> God to remove his ways from human sense,
> Plac'd Heav'n from Earth so far, that earthly sight,
> If it presume, might err in things too high,
> And no advantage gain.

(8.119–22)

When Adam (8.15–38) and Eve (4.657–58) question the stars' purpose, danger is afoot. One of Satan's most subtle temptations of Eve is a reversal of this desire; for, in her dream (5.44–45), the stars wish to know more about Eve. In book 12, Milton ties the threads of this skein together in the person of Nimrod. By equating Nimrod with inordinate desire for power over his fellow man and by making him the builder of the Tower of Babel (12.24–47), the desire to dominate one's equals is seen to be a reaching toward God's power. Nimrod repeats Satan's rebellion in the reduced circumstances of fallen earth, and the ensuing confusion of tongues is the earthly equivalent of the "endless mazes" into which speculative demons wander, just as the fruit which changes to ashes in the mouths of hell (10.560–67) is the emblem of their unity with Eve's sin. God's response to the overreaching of Nimrod is not anger but derision (12.52). The Faustian pact by which Adam's sons seek heaven through knowledge is no threat to God. The irony is supreme, for man's impious approach to God distances the deity.

The pattern of man's temperance is complex, and the signals for man are not always clear. Mammon's arguments for a middle way (2.229 ff.) might seem to advocate temperance, but they are really an argument for self-indulgence. Abdiel's "rebellion" against his commander, Lucifer, indicates that authorized order can sometimes err and must be resisted intemperately. How then is man to judge? Milton's lesson is everywhere the same: only the service of God is lawful. Yet, in the problems of temperance, Milton finds a means to drama. Strategically, the fall is an absolute, mythic act; tactically, it is the result of intemperance. The intemperance of Adam in doting on Eve permits her intemperance is straying from his side. And, at the same time, the fall is not a fall until intemperance of thought has led to an act of disobedience. The immediate result of the fall is an intemperance so gross that it constitutes the substance of sin.

With Eve's first bite of the fruit, she introduces the seven deadly sins in their myriad manifestations. The first to appear is gluttony: "she ingorg'd without restraint" (9.791); soon she is drunk. Once sated, she breaks the first of the Ten Commandments as she does

obeisance to the tree and promises to worship it daily (9. 800–01).
When she renames God the "great Forbidder" (9. 815), she takes
His name in vain. Next, she becomes avaricious and miserly as she
considers keeping the powers of the tree for herself rather than
sharing them with Adam. Jealousy at the thought of Adam with a
second Eve leads her to a parody of the love of Christ: "So dear I
love him [Adam], that with him all deaths / I could endure, without
him live no life" (9. 832–33). *PIG LAWE* will reign supreme: *P*ride,
*I*ndolence, *G*luttony, *L*echery, *A*varice, *W*rath, and *E*nvy. Her
morning cycle is complete. Eve broke from Adam to establish her
own power; she rejoins him to destroy his.

## XIV   *The Fall of Adam*

*Paradise Lost* is a closed system, for none of God's creatures can
escape the confines of omnipresence. When Satan seeks to establish
his independence, he succeeds only in creating an unintentional
parody of himself. Thus hell is not something new; it is merely the
perversion of eternity, and the analogy with a mirror is again useful
since evil is the reversed shadow of good. When Eve went to work
by herself, she was yet operating upon the heavenly pattern; if the
son's separate existence from God provided more active good, why
should not Eve's separation from Adam do the same? Had she re-
sisted Satan's blandishments, a cubit would have been added to her
moral stature. But, in her debate with Satan (9. 647–732), she leaves
Raphael's divine pattern and accepts its perverted image in Satan.
Thus, when she returns from the tree, she has chosen to model her
existence, not upon the heavenly pattern, but upon Satan's distor-
tion of it. Earth was created the "shadow of heaven"; Eve's act opens
the way for earth to become the image of hell.

Although the artifice of Eve's first fallen speech to Adam
(9. 856 ff.) is so transparent as to be almost charming, the pattern
she follows is familiar: Satan's meeting with Sin and Death, his
deception of Chaos, his hoodwinking of Uriel, and his unsuccessful
attempt to justify himself to Gabriel. The immediate pattern is her
own seduction; the original is Lucifer's temptation of his host
(5. 772 ff.). First, she takes the offensive, noting that she has missed
Adam, that separation has been an "agony of Love," and that she
will never leave him again. Second, in one rushing sentence, she
tells Adam of her adventure, beginning with the conclusion that the

forbidden tree is not a tree of death, but the way to a fuller life—the tree is "of Divine effect / To open Eyes, and make them Gods who taste" (9. 865–66). The same dramatic irony which shadows Satan's speeches follows Eve's: her characterization of her separation as "rash" and filled with "pain" and "agony" is, despite her intent to lie, an exact description of disobedience.

The demonic pattern continues when she tells Adam that it was chiefly for him that she ate the fruit (9. 877–78). When she claims, "For bliss, as thou hast part, to me is bliss, / Tedious, unshar'd with thee, and odious soon" (9. 879–80), she suggests that he should be willing to share her lot; but she also parodies her own hymn to him ("Nothing without thee is sweet"). Not content with suggesting his damnation, she spells out mutual sin:

> Thou therefore also taste, that equal Lot
> May join us, equal Joy, as equal Love;
> Lest thou not tasting, different degree
> Disjoin us, and I then too late renounce
> Deity for thee, when Fate will not permit.
>
> (9. 881–85)

The irony is thick enough to cut. The different degrees are there, but rather than Eve's being above Adam and inviting him to climb to her level, she asks that he surrender his "deity." We note also that she has taken over the demonic distinction between God and fate. Only by such division is rationalization of her act possible.

Adam, however, is yet unfallen; his "umpire conscience" is so wide-awake that he stands "astonied" while "horror chill / Ran through his veins, and all his joints relax'd" (9. 890–91). The earth, too, recognizes Eve's sin, for the garland of flowers Adam had prepared for her fades and sheds its petals. The center of the relationship between Adam and Eve, both before and after the fall, is the love of husband and wife ("Hail wedded love" [4. 750 ff. ]), and Adam's response to Eve's invitation to death pivots on that relationship. He has found her "Holy, divine, good, amiable . . . sweet" (9. 899); and, although he now recognizes that she is stripped of the first three adjectives, she is to him yet "amiable" and "sweet," and he chooses her love rather than that of God. And he does not choose in ignorance, for he knows that she is "defac't" (God's image is marred) and "deflow'r'd" (she has betrayed him).

As Adam accepts Eve's new status as his own, his perception of

Eden changes; the garden, without Eve, would be a "wild Woods forlorn." Just as Eve is no longer personified fancy, Adam is no longer personified reason; his humanness has come to the fore: "Flesh of Flesh, / Bone of my Bone thou art, and from thy State / Mine never shall be parted, bliss or woe" (9. 914–16). The sentiment is neither new nor evil; it is simply misplaced because Adam speaks Eve's lines. The struggle between his primary consciousness and his anima has, for the moment, been settled. His will has chosen to follow feminine eros, not masculine logos. In his perversion of roles, Adam forms the pattern for Petrarchan lovers who will sing in pain and despair to Eve's daughters. However, Adam's reason is quite unfallen. He reviews evidence, tests Eve-Satan's argument, and is unconvinced. Eve's physical argument, not her nice reasoning, tips the balance:

> However I with thee have fixt my Lot,
> Certain to undergo like doom; if Death
> Consort with thee, Death is to mee as Life;
> So forcible within my heart I feel
> The Bond of Nature draw me to my own,
> My own in thee, for what thou art is mine;
> Our State cannot be sever'd, we are one,
> One Flesh; to lose thee were to lose myself.
>
> (9. 952–59)

Adam now speaks of causation in terms of "lot" (chance) and "doom" (fate); providence is nowhere in the speech. Even "Consort" bows to fate, for it literally means "with-chance"; but, at the same time, the word carries a sexual connotation. Eve has cuckolded Adam; her lover is Death. Clearly, the "Bond of Nature" is flesh, not the chain of being leading upward to God. Milton has presented two archetypes relevant to this scene: the love between God and the Son, and its parody in the lust between Satan and Sin. The separation between Father and Son will end when the Son returns to the Father. The separation between Satan and Sin is healed by Satan's becoming Sin. Adam chooses to follow the demonic inversion of the divine archetype. When he proclaims "Death is to mee as Life," his model is "Evil be thou my Good."

In this new upside-down world, the eating of the forbidden fruit becomes, not the desertion and betrayal of love, but its test and seal. Drunkenness and lust are, in that reversal, desirable goals.

Adam's "rewards" are thoroughly physical: "that Fair enticing Fruit" is the cup of Comus, the voice of the sirens, the pomegranate of Persephone, the potion of Circe, the pact of Faustus, the lust of Pasiphae, the box of Pandora, and the mocking viper of wine. Although Nature must follow her master, Adam, into the domain of death, she celebrates the new dispensation with an anticipation of her response to the crucifixion: "Nature gave a second groan, / Sky low'r'd, and muttering Thunder, some sad drops / Wept at completing of the mortal Sin" (9. 1001–3).

Adam, himself, is "not deceiv'd, / But fondly overcome with Female charm" (9. 998–99); for Milton's editorial comment removes all trace of equivocation from Adam's fall: he knew better, and he ate anyway. We understand, perhaps even admire, Adam's act, and in so assenting to Adam's fall, we acknowledge our parents (as Sin and Death acknowledge Satan). We convict ourselves of original sin; and, in so doing, we justify God's ways with men. In the Biblical division of the fall into a male and a female act, Milton found the distinctions necessary to explain the paradox of evil. Adam knew good; he could have remained faithful to God; but, in his humanity, he remained faithful to Eve and chose evil. Whatever the Benthamite might say, humanity applauds Adam's decision even while labeling him a fool.

## XV *The Discursive World*

When Adam eats the apple, he ratifies the separation from God that Eve has negotiated and so moves from myth to history. In the mythic world, name and thing are not divided, nor are man and woman, nor human and divine. Before the fall, all creation was a continuum, differing in degree, not kind. In history, all the separations obtain, and the differences are in kind rather than in degree. God's language is plain, radically referential; but Satan works with simile, analogy, and parody; and Eve has chosen to enter the demonic, semantic maze. Adam, poor Minotaur, follows the thread she lays down. Eden fades slowly; there will yet be visits between the creator and the created; but "No more of talk where God or Angel Guest / With Man, as with his Friend" (9. 1–2). Raphael, the affable, is replaced by Michael of the two-handed sword. Adam, in choosing unification with Eve, chooses to separate all things; and the archetype of his choice is Satan's choice of Sin.

The center of the vast cosmic choice, from which division will
spread throughout the universe, is human. The first fruit of dis-
obedience is a drunken sex orgy; the second, a hangover. Eve's
brave new vision turns out to be the familiar domestic nightmare:

> since our Eyes
> Op'n'd we find indeed, and find we know
> Both Good and Evil, Good lost, and Evil got,
> Bad Fruit of Knowledge, if this be to know,
> Which leaves us naked thus, of Honor void,
> Of Innocence, of Faith, of Purity,
> Our wonted Ornaments now soil'd and stain'd,
> And in our Faces evident the signs
> Of foul concupiscence; whence evil store;
> Even shame, the last of evils; of the first
> Be sure then.
>
> (9. 1070–80)

Satan's mirrors are operating; for, rather than elevating man's vi-
sion, the fruit turns it downward and inward. Now Adam sees
through Satan's eyes, but he still has enough of his original percep-
tion to recognize the change. He begs the trees to cover him, as the
defeated angels begged the mountains, as sinners at the judgment of
Christ will do. Milton's essay on shame (9. 1053–65) illustrates per-
fectly the reversal of Eden. The more Adam is covered with shame,
the more naked he becomes. Man is still a microcosm; but now,
rather than representing the created universe, he represents chaos
and the inversions of hell. After sewing girdles of leaves, Adam and
Eve bewail their new "freedom" and find that chaos has come within
(9. 1122–31).

Ironically, the next event is sadly predictable, not because we
know its demonic archetype (devil with devil works in full accord),
but because we, as Adam's sons, have been there. Adam and Eve
begin to blame each other. Adam's sententious pronouncement,
though true, is utterly without charity: "Let none henceforth seek
needless cause to approve / The Faith they owe; when earnestly
they seek / Such proof, conclude, they then begin to fail"
(9. 1140–43). Although Adam speaks in abstract terms, he clearly
means to condemn Eve, and she will have none of his preaching.
Despite her recent assertion that she will never move from his side,
she at once rebels at the limitation. Then, coherence thrown to the

winds, she complains that he had granted too much freedom: "Hadst thou been firm and fixt in thy dissent, / Neither had I transgress'd, nor thou with mee" (9. 1160–61). Adam's only defense is the antifeminine complaint that echoes through Western literature: *Mulier est hominis confusion* (Woman is man's confusion). Book 9 ends with mankind's having achieved an earthly version of hell:

> Thus they in mutual accusation spent
> The fruitless hours, but neither self-condemning,
> And of thir vain contést appear'd no end.

They have invented human history.

## XVI  *The Offspring of Sin*

The structure of *Paradise Lost* is like a doubled funnel. For nine books things invisible to mortal sight are revealed as we watch the particularities of hell and heaven focus upon earth. Setting, character, and action—divine and demonic—have served to demonstrate the contrary possibilities that are open to mankind. All that has come before is gathered in Eve's choice at the tree. It is as though two immeasurable empires warred through all the dimensions of existence only to have the issue settled for want of a horseshoe nail. The act of eating the fruit is the final flake of snow that loosens an avalanche. From the opening of the poem through book 9, all existence flows into Eden. With the fall, the tide changes; now, the combinations and reversals that Adam and Eve have made their own flow from the nexus of Eden back upon the universe.

Messengers from both sides carry the news of the decisive skirmish back to the great capital seats. The parallels are strong, for both heaven and hell have a kind of omniscience. God knows the event timelessly, but Sin and Death have an immediate knowledge of Satan's success. Like carpetbaggers, they set out to claim the spoils; for as the angelic guard leaves Eden to report failure, the guards of hell's gate move to replace them. However, there is an important difference; for a devil, existence is sequential; for God there is neither sequence nor movement. This abstract distinction between demonic and divine is signaled dramatically. Satan, wishing to rival God, must fill the roles of both cause and agent. Gabriel returns to heaven to report to his commander; Satan returns to hell to report to his subordinates. Thus, the parallels are really inversions. The "bad" news is accepted calmly in heaven; the failure of Eden's guard is forgiven; and God sends Christ (obedience and life) to earth before Sin and Death arrive: "the speed of Gods / Time counts not, though with swiftest minutes wing'd" (10. 90–91).

What seemed to Satan, and to the reader, a final victory is nothing of the sort; for God still rules Eden. The alterations which sever the original bond are not, ultimately, to Satan's advantage; for rebellion chose, ironically, the punishment that fits the crime. Tactical freedom still falls within God's strategic plan.

## XVII   *The Judgment of Mankind*

Since the judgment scene is perhaps the most vividly dramatic event in Genesis 3, Milton had but to transcribe and embellish a clearly defined exchange. Implicit in Genesis is Adam's attempt to shift the blame: Eve gave him the fruit; it's her fault; God gave Eve to Adam; it's His fault. Christ disposes of this shuffling with dispatch: "Was shee thy God . . . ? to bear rule . . . was thy part" (10. 145–55). In setting Eve above himself, Adam has implicitly set her above God. Because Adam is the central link in a chain, his action is not independent, nor does his free will permit choice without responsibility. Eve, following her husband, also attempts to shift blame: "The Serpent me beguil'd and I did eat" (10. 162). Genesis 3 makes no connection between the serpent and Satan; but Milton, following tradition, does so. In *Paradise Lost* Christ, in pronouncing sentence, seems to accept some part of Eve's plea of mitigating circumstances. In the promise that her seed will bruise the serpent's head, Christ looks forward in time to the moment when he will utterly defeat Satan, Sin, and Death.

Just as Eve has been the gate through which Sin and Death entered Eden, she will be the entrance (as Mary, the second Eve) by which the "greater Man" will come into history. Eve is sentenced to pain and subjugation; Adam, to labor and death; the earth, to discord and mutability. The final act of the judgment, however, is to clothe Adam and Eve, not only with the skins of animals, but their "inward nakedness . . . / With his Robe of righteousness" (10. 221–22). The judgment has, strategically, finessed history, and a new tactical dispensation obtains.

Christ's creative judgment is mocked by Sin and Death. As they leave hell's gate, they build the famous broad and easy way to destruction. Their creative act is miscreative, for they give chaos form without giving it life. Death's mace, like some sort of gorgon's head, is "petrific," freezing asphaltic slime for a path. The meeting of Sin and Death with Satan parodies Christ's three triumphant returns to heaven: after creation, after judgment, and after victory over Satan.

Satan, who is still playing childish games, disguises himself in order to sneak past his own guards. But, when he sits on hell's throne, "fulgent" and "Star-bright," his glory is only "permissive" (10. 449–50). His grand effort to separate appearance and reality and to live between them is defeated: he and his followers become the serpent form in which he had chosen to disguise himself. Satan believes that he has come home in triumph; but, since hell is an inversion, his triumph is defeat. Beneath the grandeur of Ophion-Eurynome (10. 581) which demons will claim as the true version of Satan's temptation of Eve, is the base and abortive malformation of Satan-beast.

Yet, on earth, Satan's victory seems very real, for earth is now a place of tactics, not strategy. Sin and Death reach Eden and prepare to devour all living things. The reality behind Satan's boast that the mind is its own place is much reduced in Death's version: "To mee, who with eternal Famine pine, / Alike is Hell, or Paradise, or Heaven" (10. 597–98). Outside God's providence, nothing exists, not even chaos. Satan's son-grandson is the closest thing to nothingness, and thus an emblem of the equation of being and life. Death is a black hole that nothing except utter negation can fill. Satan, Sin, and Death, the demonic trinity, are scourges wielded by God to purify creation of its willful malformations. When they have cleaned away the offal and excrement, they will be returned to hell. Then, "Heav'n and Earth renew'd shall be made pure / To sanctity that shall receive no stain" (10. 638–39). Before that will happen, history must run its course, and so God sends angels to re-create the world. The earth is tilted on its axis; animals are set against each other and against man.

Having followed the event of man's sin to heaven, to hell, and thence back to earth, Milton returns to the nexus of Adam and Eve. The father of mankind does not approve his own actions, and Adam's speech (10. 720–844) is filled with recriminations, rationalizations, and the despair of a being separated from God. The kinship between

Adam and his "new" archetype, Satan, is striking. His response to Eden recalls Satan's response to hell: "Is this the Region, this the Soil, the Clime" (1. 242). The glory of God is no longer Adam's element, as the sun's glory is no longer pleasing to Satan: "O Sun, to tell thee how I hate thy beams" (4. 37). Adam's noble wish to accept the logical consequence of his action echoes Belial: "To suffer, as to do, / Our strength is equal, nor the Law unjust" (2. 199–200).

But the children of Adam will not be such allegorical figures as Satan's offspring Sin and Death. Cain and Abel will share Adam's free will and the resulting complexity of decision and responsibility. For Satan's family there is no possibility of salvation, but for mankind there may yet be, through Christ, a second Eden, a paradise within. However, Adam continues to repeat his dim shadowing of Satan's experiences. When he complains that he did not ask to be born, he echoes Satan's soliloquy: "O had his powerful Destiny ordain'd / Me some inferior Angel, I had stood / Then happy" (4. 58–60). But, unlike Satan, Adam would render the gift of life back to his maker since the terms are "too hard, by which I was to hold / The good I sought not" (10. 751–52). Adam's middle position makes him both the ectype of Satan and the first type of Christ, for he is a prediction of the complex, mixed nature of good and evil in the world. When he considers the effect of his sin upon future generations, he is more like Christ than Satan. As he leaves the egocentricity of despair, he begins his return to God. His "Be it so, for I submit, his doom is fair" (10. 769) constitutes the first of four traditional steps to salvation; he admits his sin. But his conviction of sin lacks patience; he would have the pain finished:

> How gladly would I meet
> Mortality my sentence, and be Earth
> Insensible, how glad would lay me down
> As in my Mother's lap!
>
> (10. 775–78)

His conviction becomes almost a matter of pride. If Adam's sin is truly cosmic, is it not too great for God to forgive? Adam lapses into Satan's inverted pride:

> Satan: So farewell Hope, and with Hope farewell Fear,
> Farewell Remorse: all Good to me is lost;
> Evil be thou my Good.
>
> (4. 108–10)

Adam:                    Thus what thou desir'st,
            And what thou fear'st, alike destroys all hope
            Of refuge, and concludes thee miserable
            Beyond all past example and future,
            To *Satan* only like both crime and doom.
            O Conscience, into what Abyss of fears
            And horrors hast thou driv'n me; out of which
            I find no way, from deep to deeper plung'd!

                                        (10. 837–44)

Despite the closeness of the parallel, there is a saving difference.
Satan's despair leads to a hardening of the heart; his pride, to an
inversion of good and evil. Adam has stopped short of "Evil be thou
my Good."

Both Adam and Satan lay prostrate in despair; but, whereas Sa-
tan's pride and hate raised him from the fiery lake, it is Eve who
comes to raise Adam. Adam is hardly ready to forgive her; his re-
sponse to her soft words is natural, just, and completely self-cen-
tered:

            Out of my sight, thou Serpent, that name best
            Befits thee with him leagu'd, thyself as false
            And hateful; nothing wants, but that thy shape,
            Like his, and color Serpentine may show
            Thy inward fraud, to warn all Creatures from thee
            Henceforth; lest that too heav'nly form, pretended
            To hellish falsehood, snare them.

                                        (10. 867–73)

Adam, in equating Eve with Satan-serpent, makes her a lamia—part
snake, part woman. For him, at the moment, she is both the parent
of sin and sin itself; and, if that allegorical unity holds, all will be
lost. The narcissistic lust of Satan and Sin produced Death; but,
since no children have been born to Adam and Eve, the outcome of
their relationship is ambivalent.

This scene is crucial to the divine comedy. If Adam and Eve
continue in the hellish pattern, their child will be Death; but, if they
regain something of heavenly love, hope for a better son remains.
Adam concludes his bitter, adolescent tirade against Eve with an
unwitting invitation for comfort. When Eve takes the cue perfectly,
human love returns to Eden for the first time since the fall.[32]
Eve's "Forsake me not thus, *Adam*" (10. 914) begins a remarkable

readjustment of values. Original harmony has been overturned by the fall, but the universe remains. Adam and Eve have sought to recast their world in the image of hell, and Eve will yet suggest the demonic solutions of suicide and barrenness, but both humans stop short of "Evil be thou my Good." The pattern of hell is rejected, the pattern of heaven is unobtainable, but the shadow of unfallen Eden remains. Eve's reach is short of divine myth, but she remembers her own history. Adam was created "for God only, shee for God in him" (4. 299), and Eve now proclaims a fallen version of that relationship: both have sinned, but Adam "Against God only, I against God and thee" (10. 931). Eve's despair, in naming herself "sole cause" of all their woe, restores Adam by giving him something to do; he is yet Eve's tutor, for "his life so late and sole delight" (10. 941) is again submissive; and she needs help. As he raises her from suppliant posture, they achieve a diminished version of their original form: "Two of far nobler shape erect and tall" (4. 288).

Adam has taken the first step on the long Platonic ladder that leads to God. Having accepted the reality of his own guilt, having ceased to blame God or Eve, he now looks to the future and regrets that the "long day's dying" must pass on to his "hapless Seed" (10. 964–65). In their fumbling attempts to reestablish a pattern forever lost, Adam and Eve create a new pattern. For the first time in *Paradise Lost*, a being who has been wronged forgives his adversary without condition; and mankind is, therefore, on the long road to a paradise within. As Eve proposes suicide and celibacy, she gives Adam a chance to restore something of their unfallen state: his reason can balance her passion. Eve's "solutions" are the product of despair, and Adam's "hope" is for revenge, not salvation. As yet they do little but huddle for warmth as Eden fades, but a beginning has been made.

Slowly Adam realizes that the new earth fits the new man: for the pain of childbirth, Eve will gain the joy of children; Adam's punishment, labor, is after all a boon. Christ has already clothed them; perhaps he will teach them more. The fire that Adam now desires is not the forbidden flame Prometheus stole from Olympus; rather, it is the homely, useful, day-to-day fire that Hephaestus brought without jealousy or condition to mankind. Through Christ, God may teach Adam and Eve to live "commodiously this life," until they "end / In dust, our final rest and native home" (10.1081–85). Book 10 ends with a new pattern in progress, for Adam and Eve are the first sinners to escape despair; in "sorrow unfeign'd, and humiliation meek," they go to confess their errors.

### XVIII  *Adam's History Lesson*

The traditional details which comprise the first ten books of *Paradise Lost* are varied and rich; but, because the Biblical narrative into which they fit is spare, Milton enjoyed great freedom in creating details. When he came to write the last two books, the situation was reversed; for, rather than choosing image and incident to flesh out a spare narrative, Milton had to force order upon the myriad details which comprise the Old Testament. Perhaps the chief traditional means of fitting details to pattern was typology, the reading of the Old Testament as at every point a prediction of the New Testament. Typology showed historical detail to be a gradual revelation, through time, of the timeless divine. To the degree that Milton follows this tradition, we can expect the chief pattern of books 11 and 12 to be a tracing of anticipations of Christ.

But other patterns may also be discovered. In some measure, Milton's Adam and Eve establish, in their reconciliation, a new pattern: the mutual forgiveness of mutual wrongs. To the eternal bipolarity of heavenly justice and demonic injustice—selfless love and selfish hate—a middle ground has been added that makes of man's soul the continuing battlefield of good and evil.

As Michael shows Adam's descendants falling from Eden and climbing toward Calvary, he discovers patterns in history that constitute "triple equations": three modes of being are shown to be interdependent; Christ—the eternal; Adam—the mythic; Everyman—the experiential. The lesson Michael teaches with these equations is twofold: in the fullness of time, Christ will defeat Satan and so save mankind; no salvation of any kind is possible without Christ. The complexities in point of view are considerable; for, as Adam sees the future, the reader recalls the past. For the reader, the process involves a kind of omniscience and a sense of irony. As Adam gropes to fit proleptic history into the pattern of divine and demonic which makes up his being, the reader is reminded of the seemingly endless repetition of conflict in human history.[33]

When book 11 begins, Adam and Eve, their stony hearts softened by prevenient grace, are praying. When Milton compares them with Deucalion and Pyrrha who prayed before the throne of

Themis, he unifies Biblical history with Classical myth; but, properly understood, Deucalion's flood is a distortion of Noah's flood. Here, the triple equation reads Adam, Noah, and Everyman. But Adam's repentance and his prayer are also human iterations of Christ's prayer for man in book 3; hence, Adam as mythic man forms a link between the archetype Christ and the historical Noah.

The human prayers "Flew up, nor miss'd the way, by envious winds / Blown vagabond or frustrate" (11. 15–16). Christ's aid prevents the prayers from becoming

> The Sport of Winds: all these upwhirl'd aloft
> Fly o'er the backside of the World far off
> Into a *Limbo* large and broad, since call'd
> The Paradise of Fools.
>
> (3. 493–96)

Paralleling the divine triple equation is a demonic pattern, and the punishment of those of Adam's sons who choose evil is to be an object lesson for faithful angels: Milton thereby maintains an eternal perspective for the temporal drama.

The judgment of Adam and Eve has a codicil: disobedient man must be removed from the garden before he eats of the Tree of Life. Since Milton dodges the nice question of whether God's "magic" in the Tree of Life could have reversed the death sentence—"And live for ever, dream at least to live / For ever" (11. 95–96)—the reader may wonder why Adam has not already eaten of the Tree of Life. Milton's God seems, however, to have anticipated the question:

> I at first with two fair gifts
> Created him endow'd, with Happiness
> And Immortality: that fondly lost,
> This other serv'd but to eternize woe.
>
> (11. 57–60)

Two more of God's comments cast an interesting light on the post lapsarian dispensation. Since God says that the soil outside the garden is "fitter" for Adam's tillage and since Adam was created outside the garden, Adam had seemingly advanced one stage on the ladder to God before the fall; therefore, his disobedience has returned him to the starting point. More importantly, God settles the *felix culpa* question. Christ notes that the "fruit" of man's repentance is more

pleasing to God than any effort of unfallen hands (11. 26–30).
Perhaps Satan's argument to Eve (9. 696–97) is therefore valid?
Perhaps man's sin is necessary to complete God's creation? God
flatly denies the whole intricate argument: Adam would have been
"Happier, had it suffic'd him to have known / Good by itself, and
Evil not at all" (11. 88–89). Whatever theologians may think, God
has no doubt that an obedient Adam is superior to a disobedient
Adam.

In book 10, the children of Satan journey to possess the domain
conquered by their father; and God sends Michael to balance the
demonic intrusion—just as he had sent Raphael to counter Eve's
demonic dream. Michael must do two things: (1) expel man from the
garden and (2) provide Adam with a vision that will give him hope.
The net effect of the extrahuman comings and goings in Eden is to
reestablish earth as a balance point. The new equilibrium is cer-
tainly not the high balance of unfallen Eden, for man's will is no
longer sufficient to move him toward God. Free will remains, but
man's power to achieve the action dictated by his will is much
reduced. When Adam sees an eagle chase two birds of "gayest
plume" and a lion chase a brace of deer, the significance is clear:
Michael, the "bird of *Jove*," will remove Adam and Eve from Eden.
But how different is the "mute" sign of nature from the easy con-
verse between Adam and Raphael, and Adam's timid approach to
Michael contrasts strongly with his confident greeting of Raphael.

Yet in both of Adam's lessons with an angel, the first precept is
that love is superior to fear. Michael, like Raphael before him,
promises that man can move toward God through faith, grace, and
good works. When Michael banishes Adam and Eve from the gar-
den, he is intolerant of their complaints: wherever Adam goes will
henceforth be Eve's native soil; God is not bound to a single place.
Still, the loss of Eden is tragic, for what might have been easy will
now be hard.

Michael's lesson for Adam is filled with confusing detail, but the
theme is simple—the nature of Christian patience:

> To show thee what shall come in future days
> To thee and to thy Offspring; good with bad
> Expect to hear, supernal Grace contending
> With sinfulness of Men; thereby to learn
> True patience, and to temper joy with fear
> And pious sorrow, equally inur'd

By moderation either state to bear,
Prosperous or adverse: so shalt thou lead
Safest thy life, and best prepar'd endure
Thy mortal passage when it comes.

(11. 357–66)

The dynamic of the lesson is also straightforward: "supernal Grace contending / With sinfulness of Men."

To prepare Adam for vision, Michael anoints Adam's eyes with Euphrasy, Rue, and three drops from the Well of Life; for, at the eating of the forbidden fruit, a film had fallen over Adam's eyes. Henceforth, he can know good only by knowing evil; and the grim tableaux are ample evidence of man's diminution. *Paradise Lost* demonstrates, therefore, a hierarchy of understanding. At the top is intuitive knowledge; at the bottom, time-bound experiential knowledge; between the two extremes are, in descending order, myth, allegory, and history. Unfallen Adam knew intuitively many things; fallen Adam must search the chaos of daily life for knowledge. As the history unfolds before him, Adam moves down the hierarchy of perceptive modes.

His first vision (11. 429–47) is mythic. In the center of a field evenly divided between cropland and pasture stands an altar. The action of Adam's first vision, sacrifice and murder, has the stark clarity of ritual and dream. The events are both historical and symbolic; together, they form an icon of man's future: "supernal Grace contending / With sinfulness of Men." Cain represents Satan, Sin, and Death: darkness and fall. Abel stands for God, Christ, and grace: light and obedience. The entirety of Michael's lesson is embodied in the tableau; but since Adam can no longer understand myth, his reaction is outrage at the absence of poetic justice. When Michael explains that Cain will, eventually, be punished and that Abel will be rewarded, Adam still misses the point; he focuses upon the details of death.

Michael, like Raphael before him, allows Adam's questions to guide the progress of the lesson. Although the point is to teach the nature of true life, Michael permits Adam to search the opposite question—the nature of death. Since Adam fails to understand the lesson through a mythic vision, Michael shifts the mode down one step—to allegory. There are many "ways that lead / To his [Death's] grim Cave, all dismal" (11. 468–69). It is an ironic measure of love that Michael binds himself to Adam's chosen mode of knowledge, to know good only through knowing evil. In this case, Adam can know life only by knowing death, and such will be the pattern of Christ and Every-Christian.

Adam's second vision (11. 477–93) shows the extent of the allegorical limitation, for he does not see men dying from the catalogue of diseases; rather, he sees a physical embodiment of each infirmity. The nurse is Depair; the warden, Death. Adam is so interested in the details that he seemingly misses all metaphysical implications and misreads allegory. Having failed to understand the significance of Abel (light and obedience), Adam cannot see beyond despair. He falls back to a juvenile complaint: he has not asked to be created. Death will be welcome to Adam, not because it is the gate to a new life, but because it brings an end to earthly pain.

Adam's understanding is, at best, that of a pagan stoic. Actually, Adam has not even reached that limited wisdom, for he shifts the blame and the disgrace to God. Since man is created in God's image, why would God deface Himself? Michael, of course, will have none of such equivocations; for, since Adam has already defaced himself by following Eve's intemperate example, and since the diseases in the lazar-house result from man's excesses, his "gluttonous delight" (11. 533), man's degeneration does not affect God. The corrective for gluttony would seem to be temperance; but even if man avoids intemperance, his dropping like ripe fruit into his "Mother's lap" (11. 536) will be accomplished through crude old age. Adam so thoroughly misunderstands the import of his second vision that he becomes half-enamored with death, and is studious about how he "may be quit / Fairest and easiest of this cumbrous charge" (11. 548–49). Although Adam has missed the point, Michael corrects even that misapprehension: "Nor love thy Life, nor hate; but what thou liv'st / Live well, how long or short permit to Heav'n" (11. 553–54). Here, then, is a proper stoicism; Adam has failed to reach this lesser wisdom without Michael's aid.

Neither the mythic vision of Cain and Abel nor the allegory of the lazar-house teaches Adam that death is the means to life. A third version of the single lesson, history, lacks both the presentative clarity of myth and the one-to-one precision of allegory. But history is the only mode that Adam and his sons may henceforth employ in their search for God until the "greater man," Christ, is born.

The movement through differing modes of preception in books 11
and 12 may be represented schematically:

```
                        Intuitive Presence (God)
        Unfallen Adam -- Myth   ------¡
                         Allegory     ¦— Patterns
                         History-----¡
          Fallen Adam --- Experiential Process (mortals)
```

Unfallen Adam lived in the world of myth, shaded by allegory; and
his reach was for the ultimate mode of knowing—intuitive presence.
Fallen Adam lives in a world of experiential process, and his reach
toward God must be through history. The pattern of hierarchical
modes is parallel to the chain of being and to the Platonic ladder;
for, since Adam has fallen several steps from all three perspectives,
he must begin the laborious climb back toward God. Should he
overreach, his knowledge will be self-defeating, even demonic, for
Satan too may be found in the patterns of history, allegory, and
myth. The chart of perceptive modes has a mirrored perversion,
reaching from experiential process to hell.

As we have noted, the remainder of Adam's lesson is historical,
and he sees in his third vision (11. 556–92) the varied human activity
of man obsessed with the things of this world. When the Sons of
God wed the Daughters of Men (Cain's descendants), invoking not
the Holy Spirit but the pagan Hymen, Adam has his first opportu-
nity to read the pattern of history. His judgment is that of Mammon:
"What can Heav'n show more?" (2. 273). Michael corrects Adam's
misreading with a grim pun: "these fair Atheist, and now swim in
joy,/ (Erelong to swim at large) and laugh; for which / The world
erelong a world of tears must weep" (11. 625–28). Adam still does
not understand, for he returns to the blame-shifting of the judgment
scene: "But still I see the tenor of Man's woe / Holds on the same,
from Woman to begin" (11. 632–33). Adam looks for patterns in
history and finds himself. Michael's response is a curt reminder of a
lesson Adam should have, by now, learned: "Man's effeminate
slackness" leads to sin.

The fourth vision (11. 638–73), "Sword-Law," moves the lesson
from a definition of the faces of death to an illustration of the path to
salvation. The "one good man" archetype, the "greater man" who
will regain the blissful seat, is Christ. The first ectype of Christ is

Abdiel who remained faithful to God in the war in heaven; and Adam, who should have perceived the pattern in the conduct of his son, Abel, failed to do so. Now, in history, the pattern begins to emerge. Enoch, "eminent / In wise deport, spake much of Right and Wrong"; but, since mankind would not receive the lesson, "a Cloud descending snatch'd him thence" (11. 665–70).

When Adam again fails to understand, Michael explains that the vision is meant to show both "what reward / Awaits the good, the rest what punishment" (11. 709–10); and the lesson is then repeated in the history of Noah. To Adam, the destruction seems so total that he cannot see its bright promise: he beholds the end of all his "Offspring, end so sad, / Depopulation" (11. 755–56). The lesson Adam draws is that peace, like war, leads to sin and destruction. When Adam finally requests help in interpretation, Michael repeats the tale of destruction, adding that the Garden of Eden will be washed away to become "an Island salt and bare, / The haunt of Seals and Orcs, and Sea-mews' clang" (11. 834–35). Adam should note that the garden is replaced by the ark, just as Adam himself is replaced by Noah.

The new equation that Michael has established is typological rather than moral. Christ-Adam-Everyman is changed to Adam-Noah-Christ. The archetype becomes the antitype, as Christ the heavenly pattern comes to earth to establish the heavenly pattern in time. In the birth of Christ, intuitive presence and experiential process will be rejoined, and the world will be recreated in the hearts of the faithful. These metaphysical implications are signaled by the rainbow, and Adam, for the first time, reads his lesson correctly. The first half of the total lesson concludes with a restatement of the "one good man" theme, but the comforting promise of "Day and Night," "Seed-time and Harvest," is shadowed with the grim promise of destruction by fire. History has much to play out before the just will have full opportunity to possess a new heaven and a new earth.

Michael pauses between the world destroyed and the world re-made to give Adam a chance to ask questions or to make observations. But Adam is silent, apparently exhausted by the demands that have been placed upon his mortal sight. Since the visions of history, inferior to heavenly visions, have been too difficult for Adam, he is reduced to listening; and such will be the condition of mankind. Not only is God's face beyond fallen capacity, so too is history. The "visions" of book 12 are verbal.

Book 11 has ended upon a hopeful note—the one just man can be victorious—but book 12 introduces his antithesis: the one evil man, the overreacher, the rebel against God. Just as Abdiel, Enoch, and Noah are patterned upon Christ, Nimrod is patterned after his adversary:

> Hee with a crew, whom like Ambition joins
> With him or under him to tyrannize,
> Marching from *Eden* towards the West, shall find
> The Plain, wherein a black bituminous gurge
> Boils out from under ground, the mouth of Hell;
> Of Brick, and of that stuff they cast to build
> A City and Tow'r, whose top may reach to Heav'n.
>
> (12. 38–44)

Here, in history, is a demonic ectype. The scale is different, for compared to the mighty towers of Pandemonium, Babel is a toy, but the pattern, the will to evil, is the same; and God responds with the same derision and irony that characterized His "fear" of Satan's rebellion. The punishment, too, is consonant with that visited upon Satan:

> Forthwith a hideous gabble rises loud
> Among the Builders; each to other calls
> Not understood, till hoarse, and all in rage,
> As mockt they storm.
>
> (12. 56–59)

Adam's indignation is proper; man was given dominion over the animals, not over other men. But the tower reaching toward God seems, to Adam, wrong for logistical reasons: how could Nimrod have expected to carry food that high, or to breathe at such an altitude? Since Adam but half understands the lesson, he misses the central point: Nimrod is not just stupid; he is sinful.

God has promised that Sin and Death will serve Him by licking up drab and filth so that the world may be renewed, and Michael tells Adam that the "one bad man" will follow his archetype in similar degrading service to God. When potentially good men are ruled by passion, "violent Lords" will be allowed to rule them: "Who oft as undeservedly enthral / His outward freedom: Tyranny must be, / Though to the Tyrant thereby no excuse" (12. 94–96).

The contest between Satan and Abdiel, between Adam and Eve, and between Cain and Abel is to be continued throughout time. The one good man becomes the "one peculiar Nation" (12. 111) as the sons of Abraham endure purification in a hostile and godless world. Yet always a Moses is born to correct the errant and to lead the chosen toward a promised land.

At last, Michael tells Adam that the Messiah will be born who "shall ascend / The Throne hereditary" (12. 369–70). When the narrative has reached this great period, Michael again pauses to allow Adam to recover and respond. Adam does quite well; he sees, at last, the meaning of the prophecy that the seed of woman shall bruise the serpent's head; and he remembers that the serpent is to bruise the seed's heel. Adam is eager for the fight to begin; patience is a difficult lesson. Michael corrects him at once: "Dream not of thir fight, / As of a Duel, or the local wounds / Of head or heel" (12. 386–88). Christ will win by accepting the consequence of Adam's sin, not by destroying Satan in combat, and thus the way to life is through death. Here, at last, is the connection between Adam's question, "What is death?" and the lesson Michael has been instructed to give, "What is Life."[34]

The time from the resurrection of Christ to the last judgment is covered very swiftly. Lines 446 to 465 echo with phrases drawn from the Psalms, from the Four Gospels, and from the Apostles' Creed. The faithful will be received in bliss: "Whether in Heav'n or Earth, for then the Earth / Shall all be Paradise, far happier place / Than this of *Eden*, and far happier days" (12. 463–65). Raphael's promise of divine mutability is, here, translated from the unfallen garden to the fallen earth. It is small wonder that Adam misconstrues the relative merits of God's two plans. He sees the happy end of fallen man in Michael's words; he has lived only the beginning of unfallen man. Raphael's promise is forgotten as Adam, overcome by the symmetry and finality of history, wonders if perhaps his sin is necessary:

> full of doubt I stand,
> Whether I should repent me now of sin
> By mee done and occasion'd, or rejoice
> Much more, that much more good thereof shall spring,
> To God more glory, more good will to Men
> From God, and over wrath grace shall abound.
>
> (12. 473–78)

Adam's *felix culpa*, although an assent to the ways of God, is quite illogical.[35] A necessary element in the pattern that he approves is the repentance that he considers retrieving; hence, no more convincing evidence of his limited vision could be presented. Adam has much to learn before he will be ready for a return to Eden.

Something of that lesson in patience is contained in Michael's description of the tribulation of Christians (12. 485–551), and Adam at last realizes his own limitations; he has his "fill / Of knowledge, what this Vessel can contain." When he summarizes his lesson, the inverted pride of *felix culpa* finds no place. The obedient conduct he hopes to achieve has the same goal, the same imperatives, that should have governed Eden before the fall. God has not changed; Adam has. The end remains, only the distance and the pain of the journey are different:

> Henceforth I learn, that to obey is best,
> And love with fear the only God, to walk
> As in his presence, ever to observe
> His providence, and on him sole depend,
> Merciful over all his works, with good
> Still overcoming evil, and by small
> Accomplishing great things, by things deem'd weak
> Subverting worldly strong, and worldly wise
> By simply meek; that suffering for Truth's sake
> Is fortitude to highest victory,
> And to the faithful Death the Gate of Life;
> Taught this by his example whom I now
> Acknowledge my Redeemer ever blest.
>
> (12. 561–73)

This passage deserves close attention for it contains Milton's answer to THE question, "What shall a man do to be saved?" Michael's approval is unrestrained, for Adam has "attain'd the sum / Of wisdom." If he can practice this wisdom, he will hardly miss the physical paradise; for the Christian may possess a paradise within that is "happier far" (12. 585–87). Blessed is he who knows that true freedom lies in pure obedience and lives by that knowledge, for all else is vanity. Such is the lesson of *Paradise Lost*.

The simplicity of the lesson, after all that poetry, drama, and learning, is devastating. Adam descends to Eve who has been tutored in a gentle dream "Portending good, and all her spirits compos'd / To meek submission" (12. 596–97). Eve's last speech is meant to contrast with her earlier willfulness; the truth of her final dream clears away the tears and pain of her Satanic dream. In sketching her relationship with Adam, she teaches him, once more, his relationship to God:

> now lead on;
> In mee is no delay; with thee to go,
> Is to stay here; without thee here to stay,
> Is to go hence unwilling; thou to mee
> Art all things under Heav'n, all places thou.
>
> (12. 614–18)

The final lines of *Paradise Lost* are perfect:

> The World was all before them, where to choose
> Thir place of rest, and Providence thir guide:
> They hand in hand with wand'ring steps and slow,
> Through *Eden* took thir solitary way.

There is available the sense of an ending, a catharsis, all passion spent. The mood is sadly tranquil, yet tinged with hope.

### CHAPTER 7

# The Perfect Pattern:
# Paradise Regained

WHEN, in 1671, Milton published *Paradise Regain'd. A Poem in IV Books. To Which is added Samson Agonistes*, he provided contrasting conclusions for the great poetic and theological vision we have traced. *Paradise Regained* shows us a perfect, sinless man who utterly rejects the world, the flesh, and the devil. Since *Samson Agonistes* is the tale of a man guilty of both original and personal sin, a man who struggles mightily toward the perfection which is the given essence of Christ, Samson is closely akin to fallen Adam, to the uncouth swain of "Lycidas," to the groping voice of the nativity ode, and even to the Satan of *Paradise Lost* (book 1). Although Samson is a man greatly gifted by God, a man high above the common route, his temptations are heightened versions of our own, his failings are prompted by universal human weaknesses, and his salvation requires that loss of self that every Christian must endure.

Of all Milton's personae, only the Lady of *Comus* and the Christ of *Paradise Regained* pass through their trials unaltered. However, the Lady requires superhuman aid to escape; only Christ requires nothing beyond himself. When the action of *Paradise Regained* begins, Christ is in full possession of the lesson learned by Adam at the close of *Paradise Lost* and is filled with the "rousing motion" that leads Samson back to his God. If Christ's almost effortless rejection of the world as it is offered to him by Satan is Milton's final word, the reader, like Moses, has been shown a region of experience forever beyond his grasp.

Such an exposure may have been Milton's purpose, for after all the partial glimpses of perfection, after all the terrible struggles with human imperfections, he may have wished, for once, an unequivocal victory. And yet the individual poems do not follow such a pattern; for, despite the religious fervor of Milton's art, he is by no means a mystic bent upon escape from the fallen world. Each of his major poems descends at its close from the mountain of vision, almost as though Milton viewed ecstasy as an abdication of responsibility. Compared to the poems of Richard Crashaw, Henry Vaughan, or even George Herbert, *Paradise Regained* keeps both feet firmly planted on the ground; for, at the close of the sequel to *Paradise Lost,*Christ leaves magical banquets, visionary mountains, and temple levitation to return to his mother's house and to the work of his mission in the world.

Since external evidence is inconclusive, the long and complicated question as to whether the epic, *Paradise Regained,* or the drama, *Samson Agonistes,* is Milton's concluding statement is likely to remain unsolved.[1] For our purpose, it may be enough to note that the epic presents the archetype of man's true nature, and that the drama shows us a type who is struggling toward an unknown perfection. I prefer the traditional ordering which shows Milton, in *Samson,* fully engaged, bloodily cognizant of man's condition as he completes the good fight. Metaphysically, neither is "final" so long as the binding of Satan and the final judgment lie in the future, for the archetypal pattern of Christ is timeless and the struggle of Samson is diurnal.

## I  *Resumé*

The four books of Milton's brief epic, *Paradise Regained,* are an ingenious expansion of the Biblical narratives of Christ's temptation in the wilderness. The poem's action begins with John's baptism of Jesus, at which a dove descended and a voice acknowledged Jesus' divinity. Satan, who had watched the baptism, fled to a council of demons to plan a response to this new "son" of God. A demonic plan—to ensnare Jesus in sin and so discover the relationship of Christ to the prophecy that the seed of Eve would bruise the serpent's head—was formed. God smiled at Satan's plan, and He told Gabriel that Christ's temptation constituted a preparation, through suffering, for his final victory over Satan, Sin, and Death.

Jesus wandered into the desert to meditate upon his future and recalled the signs he had been given, early in life, of his divine nature. He waited for forty days, fasting, the further revelation of God's will. At last he grew hungry, and to him appeared an old man who claimed to recognize Jesus as he whom the voice had acknowledged at baptism. He asked that Jesus turn stones into bread that they both might eat. Jesus refused, citing precedents from Hebrew history, and he saw through Satan's disguise. Satan claimed, by precedent, the right to tempt a man of God and denied that he was the enemy of mankind. Jesus called Satan a liar, asserted that all Satan's supposed service to man was performed in unwilling obedience to God, and reminded Satan that the boasted oracular voices were now silent. Satan claimed the right of all sufferers to rebel against their torments through lies. Since God, he argued, allows hypocrites and atheist priests in holy places, why should Satan not be granted an audience with Jesus? When Christ ended the discussion by reminding Satan that they both operated only with God's permission, Satan bowed and disappeared as night fell.

Meanwhile, in book 2, those who were baptized with Jesus and who believed in him sought their savior without success. For a time, they doubted his divinity; but, recalling prophecies of the Messiah, they waited in patience for his return. Mary, who also missed her son, mused over the prophecies, the birth, and the youth of Jesus; and, although she feared the sword in her heart, she gathered patience and waited. And Satan, after being dismissed by Christ, returned to his council for advice about further temptations. When Belial suggested that Satan set a woman before Christ, Satan rejected the idea and instead chose to offer Christ honor, glory, and popular praise. Since he knew that Jesus hungered, he took a subtle band of spirits with him to prepare and serve a banquet in the desert.

Jesus, who had dreamed of sharing Elijah's and Daniel's food, awoke and went to a beautiful grove where Satan appeared to him in the guise of a cosmopolitan. He reminded Jesus of God's ability to feed His chosen in the desert and suggested that Jesus had been forgotten. When Jesus assured Satan that God would provide all necessary things, Satan asked if Jesus would accept a gift of food. "As I like the giver," Jesus replied. Satan, saying that he represented Nature who was shamed by the hunger of her master, set a rich table and urged Jesus to eat. Jesus answered that he, too, could call forth a banquet if he wished, but he wondered why Satan wished to aid his enemy, the Son of God? Angered at the repulse, Satan dismissed the banquet to the sound of harpie wings and talons.

Although Satan felt himself defeated, he renewed, in book 3, the temptation by offering Jesus wisdom and fame. If, he said, Jesus was wise, why was he so little known? By the time Alexander was Jesus' age, he had conquered the world; Scipio had won fame at Carthage; Pompey had ridden in triumph through Rome; and, the older Julius Caesar became, the more glory he sought. Jesus rejected Satan's offer of wisdom and fame, saying that he desired neither wealth for empire's sake, nor empire for glory's sake. True glory, he said, lies in goodness, not in a mob's adulation, and conquest begets corruption: Job and Socrates have greater fame than any military man.

When Satan rebuked Jesus for rejecting glory and asserted that even God the Father seeks glory, Jesus reminded him that all glory is God's; that those who seek glory for themselves attempt to take it from the Father; and that God shares glory with those who seek to honor God. The argument abashed Satan, for he remembered his own lost glory, but he asked Christ why he did not hasten to fulfill Biblical prophecies of the Messiah. Christ answered that the timetable was in God's hands, and that those who obey best can command best. Again he asked why Satan wished to hasten his own destruction, since even Satan must know that the demonic kingdom would fall when the Son's kingdom was established. Satan answered that he wished to end the suspense; since he must eventually be "worst," he would be so now.

For a moment the tables were turned, the tempter became the tempted, and Satan almost wished to ask forgiveness, but he at once hardened his heart and renewed the temptation of Jesus. He began by asking why Jesus was so slow in moving toward the good. Perhaps he was shy? Satan would be glad to help. He offered to show Jesus the glory of the world and to give him the knowledge necessary to defeat the world's rulers. Taking Christ to a high mountain, he showed him the hosts of Parthia. With these troops, which Satan would give him, Jesus could defeat Rome and restore the ten tribes of the Jews. Jesus answered that the tribes had not yet completed their punishment and that the Son of God would await the workings of his Father.

Although Satan had been defeated in every attempt, he continued the temptation in book 4 by showing Jesus the grandeur of Rome. With the proper ruler, he asserted, Rome could make the entire world a much better place; Jesus would be the perfect benevolent monarch. Jesus contrasted the decadence of Rome with the glory of his own future kingdom. But Satan was so overcome by the grandeur of his own temptation that he proceeded, despite the Son's categorical refusals, by offering Jesus the whole world if he would

but worship Satan. Such a gift deserved such gratitude. Christ told
Satan to get behind him and be forever damned.

Satan was surprised at Jesus' anger since the temptations had
harmed no one; and he argued that, since his and Jesus' fates were
linked, he had a right to test Jesus. As Satan recalled Christ's preco-
cious display of wisdom, he offered the Son both the learning and
the art of Greece since Hebrew lore was incomplete and unsophisti-
cated. Since Christ must know gentile ways in order to rule the
gentiles, Satan offered the beauty of art, the wisdom of philosophy,
and the skill of oratory. With such gifts, Jesus would be prepared to
rule the world.

Jesus replied that he already knew everything the Greeks had
learned, for to seek truth in pagan lore was to be a deluded child
gathering pebbles upon a beach. Hebrew art, because it was true,
was greater than the art of Greece; and, since Christ knew God who
is truth, he had no need for the dim, secondhand knowledge of
pagan sages. This rejection angered Satan, and he predicted the
pain in store for Jesus, adding that the stars showed no date for the
advent of Christ's kingdom. He returned Jesus to the desert, pre-
tended to disappear, and left Jesus in darkness.

That night, as Christ slept, Satan sent ugly dreams and a fierce
storm, but the Son slept peacefully throughout the night. When
dawn came, Satan returned to find Jesus no worse than wet. Al-
though Jesus told Satan to stop his vain temptations, Satan asserted
that there was yet a final test which would reveal the exact nature of
Jesus' Sonship, and he carried Christ to the pinnacle of the temple
in Jerusalem. Setting Christ on the dizzy height, Satan told him to
either stand or cast himself down that the angels might catch him.
Christ answered, "Tempt not the Lord thy God," and stood on the
pinnacle. Satan, however, fell and fled in consternation to carry the
news of his defeat to his demons.

Angels came and carried Christ to a beautiful feast where he
dined on fruits from the Tree of Life and drank of the Waters of Life.
The angels sang Jesus' praise, acknowledging him to be the Son who
had driven Satan from heaven. Thus Adam was avenged; for, by
vanquishing temptation, Jesus had regained paradise for all men.
Since the new paradise was within Christ, it would henceforth be
beyond Satan's influence. When the song ended, Jesus returned,
unobserved by men, to his mother's house.

## II  *A Sequel to* Paradise Lost?

To a reader fresh from *Paradise Lost, Paradise Regained* is puzzling, for the first 182 lines seem designed to connect the two poems in mode, theme, and structure. "One man's firm obedience" in the brief epic is to recover the Eden which was lost in the great epic by "One man's disobedience." Both poems use the triple stage of heaven, earth, and hell; both give us three perspectives (human, demonic, and divine) through which to judge events. Satan is again the malcontented tempter, and the bait he offers Christ is a masculine version of that which seduced Eve.

The typological predecessors which both Satan and Christ recall are those same types revealed to Adam by Michael in the future history which constitutes the last two books of *Paradise Lost.* Up-down, black-white, light-dark, separation-unity bear their accustomed symbolic dimensions. As the opening of *Paradise Lost* established the epic genre by allusions to Classical epics, so the opening lines of *Paradise Regained* echo Virgil's "I sing of arms and the man," and in both poems Milton asserts the superiority of Christian epic to those of the pagan masters. The muse invoked, "Thou Spirit," links Milton's inspiration to Christ's and so makes of poetic composition a struggle comparable to Christ's temptation, just as the composition of *Paradise Lost* is linked to the creation of the universe. When Milton promises to "tell of deeds / Above Heroic, though in secret done" (1. 14–15), we are to remember the higher argument of "Patience and Heroic Martyrdom" (*PL*, 9.33) which signals the superiority of *Paradise Lost* to martial epic and romance.[2]

Certainly the theology of *Paradise Regained*, the structures which I have called "strategic," are close kin to those of *Paradise Lost;* the differences are in textures, in "tactics," in the surface experiences of the poems as drama. Underlying both poems is the serene sameness of God; but, whereas *Paradise Lost* presents us with seemingly radical rearrangements of the manifest nature of existence, the surface of *Paradise Regained* is entirely congruent with strategic imperatives: Adam and Eve plunge into a flood of emotions; Christ is never "worse than wet." Thus, if we read *Paradise Regained* as drama, we are bound to be disappointed.[3]

Had Milton wished to celebrate Christ's power, the Bible offers the resurrection, the ascension, and the last judgment. Had he wished to demonstrate Christ's obedience, he might have chosen Gethsemane or the crucifixion. Instead, he chose the triple temptation of Christ in the wilderness as recorded by Matthew and Luke.[4] Certainly there is dramatic potential in the episode, for Christ might have suffered terribly from hunger and thirst; he might have felt a patriot's frustration at Rome's complacent tyranny; he could have burned with a desire to destroy the adversary, Satan; he might have felt himself deserted, and very humanly have sought another miracle to reassure himself of God's favor. Although Milton seems to be aware of the dramatic potentials, each of the possible crises occurs only retrospectively in *Paradise Regained*; for Christ remembers having entertained and then dismissed the various possibilities of self-aggrandizement through worldly wisdom and power.

As I have suggested, the key to understanding *Paradise Regained* is to recognize that it is a *demonstration* of the perfection of Christ, not the *drama* of achieving that perfection: it is cognitive, not sensuous. One character, Christ, is aware of this distinction; the other character, Satan, is not. Satan proceeds as if the temptations were a genuine conflict through which both loser and winner could be changed. But in *Paradise Regained* little play exists in the strategic rope, and Satan has only the faintest shadow of tactical freedom. At every point the actions of Christ are in perfect concord with the will of the Father. Christ scarcely interacts with Satan at all, and then it is to brush him away like a persistent gnat.

We are confronted, therefore, by a singularly undramatic spectacle, the spectacle of Satan's ramming his head again and again against the unmoving wall of Christ until the wall sends him away. Even Satan's final rationalization for the temptation, his desire to discover if Jesus is not only a son of God but the Son of God who is to bruise Satan's head, is undercut, for Satan already knows the answer:

> Long the decrees of Heav'n
> Delay, for longest time to him is short;
> And now too soon for us the circling hours
> This dreaded time have compast, wherein we
> Must bide the stroke of that long threat'n'd wound.
>
> (1. 55–59)

Likewise, Satan has nothing of real value to offer Christ, and knows it: Christ already displays "All virtue, grace and wisdom to achieve / Things highest, greatest" (1. 68–69). As a drama of discovery *Paradise Regained* offers little more than a series of abortive feints, for Satan cannot offer even the genuine opportunity to reject his offers since Christ has already come to terms with temptation (1. 196–293), since he knows that "what concerns my knowledge God reveals." The negative is also closed to Satan, for he cannot offer the bitter cup of Gethsemane nor the terrible exclusion of "My God, My God. Why hast Thou forsaken me?" because those "gifts" also come from the Father.

### III  *Dramatic Demonstration*

Although the Christ of *Paradise Regained* has already learned the lessons which the poem demonstrates, the reader has not.[5] And Milton is able to generate considerable tension in the brief epic by playing off the reader's presumed response to Satan's offers against those of Christ. The poem presents two contrary readings of Christ's passive resistance—to Satan, inactivity is sloth; to Christ, it is patience—and the driving force of the two characters makes such diversity of judgment inevitable. Satan is always motivated by pride; Christ, by magnanimity. Pride is generated by insecurity; magnanimity, by confidence. Pride and sloth are antithetical; magnanimity and patience are complementary. As the two great antagonists thrust and parry, the reader is exposed alternately to Satan's desperate activity and to Christ's confident patience. The temptation of the reader is to judge Christ by the standards of Satan. The devil himself says it best as he responds to Belial's suggestion that the way to catch Christ is to "Set women in his eye and in his walk" (2. 153): "*Belial*, in much uneven scale thou weigh'st / All others by thyself" (2. 173–74). As we experience the poem, we come to realize that Satan is doing exactly what he faults Belial for doing, and we may even find ourselves guilty of the charge.

The tale of Christ in the wilderness is traditionally divided into three sections: the temptation of bread; the temptation of the world; the temptation of the temple. Although Milton treats the first and third temptations in brief and expands the second to fill the body of his poem, the dynamics of *Paradise Regained* are such that the first

and third temptations are linked; both are temptations to supersede
the laws of nature and so elevate Christ at the expense of God. To
this basic temptation, Satan adds a humanitarian note:

> But if thou be the Son of God, Command
> That out of these hard stones be made thee bread;
> So shalt thou save thyself and us relieve
> With Food, whereof we wretched seldom taste.
>
> (1. 342–45)

The fundamental nature of the temptation is disguised beneath the
desire to preserve self and to perform a good work.[6] As with Eve in
*Paradise Lost,* Satan suggests that Christ's duty requires a selfish
act. At once Christ picks up the food metaphor: "Man lives not by
Bread only, but each Word / Proceeding from the mouth of God"
(1. 349–50). As it was in Eden, the choice is still between physical
and spiritual food, and the same precept holds: Seek first the food of
heaven and earthly food will be provided. A major goal of *Paradise
Regained* is to reverse Eve's action at the tree of knowledge of good
and evil. Christ has passed the first and most obvious test, but
Satan, in book 2, sophisticates the temptation. Since Christ will not
miraculously make food, Satan makes it for him (2. 337–67). Unwit-
tingly, Satan is still parodying his heavenly original, for the banquet
he sets in the wilderness is the demonic equivalent of the feast
provided for Christ when the ordeal is finished (4. 586–95). Had
Christ made bread of stone or accepted Satan's feast, he would have
repeated Eve's fall; by patiently awaiting God's true spiritual feast,
he reverses Eve's sin.

But there was a good deal more to Eve's sin than a yielding to
physical hunger; mankind's original hunger was also for knowledge
and power. Milton's expansion, in *Paradise Regained,* of the tempta-
tions which may be called "the world" constitutes book 3 and the
first half of book 4; the poet sets before Christ and the reader the
considerable temptation to the knowledge and the power that was
implicit in Adam's and Eve's curiosity about the stars. The tempta-
tion of the world may be broken into three parts: raw, military
power; power through governmental organization; and power
through art and learning. Each temptation is cloaked with the same
rationalization that disguised the first: Christ, by serving himself,
can benefit mankind. With the military power of Parthia, Christ

could become an Alexander the Great and at the same time free the Jews from their hated Roman masters. Christ's response to the temptation is filled with magnanimous patience:

> My time I told thee . . .
> . . . is not yet come;
> When that comes think not thou to find me slack
> On my part aught endeavoring, or to need
> Thy politic maxims, or that cumbersome
> Luggage of war there shown me, argument
> Of human weakness rather than of strength.
>
> (3. 396–402)

As for the Jews, "To his due time and providence I leave them" (3. 440).

When Christ is offered the dictatorship of Rome, Satan has sophisticated the temptation of Parthia, for the military battles have been won and a political structure established. As Emperor of Rome, Christ would aid not just the Jews but all civilization: "expel this monster from his Throne / Now made a sty, and in his place ascending / A victor people free from servile yoke" (4. 100–103). For Christ, the temptation is no greater than was the offer of Parthian armies; but, for the reader, the ante has been raised in that the grandeur that was Rome is both a personal temptation to become godlike Caesar and a humanitarian temptation to use Rome's power for the good of man. Since we do not have Christ's confidence, his answer to Satan, "of my Kingdom there shall be no end," is unlikely to be ours. Satan, likewise, is overcome by a temptation which he cannot imagine anyone refusing, and he bares the hook beneath the bait: the gift is Christ's "if thou wilt fall down, / And worship me as thy superior Lord" (4. 166–67). The reader, who may have been tempted, can retreat into the security of Christ's response, "Get thee behind me" (4. 193), and the temptations would seem to be over.

Yet the third of the worldly temptations is the greatest, both for Milton and for the sort of reader he desired. When Satan catalogues the accomplishments of Classical Greece, of Plato, Aristotle, Zeno, Homer, and Socrates, he sets forth the very roots which nourished Milton's intellectual development, and they are the more attractive in that Satan does not offer the finished product, but only the opportunity: "These here revolve, or, as thou lik'st, at home, / Till time

mature thee to a Kingdom's weight" (4. 281–82). Christ, like Milton
and the reader, recognizes the temptation of wisdom as the most
dangerous of all, and he does not reject it out of hand as he has the
power of Parthia and the organization of Rome. Instead, Christ
catalogues Classical accomplishments, finds them inferior to He-
brew learning, and ends by divorcing their excellence from Satan:
the wisdom of the Classics is to be dismissed "Unless where moral
virtue is express'd / By light of Nature, not in all quite lost"
(4. 351–52). As we have seen in examining Milton's earlier poems,
the light of nature can lead a devout student a goodly distance on the
path to God; only when priorities get confused does learning lead to
sin.

Christ's rejection of the world-as-end is complete, and a baffled
Satan summarizes the patient triumph of the Son:

> Since neither wealth, nor honor, arms nor arts,
> Kingdom nor Empire pleases thee, nor aught
> By me propos'd in life contemplative,
> Or active, tended on by glory or fame,
> What dost thou in this World?
>
> (4. 368–72)

Throughout the temptations Satan makes the same three errors: he
assumes that Christ's goals, like his own, are egocentric; he fails to
realize that "By me propos'd" vitiates any good in the gift; and he
assumes that Christ's kingdom is "in this World."[7] Having
exhausted the "natural" gifts at his disposal, Satan now turns to
threats as he reads Christ's earthly fate in the stars: "Sorrows, and
labors, opposition, hate, / Attends thee, scorns, reproaches, in-
juries, / Violence and stripes, and lastly cruel death" (4. 386–88).
Satan's duplicity is clear: if he believes the stars, then his offers of
glory are lies; if he does not believe the stars, his threats are lies.
Satan, a creature of time, cannot understand the infinite:

> A Kingdom they portend thee, but what Kingdom,
> Real or Allegoric I discern not,
> Nor when, eternal sure, as without end,
> Without beginning; for no date prefixt
> Directs me in the Starry Rubric set.
>
> (4. 389–93)

Satan understands well enough a historical kingdom; he can even posit an allegorical kingdom; but a mythic kingdom in which the real and the allegorical are joined in timeless congruity of pattern and example is beyond his wildest dream since such a kingdom is exactly that against which he rebelled in heaven.

The night of storm and evil dreams which Satan visits upon Christ is the Satanic version of Christ's passion; it represents Satan's attempt to control existence by following his own incomplete understanding of the future he has read in the stars. But, since the stars reflect God's will (in this case, they mirror Gethsemane and the crucifixion), Satan's effort to fill a pattern beyond his understanding is futile. When he discovers that Christ is "no worse than wet," Satan's agile mind changes the real storm to allegory. If he has been unable to reify the dire predictions signed in the stars, he has, at least, constructed an omen equal to God's: "this ominous night that clos'd thee round, / So many terrors, voices, prodigies / May warn thee, as a sure foregoing sign" (4. 481–83). Satan's storm demonstrates the vast gulf which separates his being from that of Christ, for the most physical of Satan's creations is, at best, merely an omen of an omen.

All that remains for Satan is brute force, the suicidal plunge into the vortex of God's power which all of the demons except Moloch have rejected. All the boasted subtleties are forgotten as Satan sets Christ on the pinnacle of the temple with a command that he believes Christ unable to disobey;

> There stand, if thou wilt stand; to stand upright
> Will ask thee skill; I to thy Father's house
> Have brought thee, and highest plac't, highest is best,
> Now show thy Progeny; if not to stand,
> Cast thyself down; safely if Son of God.
>
> (4. 551–55)

Satan entertains but two possibilities: Christ must either stand or not stand. In either case, Christ will have obeyed Satan's command, and so there seems to Satan no way for Christ to solve the problem without sin. Confronted with the demonic either/or, Christ responds with both/and. Christ stands; Satan falls; and the angels carry Christ safely from the height to a feast.

The conclusion of *Paradise Regained* demonstrates the fulfillment of the perfect pattern, for Christ as ectype has joined with Christ as archetype; all the types of the Old Testament (from Adam to John the Baptist) are fulfilled in Christ the antitype—as the choir of angels celebrates the demonstration that all tactics are subordinate to divine strategy.[8] Christ returns to his mother's home quite unaltered by Satan's machinations, but the reader has been given a glimpse of perfection against which to measure his own life.

CHAPTER 8

# *Coda:* Samson Agonistes

I N *Paradise Regained,* Milton showed us the "one greater Man"
promised in line 4 of *Paradise Lost,* and in the story of Christ's
temptation he demonstrated the nature of the "paradise within"
promised to repentant Adam, for Christ knows

> that to obey is best,
> And love with fear the only God, to walk
> As in his presence, ever to observe
> His providence, and on him sole depend,
> Merciful over all his works, with good
> Still overcoming evil, and by small
> Accomplishing great things, by things deem'd weak
> Subverting worldly strong, and worldly wise
> By simply meek . . .
>
> (*PL,* 12.561–69)

But *Paradise Regained* does not demonstrate the final three lines of
Adam's lesson:

> that suffering for Truth's sake
> Is fortitude to highest victory,
> And to the faithful Death the Gate of Life.

Thirty-three years earlier, in "Lycidas," Milton had discovered
death to be the gate of life; but "the better fortitude / Of Patience
and Heroic Martyrdom" (*PL,* 9.31–32) remained unsung. A poem on
the crucifixion would seem to have been the obvious choice; in-
stead, for whatever reasons, Milton gave us *Samson Agonistes.* Yet
it is a mistake to read Samson as a "Christ figure," for the place of
*Samson Agonistes* in Milton's total vision is ambiguous, not only

169

because the date of the poem remains in question, but also because of two seemingly contradictory pieces of evidence.

First, Samson does not discover death to be the gate of life in a Christian sense; at best, he discovers death to be the gate of fame. Because Samson lived centuries before the Christian dispensation, he is an *anticipation* of Christ, not an *imitation*. Like all the Old Testament types of Christ, Samson is ignorant of his relationship to God's ultimate design; he is a *type* blundering toward an unrevealed *antitype*; he is not an *ectype* reaching upward toward a revealed *archetype*. Thus, Samson's relationship to providence is qualitatively different from the relationship available to the Christian.

Second, there are parallels between Samson and Milton (both are blind, both have been betrayed by their nations, both seem to have failed in leading the chosen few) that are so strong as to suggest that *Samson Agonistes* is a thinly disguised autobiography of Milton. In this case, since Milton is a Christian, seeking to perfect his ectypal relationship to the revealed archetype, Samson-as-Milton is a Christian whose struggles and failings are precisely those of Every Christian. Put simply, *Samson Agonistes* can be read as either a Christian or a pre-Christian work, and both readings are congruent with Milton's grand design. The best solution is to read it both ways: internally, the play is pre-Christian, both in its Classical Greek form and in its doctrine; affectively, since both the reader of Milton and Milton himself are keenly aware of the completed antitype, the play is Christian in the same sense that the Old Testament is Christian.[1]

## I   The Biblical Samson

The hero of Milton's closet drama is very different from the swaggering folk hero who storms through Judges 13–16. The Biblical Samson's life began with great promise, for an angel had appeared to the barren wife of Manoa, had promised her that she would bear a child who would begin the delivery of the Israelites from Philistian captivity, and had directed that the child be reared a Nazarite. When Manoa and his wife made a burnt offering in thanksgiving to God, the angel ascended in the flames. The annunciation of Samson bears strong typological relationships to the annunciation of Christ.

But the exploits of Samson are without dignity. He began by contracting marriage to a Philistian woman and then trapping her friends in a riddle game. When they solved the riddle by coercing

Samson's wife, he killed thirty of them and gave his wife to a friend. Later, Samson returned and demanded to sleep with the woman; and, when her father refused him the privilege, Samson tied the tails of 300 foxes together, set them on fire, and chased them through Philistian crops. Samson responded to their protests by slaughtering all within reach and by then running away. Not surprisingly, a Philistian army moved against the Israelites who, to save themselves, delivered Samson, bound, to the enemy. He broke the bonds and slew a thousand Philistines with the jawbone of an ass. Later he visited a harlot in Gaza and carried off the city gates. Typology is sufficiently elastic to read each of these adventures as anticipations of events in Christ's life, but Samson's most famous episode ties him, not with the perfect Christ, but with the imperfect Adam.

At the order of the Philistines, Dalila seduced Samson to learn the secret of his great strength. Three times he deceived her and seized the occasions to destroy more Philistines, but she persisted until he at last told her that his strength lay in his hair. Dalila caused him to fall asleep in her lap, called a barber who cut off the seven locks of his hair, and delivered him to the Philistines. They put out Samson's eyes, bound him in brass fetters, and set him to work grinding grain. To celebrate the capture of Samson, a feast was held in honor of the god, Dagon. When Samson was put on display at Dagon's temple, he prayed to God for strength that he might avenge his blinding. His prayer was granted, Samson pushed over the two pillars which supported the temple, and Samson and 3,000 Philistines were killed in the crash. The Biblical Samson is an egocentric, insensitive bully whose character and adventures are like those of a pagan sun-god.

## II  *Milton's Samson*

Although the Biblical Samson is neither sensitive, moral, nor intelligent, typologists had interpreted his adventures as an anticipation of Christ's life. Following that tradition, Milton makes his Samson eloquently introspective and gives him the conscience of a seventeenth-century Puritan. The mutation of Samson from folk hero to saint parallels the changes that Aeschylus and Sophocles had made in raw myth in order to produce their great dramas.[2] Milton's play is, in form, just such a Classical tragedy: the unities of time, place, and action are carefully observed; there is a chorus and a

messenger; violent action takes place off-stage; and we watch a
hero enmeshed in the coils of fate. But, just as Milton conquered
the epic form in *Paradise Lost* and the elegy in "Lycidas," he
bends Aristotelian tragic principles to his own ends in *Samson
Agonistes*. Greek fate is encompassed by providence, and Samson's
epiphany reveals not the ways of man confronted with the brute
and implacable power of the universe, but the ways of God with a
sinful man.[3]

Milton's play begins with Samson blind and enslaved, and the
Biblical adventures are included only through the rueful recollec-
tions of Samson, Manoa, and the chorus. Milton makes Dalila Sam-
son's wife; inserts the giant, Harapha; and extrapolates the role of
Manoa. Nevertheless, the Biblical story is not so much contradicted
as revised; for Milton makes of the old "Ebrews" a functioning
Classical chorus without violating their historical character. The
play is a brilliant weaving of the Hebraic story on a Classical loom for
Christian purposes, a stunning exercise in syncretic subordination.[4]

Intricate image patterns move in and out of the action: seas,
storms, and ships; animals, insects, and snakes; light, darkness, and
flames; land and water. The reader accustomed to Milton's
"trustworthy" imagery is likely to be startled when he discovers that
both Samson and Dalila are compared to ships, that both Samson
and Harapha "storm," and that the victorious Samson is remem-
bered by his tribe as a dragon in a hen house. Rhyme and meter in
*Samson Agonistes* are intricately varied, and the syntax is much
more convoluted than that of *Paradise Regained*. All of Milton's
poetry is rich in sound, but *Samson Agonistes* is almost a song—a
poem best appreciated in an oral reading.

If *Samson Agonistes* is indeed Milton's final work, the body of the
poems, taken as a whole, repeats the pattern we have noted in
individual works: a struggle through the layered masks of the world
toward a clear vision of God's ways is concluded with a return to the
experiential world. I find it plausible that Milton recovered, at the
last, the freedom to use rhyme which he gave up for *Paradise Lost*,[5]
and that Classical learning, castigated in *Paradise Regained* as a bad
master, is restored in *Samson Agonistes* as a useful servant. Finally,
my belief (and hope) is that Milton's final vision is tempered to the
limitations of man in a complex world in the fashion that *Samson
Agonistes* indicates.

### III  *Samson's Progress*

Milton's tale of Samson traces a series of interrelated movements: physically, he moves from slavery to mastery; socially, his reputation changes from infamy to glory; psychologically, he grows from despair through hope to patience; spiritually, his state changes from pride through humility to magnanimity. Each of the movements is based upon the four traditional steps of salvation: conviction, contrition, confession, and conversion from evil to good. As he shifts allegiance from self to God, he gives up law and precedent in favor of revelation.[6]

These changes are summed up in the great paradoxical metaphor of the play: when Samson had outward sight, he was inwardly blind; and the sufferings of physical blindness lead him to spiritual sight. The patterns of regeneration do not occur serially, nor do they hinder each other. Each is woven into the play like a bright thread in a tapestry; they form together, just as each is formed by, Samson's trial and victory. But, unlike the Lady of *Comus*, Samson is not primarily the conflux of a complicated set of analogies; rather, he is a complete human being. The picture in the foreground of the play is that of a sinner who is finding his way through the precious distractions of the world back to his God.

When the play opens, Samson is so completely enmeshed in himself that his visitors, who offer a series of worldly alternatives to his destructive egocentricity, unwittingly torture him further: the Chorus offers love of tribe and obedience to law, Manoa offers the comfort of family love, Dalila presents the delights of sensuality, Harapha tempts Samson to return to military glory, and the messenger combines and summarizes these worldly alternatives in his two visits to the bound Samson. First, he gives Samson the opportunity to reject the lesser possibilities: personal safety and tribal liberation. Second, he allows Samson to supersede the requirements of law and precedent. By subduing his personal, tribal, and legal desires, Samson prepares himself for the rousing motion from God that signals his spiritual victory. The dominant shape that emerges from a total view of the play is a simple, strong movement from self to God.

The barometer of that movement is the Chorus.[7] Its first speech reflects the spiritual chaos that Samson has evidenced in his opening

meditation: "Strongest of mortal men, / To lowest pitch of abject
fortune thou art fall'n" (168–69). But the Chorus also teaches. When
Samson in proud despair asks, "Am I not sung and proverb'd for a
Fool?" (203), and then blames God for granting him strength with-
out wisdom, the Chorus reminds him that he must not tax divine
disposal. When it attacks Samson by asking why he had married
outside his tribe, it leads him to admit a fault and moves him,
however slightly, from self-pity: "Of such examples add mee to the
roll, / Mee easily indeed mine may neglect, / But God's propos'd
deliverance not so" (290–92). The Chorus closes this first scene with
an affirmation that contains both faith and hope: "Just are the ways
of God, / And justifiable to Men" (293–94). By externalizing Sam-
son's own thoughts, the Chorus functions as both tempter and
teacher; as Samson corrects the Chorus, he corrects himself; such is
the role of each of his visitors.

Despite Manoa's obvious good intentions, he tempts Samson to
abdicate his role as God's servant, even as he chastises his son for his
despair. When Samson's pride helps him reject his father's offer,
Manoa corrects that pride: "Be penitent and for thy fault contrite, /
But act not in thy own affliction, Son" (502–3); for Samson's present
punishment, like his past glory and future death, is in God's hands.
But the pious resignation of Manoa contains another, more insidious
temptation: perhaps God wills Samson's return to the relative com-
forts of his father's home. Again, pride protects Samson: "His par-
don I implore; but as for life, / To what end should I seek it?"
(521–22).

The first steps of salvation (conviction and contrition) have led
Samson not to hope but to despair. His faith is firm, but he does not
grant God the power to use such a sinner as himself. By assuming
that he is now worthless to God, he implies that he was once valu-
able. His pride suggests that God needs man; and Samson's de-
spair—as we have seen in Satan—is the ultimate pride. The Chorus
senses an error:

> But God who caus'd a fountain at thy prayer
> From the dry ground to spring, thy thirst to allay
> After the brunt of battle, can as easy
> Cause light again within thy eyes to spring,
> Wherewith to serve him better than thou hast.
>
> (581–85)

The imagery employed by the Chorus blends light and water in the same way that the invocation to book 3 of *Paradise Lost* does, and its hope is a clear advance over Samson's despair, but the Chrous, too, limits the scope of God's power; for it means physical, not spiritual, sight: that God might have use for a blind man does not seem possible. Samson does not share even that physical hope, for his words, "My race of glory run, and race of shame, / And I shall shortly be with them that rest" (597–98), echo Adam's desire to return to the earth which bore him. When Manoa returns to the lesser physical hope that Samson will be allowed to return home, Samson again rejects his father: "This one prayer yet remains, might I be heard, / No long petition, speedy death, / The close of all my miseries, and the balm" (649–51). Like Adam, Samson does not understand that death is the gate to life and that his end can be not a dismissal from service but a glorious use of God's instrument.

The Chorus sides with Samson and in its speech on patience mirrors both the despair of the Ebrews and the harsh vision of Sophocles: "Just or unjust, alike seem miserable, / For oft alike, both come to evil end" (703–4). Man's only real choice is the manner of meeting defeat, and the Chorus then adds its prayer to Samson's: "Behold him in this state calamitous, and turn / His labors, for thou canst, to peaceful end" (708–9). Since Samson's father wishes to return his son to childhood, and since the Chorus wishes him restored to his former self, Samson cannot move forward so long as he considers only his self, his family, and his tribe. These first two episodes (Samson and the Chorus; Samson, Manoa, and the Chorus) have stayed Samson's descent into black melancholy and (like the *mens*) have provided a balance against the destructive pull of the ego; but, until Samson can move beyond himself, beyond his own history, the future is a black pit.

The episode with Dalila occupies the middle of the play, both literally and thematically; for just as she has been the occasion for Samson's fall, she becomes the spur for his regeneration. As this pattern suggests, the parallels and the contrasts between Dalila and Eve are strikingly pertinent. She too lists mitigating circumstances: women are weak and unable to keep secrets; she wished to keep Samson all to herself; the priests of Dagon had urged her to cut his hair and so commit a private wrong for the public good; she will make it up to Samson through carnal solace. Like Eve, she desires

to hold her man's hand; but nothing in her plea is equivalent to
Eve's "Forsake me not thus Adam." Indeed, much of Dalila's pro-
test smacks not of Eve but of Satan.[8]

Samson's response is not Adam's, for he forgives Dalila only "At
distance," and by rejecting her touch, he refuses to rejoin her sin.
Finally, his last words to Dalila link her with Judas and his silver:
"Cherish thy hast'n'd widowhood with the gold / Of Matrimonial
treason" (958–59). Dalila, however, serves Samson well; for by
arousing his hate and fear, by giving him a target other than himself
or God, she helps him break from the torpor of self-pity and the sin
of despair. When he rejected the temptations of the Chorus and of
Manoa, he rejected misguided but not evil goals. Because Dalila is
outside family, tribe, and law, Samson's anger purges him like a
righteous fire. Yet, it is clear that she is still attractive to Samson;
and, for the reader, her arguments hold the same specious attraction
that tempted him to side with (or at least admire) Satan. If we are
cultural relativists, Dalila must seem to be treated unfairly, and we
may even weep for the slaughtered Philistines. But since her Dagon
is not God, Milton expects us to enjoy the dramatic irony of her
self-justification: "I shall be nam'd among the famousest / Of
Women" (982–83) is an accurate prediction, but the fame of Dagon
is the infamy of God. Dalila, like Satan, believes that the mind can
make a heaven of hell or a hell of heaven, and the Chorus signals her
demonic allegiance: "She's gone, a manifest Serpent by her sting /
Discover'd in the end, till now conceal'd" (997–98).

Dalila has led Samson to a rediscovery of the operation of provi-
dence ("God sent her"), but his recognition is still selfish ("to debase
me, / And aggravate my folly"). Samson needs yet another lesson. As
the Chorus reflected Samson's tribe, as Manoa represented his fam-
ily, as Dalila stood for his flesh, Harapha is a mirror of Samson's
desire for earthly glory. And the double standard that the reader
must recognize in order to understand Dalila is again necessary to
properly judge Harapha. Judged by worldly standards, Harapha is a
formidable, worthy adversary for Samson. Judged by the standards
of eternity, he is a *miles glorioso*, a braggadocio,[9] who must learn to
restrain himself in the presence of God. The reader should give
Harapha credit for being in an impossible situation. If he battles
Samson and wins, he will be guilty of picking on a blind man.
Should he fight Samson and lose, he would have lost everything he
holds dear to a cripple. By properly understanding the rules of

Harapha's world, the reader can make a proper evaluation of Samson's juvenile exploits. It is important that Samson see in Harapha's huff and puff an image of his own vanity. Early in the play, Samson notes that "the contest is now / 'Twixt God and *Dagon*" (461–62), but his tone implies that God will simply have to get along without Samson's considerable help. In plumbing the shallowness of Harapha, Samson realizes that the contest has always been, and always will be, between the false and the true God. God may choose to use Samson, or He may work through some other means; but, ultimately, no man is necessary to God.

As Samson gains a truer image of himself, a grim humor creeps into his speech. To the hesitant Harapha he says, "The way to know were not to see but taste" (1091), and, of course, Harapha wants, by this time, no part of Samson. Yet, for the knowing reader, the image of tasting links Samson with Eve and the fruit, with the blood-wine of communion, and with the apocalypse when all men will be pressed to wine. Samson himself will be pressed in the temple of Dagon, and the wine of his death, which temporarily frees the Ebrews from the Philistines, is a typological forecast of Christ's life-giving crucifixion. Harapha enables Samson to achieve a measure of magnanimity, for Samson learns the liberating lesson that Gabriel tried to teach Satan: "what folly then / To boast what Arms can do, since thine no more / Than Heav'n permits, nor mine" (*PL*, 4. 1007–9). Christ repeats that lesson to Satan in *Paradise Regained*: "do as thou find'st / Permission from above; thou canst not more" (1.495–96).

Samson's magnanimity is less clear, less pure than either Gabriel's or Christ's, but it terrifies Harapha: "His Giantship is gone somewhat crestfall'n," notes the Chorus; and the brave Cavaliers must have felt somewhat the same as they confronted Cromwell's army. At best, Harapha lives in L'Allegro's world; Samson, like Il Penseroso, has attained "something like Prophetic strain."

Despite the resurgence of hope in faith which Samson's visceral exchanges with Dalila and Harapha have prompted, he cannot act; for the religious law of the Hebrews yet stands between Samson and God's unrevealed plan: Samson must neither commit suicide by refusing to obey the messenger, nor sin by appearing at Dagon's feast. Without a revelation, Samson is caught. Only when he realizes that God "may dispense with me or thee . . . For some important cause" (1377–79) does he feel "Some rousing motions" as

God reclaims a willful instrument. With this miracle, Samson's internal agon is complete. The culmination of physical action, Samson's triumphant death, occurs off-stage, not simply in compliance with Classical theory, but in order to maintain the spiritual focus of the play. Samson's death is important chiefly for the Chorus, for Manoa, and for the reader.[10]

Manoa's lesson is savage: he came to ransom his great son; he leaves to carry home the broken body of all his hopes. To Samson's type of Christ, the father plays a type of Mary. The Chorus, which has dithered at the off-stage shouts and worried for its own safety, joins Manoa in setting forth the internal lesson of *Samson Agonistes*. Most of that lesson is cast in the dark mode of omens and emblems, for those who see a historical type cannot know the complete pattern toward which history aims.

Samson's vengeance is compared to a dragon and to an eagle. The return of his virtue (power as well as holiness) is like the rebirth of the phoenix. Perhaps the three metaphors represent stages in the perception of God. The raiding dragon is a primal figure, powerful and amoral. The eagle is Jove's bird, an identification strengthened by comparing his predatory dive to a thunderbolt. The phoenix, whose rebirth is a familiar emblem for the conquest of death by Christ and his saints, may indicate that Samson has achieved a diminished version of ultimate victory. But the phoenix, in *Samson*, does not relate to Samson's death but to the return of his power before death. Samson's only promised immortality is in the memory of his tribe. The reader may see in typal hints a prediction of the divine comedy; but, for the Chorus and Manoa, the play is a pre-Christian tragedy.

The lesson they draw is cast in the firm language that characterizes God's speech in book 3 of *Paradise Lost:* all events, somehow, fit God's pattern. He may appear to turn His face from the holy, but God eventually cares for His own and rains destruction upon the heads of those who seek to thwart providence. For the modern reader, this wisdom is grim; in fact, it is only better than the Greek tragic vision because it insists that the fates are sighted and benevolent. But, for Samson's age, the revelation of God's power and justice must suffice. Manoa notes that "Nothing is here for tears" (1721); and the Chorus, content with "new acquist / Of true experience," departs, "calm of mind, all passion spent." In the dim future, David will defeat Harapha's son Goliath; and the greater man, Christ, will arise from the destruction of Satan's son, Death. But the time, in *Samson Agonistes*, has not yet been fulfilled.

In *Paradise Regained*, Milton summarized the basic, simple demands that Christianity makes upon Everyman; but the purity of that vision, austere and scarcely adorned with the sensuous comforts of poetry or with a compassionate understanding of sin, is esthetically uncomfortable and theologically terrifying. If man must achieve through his own power even a diminished version of Jesus' triumph over Satan, heaven is indeed too high. Just as the persona of "Lycidas" returns us to the experiential world after his brief vision of paradise, just as Adam comes down from the mount to search the world that is all before him, so too Milton descends from the antitype Christ to the type Samson.

Samson's agony numbs us; but it is, after all, the trial of a man, not the story of a God who has emerged from a human chrysalis. In his own way Everyman may emulate Samson; for Samson's world consists of all the contrary forces that constitute diurnality. He is not only a type of Christ, he is an ectype of the great archetypes of obedience and sin (Abdiel and Satan) and a descendant of Cain and Abel. of Nimrod and Noah. As that mixture, Samson forms a comprehensible way station in the journeys of man to God and of God to man that meet in the terrible joy of Calvary.

# CHAPTER 9

# *Conclusion*

THE significance of Milton in our literary tradition can hardly be overestimated. In the eighteenth century, sensibilities as different as those of Alexander Pope and William Blake found him a master to be adapted for a diminished view of man's place in the universe (Pope) or corrected to conform to the primacy of an immanent God (Blake). The Romantic poets, particularly Shelley and Keats, found it necessary to write their way from beneath his giant shadow in order to discover their own poetic voices. In our own age, T. S. Eliot wrote *The Waste Land* in a vain attempt to provide a generation of unbelievers with a unified sensibility such as he found in Milton's meshed art; and Milton's voice can also be heard echoing in the great novels of William Faulkner. Indeed, the character of Satan ranks with the giants fathered by Shakespeare as a literary archetype to be endlessly repeated in our poetry, drama, and fiction.

But what, specifically and in brief, is the Miltonic legacy? The posing of eternal questions as to the nature of man, of his place in the universe, and of his relationships to transcendence seems to me to be Milton's most important achievement. The integration of those questions into a dialogue that is strikingly modern—despite the 300 years that have passed since Milton's death—and the testing of faith against adversaries that are much more than straw men constitute Milton's passionate intellection. And we care about his art precisely because it is earned, strenuously, in the very poems that set it forth. Always we can find in the ebb and flow of image and idea the contrarieties of poetic process, and the tranquil conclusions of Milton's poems are the more striking in that they represent an achieved catharsis for the author as well as an invitation to catharsis for the reader.

180

In closing, let me presume to set forth a brief catalogue of formal poetic accomplishments. Milton fulfilled the dream of the English Renaissance for an epic to match those of Greece and Rome. In "Lycidas," he restored the vitality of the pastoral mode. "L'Allegro–Il Penseroso" established a generalized and yet specific topographical diction that taught our poets to paint "tulipness," rather than the streaks of a tulip. *Samson Agonistes* is the only really successful Greek tragedy written in English; it proved that close adherence to a formal poetic need not diminish genius. In writing sonnets, Milton adapted, stretched, and inverted the conventions of both English and Italian models almost to destruction on topics ranging from the most public ("Avenge O Lord") to the most private ("Methought I Saw"). His example should have settled, once and for all, the complaint that form restricts genius.

The blank verse of *Paradise Lost* strains syntactical patterns to such an extent that we find it almost not English. The epic similes are so organically proleptic that each constitutes a little essay on the relationship between time and eternity. Pronoun references float among viable alternatives and tease us into recognizing "meaningful ambiguities" that mock the giant empiricism. Lines are so enjambed that the poetic unit seems the paragraph, and yet line-breaks frequently cast words backward and forward so that the history and future of an image are contained in its present. Sonorous catalogues lead the imagination beyond image, and negative similes give us simultaneously the presence and absence of sound and silence, of light and dark, of movement and stasis.

Milton's poetic vices are generally the excesses of his virtues. Many readers find that "darkness visible" provides no illumination and that "dark with excessive bright" yields no shade. Sometimes the exotic names seem tiresomely contrived, the elevated syntax on occasion seems merely pompous, and the basic imagery on occasion appears too obviously black and white. When the glistening ritual bubble bursts, we may sometimes feel with Dr. Johnson that, where so much attention is paid to artifice, there can be little sincerity. Milton's style is very easy to parody, for it occupies the uneasy border shared by the sublime and the ridiculous.

Finally, it seems to me, Milton's artistic accomplishments are inseparable from his vision. Unless the reader is caught in the great arguments—however tentatively and with whatever reservations—the grandeur may seem pomp and the sublimity seem a posing. For this reason my effort in this study has been to help the reader understand the terms of Milton's vision, not only for the sake of that vision but for the soaring song.

# Notes and References

## Chapter One

1. William R. Parker, *Milton: A Biography* (London, 1968) is the fullest modern biography. Hanford and Taaffe, *A Milton Handbook* (New York, 1970) is good for a quick survey of the materials for a life of Milton.
2. E.A.J. Honnigmann, ed., *Milton's Sonnets* (London, 1966), provides a full account of the sonnets' occasions.
3. William Haller, *The Rise of Puritanism* (New York, 1938), traces in detail the dynamics of Puritan disaffection with established religion.
4. Maurice Ashley, *England in the Seventeenth Century* (Harmondsworth, Middlesex, 1950), provides a very readable account of the war.
5. Among Milton's contributions to the controversies are *Of Reformation Touching Church-Discipline in England* (1641); *The Reason of Church-Government* (1642); and *An Apology for Smectymnuus* (1642).
6. John G. Halkett, *Milton and the Idea of Matrimony* (New Haven and London, 1970).

## Chapter Two

1. Arthur Barker, "The Pattern of Milton's Nativity Ode," *University of Toronto Quarterly*, X (1941), pp. 167–81.
2. Rosemond Tuve, *Images and Themes in Five Poems by Milton* (Oxford, 1957), pp. 37–72.
3. J. B. Broadbent, "The Nativity Ode," *The Living Milton*, ed. F. Kermode (London, 1960), pp. 12–31.
4. William G. Madsen, *From Shadowy Types to Truth: Studies in Milton's Symbolism* (New Haven, 1968).
5. Mircea Eliade, *Cosmos and History: The Myth of the Eternal Return* (New York, 1959).
6. Herbert E. Cory, *Spenser, the School of the Fletchers, and Milton* (Berkeley, 1912).
7. E.M.W. Tillyard, *The Elizabethan World Picture* (London, 1943).

183

### Chapter Three

1. D.L. Clark, *Milton at St. Paul's School* (New York, 1948).
2. D.M. Miller, "From Delusion to Illumination: A Larger Structure for 'L'Allegro–Il Penseroso,'" *Publications of the Modern Language Association of America*, LXXXVI (1971), pp. 32–39.
3. Eleanor Tate, "Milton's 'L'Allegro' and 'Il Penseroso'—Balance, Progression, or Dichotomy," *Modern Language Notes*, LXXVI (1961), pp. 585–90.
4. D. C. Allen, *The Harmonious Vision* (Baltimore, 1954), pp. 9–18.
5. Nan C. Carpenter, "The Place of Music in 'L'Allegro' and 'Il Penseroso,'" *University of Toronto Quarterly*, XXII (1953), pp. 354–67.
6. Rosemond Tuve, "The Structural Figures of 'L'Allegro' and 'Il Penseroso,'" *Images and Themes* (Cambridge, Mass., 1957) pp. 15–36.

### Chapter Four

1. Willa M. Evans, *Henry Lawes: Musician and Friend of Poets* (New York, 1941).
2. James H. Hanford, "The Chronology of Milton's Private Studies," *Publications of the Modern Language Association of America*, XXXVI (1921), pp. 251–314.
3. Eugene Haun, "An Inquiry into the Genre of *Comus*," *Essays in Honor of Walter Clyde Curry* (Nashville, Tenn., 1954), pp. 221–39.
4. Gretchen Finney, "*Comus*, Drama per Musica," *Studies in Philology*, XXXVII (1940), pp. 482–500.
5. Joan L. Klein, "Some Spenserian Influences on Milton's *Comus*," *Annuale Mediaevale*, V (1964), pp. 27–47.
6. A.S.P. Woodhouse, "The Argument of Milton's *Comus*," *University of Toronto Quarterly*, XI (1941), pp. 46–71.
7. William Madsen, *From Shadowy Types to Truth* (New Haven, 1968).
8. Sears Jayne, "The Subject of Milton's Ludlow *Mask*," *Publications of the Modern Language Association of America*, LXXIV (1959), pp. 533–43.
9. John M. Steadman, "Milton's *Haemony*: Etymology and Allegory," *Publications of the Modern Language Association of America*, LXXVII (1962), pp. 200–207.
10. John Arthos, "The Realms of Being in the Epilogue of *Comus*," *Modern Language Notes*, LXXVI (1961), pp. 321–24.

### Chapter Five

1. James H. Hanford, "The Pastoral Elegy and Milton's 'Lycidas,'" *Publications of the Modern Language Association of America*, XXV (1910), pp. 403–47.

2. Wayne Shumaker, "Flowerets and Sounding Seas: A Study in the Affective Structure of 'Lycidas,' " *Publications of the Modern Language Association of America,* LXVI (1951), pp. 485–94.

3. Jon S. Lawry, " 'Eager Thought': Dialectic in 'Lycidas,' " *Publications of the Modern Language Association of America,* LXXVII (1962), pp. 27–32.

4. Harris Fletcher, "Milton's 'Old Damoetas,' " *Journal of English and Germanic Philology,* LX (1961), pp. 250–57.

5. Caroline W. Mayerson, "The Orpheus Image in *Lycidas,*" *Publications of the Modern Language Association of America,* LXIV (1949), pp. 189–207.

6. John S. Coolidge, "Boethius and 'That Last Infirmity of Noble Mind,' " *Philological Quarterly* XLII (1963), pp. 176–82.

7. Claud A. Thompson, " 'That Two-Handed Engine' Will Smite: Time Will Have a Stop," *Studies in Philology,* LIX (1962), pp. 184–200.

8. Richard P. Adams, "The Archetypal Pattern of Death and Rebirth in Milton's *Lycidas,*" *Publications of the Modern Language Association of America,* LXIV (1949), pp. 183–88.

9. Rosemond Tuve, "Theme, Pattern, and Imagery in *Lycidas,*" *Images and Themes,* pp. 73–111.

10. Donald C. Dorian, *The English Diodatis: A History of Charles Diodati's Family and His Friendship with Milton* (New Brunswick, N.J., 1950).

*Chapter Six*

1. Ernest Sirluck, "Milton's Idle Right Hand," *Journal of English and Germanic Philology,* LX (1961), pp. 749–85.

2. J. H. Hanford and James G. Taaffe, "Milton's 'Biographia Literaria,' " *A Milton Handbook,* pp. 299–314.

3. William Haller, *Liberty and Reformation in the Puritan Revolution* (New York, 1955).

4. C. M. Bowra, *From Virgil to Milton* (London, 1945).

5. Ralph W. Condee, *Milton's Theories Concerning Epic Poetry: Their Sources and Their Influence on Paradise Lost* (Urbana, Ill., 1949).

6. Allan H. Gilbert, *On the Composition of Paradise Lost: A Study of the Ordering and Insertion of Material* (Chapel Hill, N.C., 1947).

7. Jackson I. Cope, *The Metaphoric Structure of Paradise Lost* (Baltimore, 1962.)

8. C. S. Lewis, *A Preface to Paradise Lost* (Oxford, 1942).

9. William Empson, *Milton's God* (London, 1961).

10. Stanley Fish, *Surprised by Sin: The Reader in Paradise Lost* (Berkeley, 1967).

11. Helen Gardner, "Milton's 'Satan' and the Theme of Damnation in Elizabethan Tragedy," *Essays and Studies,* I (1948), pp. 46–66.

12. John M. Steadman, "Archangel to Devil: The Background of Satan's Metamorphosis," *Modern Language Quarterly*, XXI (1960), pp. 321–35.

13. John M. Steadman, "Pandaemonium and Deliberate Oratory," *Neophilologicus*, XLVIII (1964), pp. 159–75.

14. Robert C. Fox, "The Allegory of Sin and Death in *Paradise Lost*," *Modern Language Quarterly*, XXIV (1963), pp. 354–64.

15. H. F. Robins, "Satan's Journey: Direction in *Paradise Lost*," *Journal of English and Germanic Philology*, LX (1961), pp. 699–711.

16. R. J. Zwi Werblowsky, *Lucifer and Prometheus: A Study of Milton's Satan* (London, 1952).

17. Irene Samuel, "The Dialogue in Heaven: A Reconsideration of *Paradise Lost*, III, 1–417," *Publications of the Modern Language Association of America*, LXXII (1957), pp. 601–11.

18. Thomas Kranidas, "Adam and Eve in the Garden: A Study of *Paradise Lost*, Book V," *Studies in English Literature*, IV (1964), pp. 71–83.

19. Joseph H. Summers, *The Muse's Method: An Introduction to Paradise Lost* (Cambridge, Mass., 1962).

20. John M. Steadman, "Allegory and Verisimilitude in *Paradise Lost:* The Problem of the 'Impossible Credible,' " *Publications of the Modern Language Association of America*, LXXVIII (1963), pp. 36–39.

21. William B. Hunter, "Prophetic Dreams and Visions in *Paradise Lost*," *Modern Language Quarterly*, IX (1948), pp. 277–85.

22. Patrick Mullahy, *Oedipus: Myth and Complex* (New York, 1955), treats such assumptions in relation to Oedipus.

23. Wayne Shumaker, "The Fallacy of the Fall in *Paradise Lost*," *Publications of the Modern Language Assocation of America*, LXX (1955), pp. 1185–87.

24. John M. Evans, *Paradise Lost and the Genesis Tradition* (New York, 1968).

25. Don C. Allen, "Milton and the Love of Angels," *Modern Language Notes*, LXXVI (1961), pp. 489–90.

26. Milton Miller, "*Paradise Lost:* The Double Standard," *University of Toronto Quarterly*, XX (1951), pp. 183–99.

27. C. S. Lewis, *The Allegory of Love* (Oxford, 1936).

28. Millicent Bell, "The Fallacy of the Fall in *Paradise Lost*," *Publications of the Modern Language Association of America* LXVIII (1953), pp. 863–83.

29. Esmond L. Marilla, *The Central Problem of Paradise Lost: The Fall of Man* (Cambridge, Mass., 1953).

30. Kester Svendsen, *Milton and Science* (Cambridge, Mass., 1956).

31. Howard Schultz, *Milton and Forbidden Knowledge* (New York, 1955).

32. Mother Mary C. Pecheux, "The Concept of the Second Eve in *Paradise Lost*," *Publications of the Modern Language Association of America*, LXXV (1960), pp. 359–66.

33. H.R. MacCallum, "Milton and Sacred History: Books XI and XII of *Paradise Lost*," *Essays in English Literature from the Renaissance to the Victorian Age Presented to A.S.P. Woodhouse*, ed. M. Maclure and F. Watt (Toronto, 1964), pp. 149–68.

34. John Erskine, "The Theme of Death in *Paradise Lost*," *Publications of the Modern Language Association of America*, XXXII (1917), pp. 573–82.

35. Arthur O. Lovejoy, "Milton and the Paradox of the Fortunate Fall," *English Literary History*, IV (1937), pp. 161–79.

### Chapter Seven

1. William R. Parker, "The Date of *Samson Agonistes*," *Philological Quarterly*, XXVIII (1949), pp. 145–66.

2. Merritt Y. Hughes, "The Christ of *Paradise Regained* and the Renaissance Heroic Tradition," *Studies in Philology*, XXXV (1938), pp. 254–77.

3. Stanley E. Fish, "Inaction and Silence: The Reader in *Paradise Regained*," *Calm of Mind*, ed. by Joseph A. Wittreich (Cleveland, 1971), pp. 25–47.

4. Barbara K. Lewalski, *Milton's Brief Epic: The Genre, Meaning, and Art of Paradise Regained* (Providence, 1966.)

5. Irene Samuel, "Milton on Learning and Wisdom," *Publications of the Modern Language Association of America*, LXIV (1949), pp. 708–23.

6. Howard Schultz, "Christ and Antichrist in *Paradise Regained*," *Publications of the Modern Language Association of America*, LXVII (1952), pp. 790–808.

7. John M. Steadman, "*Paradise Regained*: Moral Dialectic and the Pattern of Rejection," *University of Toronto Quarterly*, XXXI (1962), pp. 416–30.

8. Northrup Frye, "The Typology of *Paradise Regained*," *Modern Philology*, LIII (1956), pp. 227–38.

### Chapter Eight

1. Michael F. Krouse, *Milton's Samson and the Christian Tradition* (Princeton, N.J., 1949).

2. Kenneth Fell, "From Myth to Martyrdom: Towards a View of Milton's *Samson Agonistes*," *English Studies*, XXXIV (1953), pp. 145–55.

3. Martin E. Mueller, "*Pathos and Katharsis in Samson Agonistes*," *English Literary History*, XXXI (1964), pp. 156–74.

4. William R. Parker, *Milton's Debt to Greek Tragedy in Samson Agonistes* (Baltimore, 1937).

5. Claude E. Wells, "Milton's 'Vulgar Readers' and 'The Verse,' " *Milton Quarterly*, IX (1975), pp. 67–70.

6. Ann Gossman, "Milton's Samson as the Tragic Hero Purified by Trial," *Journal of English and Germanic Philology,* LXI (1962), pp. 528–41.

7. Gretchen L. Finney, "Chorus in *Samson Agonistes,*" *Publications of the Modern Language Association of America,* LVIII (1943), pp. 649–64.

8. M.A.N. Radzinowicz, "Eve and Dalila: Renovation and the Hardening of the Heart," *Reason and the Imagination,* ed. J. A. Mazzeo (New York, 1962), pp. 155–81.

9. Daniel C. Boughner, "Milton's Harapha and Renaissance Comedy," *English Literary History,* XI (1944), pp. 297–306.

10. Roger B. Wilkenfeld, "Act and Emblem: The Conclusion of *Samson Agonistes,*" *English Literary History,* XXXII (1965), pp. 160–68.

# Selected Bibliography

PRIMARY SOURCES

*The Complete Poetical Works of John Milton* (Cambridge Edition). Edited by Douglas Bush. Boston: Houghton Mifflin, 1965. Relatively few notes. Clear, clean text.

*Complete Prose Works of John Milton*. General editor, Don M. Wolfe. New Haven: Yale University Press, 1953–. New edition of the prose; likely to become standard.

*John Milton. Complete Poems and Major Prose*. Edited by Merritt Y. Hughes. New York: Odyssey Press, 1957. Standard student edition; copiously annotated. Translations of Latin and Italian works.

*Milton's Sonnets*. Edited by E.A.J. Honigmann. London: Macmillan; New York: St Martin's Press, 1966. Much historical and biographical data; little interpretation.

*The Poems of John Milton*. Edited by John Carey and Alastair Fowler. London: Longman, 1968; New York: W. W. Norton, 1972. Many notes, but significantly different from Hughes.

*The Works of John Milton*. General editor, Frank A. Patterson. 18 vols., in 21. New York: Columbia University Press, 1931–38. Standard scholarly edition.

SECONDARY SOURCES

1. Biography

BUSH, DOUGLAS. *John Milton: A Sketch of His Life and Writings*. New York: Macmillan, 1964. Good, brief literary biography.

PARKER, WILLIAM R. *Milton: A Biography*. 2 vols. Oxford: Clarendon Press, 1968. Magnificent, most recent full biography.

2. Bibliography

HANFORD, JAMES H., comp. *Milton* (Goldentree Bibliography). New York: Appleton-Century-Crofts, 1966. Well selected, inexpensive, but unannotated.

HUCKABAY, CALVIN, comp. *John Milton: An Annotated Bibliography 1929–1968.* Pittsburgh: Duquesne University Press, 1970. Most detailed of one-volume bibliographies.

3. Handbooks

HANFORD, JAMES H. and JAMES G. TAAFFE. *A Milton Handbook.* 5th rev. ed. New York: Appleton-Century-Crofts, 1970. Wealth of biographical and historical material; useful bibliography.

LE COMTE, EDWARD S. *A Milton Dictionary.* New York: Philosophical Library, 1961. Handy annotations of myths, names, and allusions.

NICOLSON, MARJORIE H. *John Milton: A Reader's Guide to His Poetry.* New York: Farrar, Straus, 1963. Especially good for beginning students.

4. Background Studies

BAKER, HERSCHEL. *The Wars of Truth: Studies in the Decay of Christian Humanism in the Earlier Seventeenth Century.* Cambridge, Mass.: Harvard University Press, 1952. Useful, detailed examination of the humanistic tradition.

BUSH, DOUGLAS. *Mythology and the Renaissance Tradition in English Poetry.* New York: Pageant Book Co., 1957. Demonstrates the uses of Classical myth from Spenser through Milton; some notice of earlier uses.

CONKLIN, GEORGE N. *Biblical Criticism and Heresy in Milton.* New York: King's Crown Press, 1949. Explains the principles available to Milton for Biblical interpretation.

CURRY, WALTER CLYDE. *Milton's Ontology, Cosmogony, and Physics.* Lexington: University of Kentucky Press, 1957. Very readable discussion of Milton's poetic universe.

HALLER, WILLIAM. *The Rise of Puritanism; or, The Way to the New Jerusalem as Set Forth in Pulpit and Press from Thomas Cartwright to John Lilburne and John Milton, 1570–1643.* New York: Columbia University Press, 1938. Useful investigation of Milton and the Puritan tradition.

SAMUEL, IRENE. *Plato and Milton.* Ithaca, N.Y.: Cornell University Press, 1947. Short, readable introduction to Milton's debts to Plato.

STEADMAN, JOHN M. *Milton and the Renaissance Hero.* London: Oxford University Press, 1967. Good on standards by which to evaluate Christ, Adam, and Satan.

TILLYARD, EUSTACE MANDEVILLE WETENHALL. *The Elizabethan World Picture.* London: Chatto & Windus, 1943. Explains the implicit system behind Milton's poetry. Essential for beginners.

WILLEY, BASIL. *The Seventeenth Century Background: Studies in the Thought of the Age in Relation to Poetry and Religion.* London: Chatto & Windus, 1934. Good introduction to the intellectual ferment of Milton's day.

5. General Studies of Milton's Poetry

ALLEN, DON CAMERON. *The Harmonious Vision; Studies in Milton's Poetry*. Baltimore: Johns Hopkins Press, 1954. Interesting essays on lesser poems.

DANIELLS, ROY. *Milton, Mannerism and Baroque*. Toronto: University of Toronto Press, 1963. Complex attempt to set Milton's syntheses in the context of esthetic movements.

LAWRY, JON S. *The Shadow of Heaven: Matter and Stance in Milton's Poetry*. Ithaca: Cornell University Press, 1968. Intelligent, well written interpretation of Milton's poetry.

MADSEN, WILLIAM G. *From Shadowy Types to Truth; Studies in Milton's Symbolism*. New Haven: Yale University Press, 1968. Examines the roots of Milton's symbolism in Biblical theories of accommodation. Excellent background.

TUVE, ROSEMOND. *Images & Themes in Five Poems by Milton*. Cambridge, Mass.: Harvard University Press, 1957. Complex and provocative readings of Milton's lesser poems.

6. Collections of Secondary Studies

a. HUGHES, MERRITT Y., gen. ed. *A Variorum Commentary on the Poems of John Milton*. New York: Columbia University Press, 1970–. In progress; volumes currently appearing. Summary and synthesis of critical study of Milton's poems. Fine for overview of critical opinion.

b. *Milton Studies*. Pittsburgh: University of Pittsburgh Press, 1960–. Annual collection of original essays.

c. The following listings are collections of essays, many previously printed. Together they form a very accessible sectioning of Milton scholarship and criticism.

ADAMS, ROBERT M. *Ikon: John Milton and the Modern Critics*. Ithaca: Cornell University Press. 1955.

BARKER, ARTHUR E., ed. *Milton: Modern Essays in Criticism*. New York: Oxford University Press, 1965.

FRANSON, JOHN KARL, ed. *Milton Reconsidered: Essays in Honor of Arthur E. Barker*. Atlantic Highlands, New Jersey: Humanities Press, 1976.

KERMODE, FRANK, ed. *The Living Milton: Essays by Various Hands*. London: Routledge & Kegan Paul, 1960.

MARTZ, LOUIS L., ed. *Milton: A Collection of Critical Essays*. Englewood Cliffs. N.J.: Prentice-Hall, 1966.

PATRICK, J. MAX, ed. *SAMLA Studies in Milton: Essays on Milton and his Works*. Gainesville: University of Florida Press, 1953.

SHAWCROSS, JOHN T., ed. *Milton: The Critical Herigage*. New York: Barnes & Noble, 1970.

STEIN, ARNOLD, ed. *On Milton's Poetry: A Selectiof of Modern Studies.* Greenwich, Conn.: Fawcett, 1970.

SUMMERS, JOSEPH, ed. *The Lyric and Dramatic Milton.* New York: Columbia University Press, 1965.

THORPE, JAMES E., ed. *Milton Criticism: Selections from Four Centuries.* New York: Rinehart & Company, 1950.

WITTREICH, JOSPEH A., ed. *Milton and the Line of Vision.* Madison: University of Wisconsin Press, 1975.

## 7. *Comus*

CAMÉ, JEAN-FRANCOIS. "Myth and Myths in Milton's *Comus.*" *Cahiers Elisabethains,* V (1974), pp. 3–24. Milton's use of pagan myths to express Christian truths.

DEMARAY, JOHN G. *Milton and the Masque Tradition*: The *Early Poems, "Arcades" and Comus.* Cambridge, Mass.: Harvard University Press, 1968. Excellent background in the genre of *Comus.*

DIEKHOFF, JOHN S., ed. *A Maske at Ludlow*: *Essays on Milton's Comus.* Cleveland: Case Western Reserve University Press, 1968. Convenient gathering of *Comus* criticism.

FLETCHER, ANGUS. *The Transcendental Masque: An Essay on Milton's Comus.* Ithaca: Cornell University Press, 1971. Intriguing speculations on the metaphysical significance of *Comus.*

## 8. "Lycidas"

ELLEDGE, SCOTT, ed. *Milton's "Lycidas"*: *Edited to Serve as an Introduction to Criticism.* New York: Harper & Row, 1966. Contains translations of Classical pastoral elegies that may have influenced Milton.

PATRIDES, C. A., ed. *Milton's "Lycidas"*: *The Tradition and the Poem.* New York: Holt, Rinehart & Winston, 1961. Best place to get a view of "Lycidas" criticism.

## 9. *Paradise Lost*

COLLINS, DAN S. "The Buoyant Mind in Milton's Eden," *Milton Studies,* V (1973), pp. 229–48. Convincing argument that Milton's prelapsarian Eden is not static.

COPE, JACKSON I. *The Metaphoric Structure of Paradise Lost.* Baltimore: Johns Hopkins Press, 1962. Complex "structuralist" perspective. Advanced students.

EMPSON, WILLIAM. *Milton's God.* London: Chatto & Windus, 1961. Provocative exposition of Satanist school.

EVANS, JOHN M. *Paradise Lost and the Genesis Tradition.* New York: Oxford University Press, 1968. Study of historical interpretations of Genesis. Recommended.

FISH, STANLEY E. *Surprised by Sin: The Reader in Paradise Lost*. Berkeley: University of California Press, 1967. "Affective" answer to Satanist school.

GALLAGHER, PHILIP J. " 'Real or Allegoric': The Ontology of Sin and Death in *Paradise Lost.*" *English Literary Renaissance*, VI (1976), pp. 317–35. Useful instances of Milton's use of Classical myth in pursuit of truth.

HILL, JOHN SPENCER. " 'Alcestis from the Grave': Image and Structure in Sonnet XXIII." *Milton Studies*, X (1977), pp. 127–39. Clear-cut demonstration of Milton's syncretic use of myth.

KELLEY, MAURICE. *This Great Argument: A Study of Milton's De Doctrina Christiana as a Gloss upon Paradise Lost*. Princeton, N.J.: Princeton University Press, 1941. Important study; flawed by forcing the epic to fit Kelley's reading of Milton's theology.

KIRKCONNELL, WATSON. *The Celestial Cycle; The Theme of "Paradise Lost" in World Literature with Translations of the Major Analogues*. Toronto: Toronto University Press, 1952. Very useful; sometimes misleading because selections emphasize similarities.

LEWALSKI, BARBARA K. "Milton on Women—Yet Once More." *Milton Studies*, VI (1974), pp. 3–20. Strong argument that Milton is not a male chauvinist.

LEWIS, C. S. *A Preface to "Paradise Lost."* London: Oxford University Press, 1942. Useful in establishing the ritualistic mode of the epic.

LIEB, MICHAEL. "Milton and the Metaphysics of Form." *Studies in Philology*, LXXI (1974), pp. 206–24. Asserts that the familiar dichotomies of body-spirit, external-internal, visible-invisible are not prelapsarian.

MACCAFFREY, ISABEL G. *Paradise Lost as "Myth."* Cambridge, Mass.: Harvard University Press, 1959. Examines modern attitudes toward myth; reads the poem in "mythic" context.

PATRIDES, C. A. *"Presidise Lost* and the Theory of Accommodation." *Bright Essence: Studies in Milton's Theology*. Ed. by W. B. Hunter *et al.* Salt Lake City: University of Utah Press, 1971, pp. 159–63. Excellent backgrounds and illustrations of the uses of accommodation.

SUMMERS, JOSEPH. *The Muse's Method; An Introduction to Paradise Lost*. Cambridge, Mass.: Harvard University Press, 1962. Traces Milton's manipulations of point of view. Very readable.

WEBBER, JOAN. "Milton's God." *English Literary History*, XL (1973), pp. 514–31. God is willing to risk chaos to give men free will.

### 10. *Paradise Regained*

LEWALSKI, BARBARA K. *Milton's Brief Epic; The Genre, Meaning, and Art of Paradise Regained*. Providence: Brown University Press, 1966. Solid, detailed examination of the background of Paradise Regained. Recommended highly.

WITTREICH, JOSEPH A., ed. *Calm of Mind; Tercentenary Essays on Paradise Regained and Samson Agonistes in Honor of John S. Diekhoff.* Cleveland: Case Western Reserve University Press, 1971. Varied essays by well-known critics.

11. *Samson Agonistes*

CRUMP, GALBRAITH M., ed. *Twentieth Century Interpretations of Samson Agonistes: A Collection of Critical Essays.* Englewood Cliffs, N.J.: Prentice-Hall, 1968. Handy collection of previously printed articles.

GROSE, CHRISTOPHER. " 'His Uncontrollable Intent': Discovery as Action in *Samson Agonistes.*" *Milton Studies,* VII (1975), pp. 49–76. Samson's internal action breaks through the Hebrews' inability to see the will of God leading in a new direction.

HONE, RALPH E. *John Milton's Samson Agonistes: The Poem and Materials for Analysis.* San Francisco: Chandler Publishing Co., 1966. Contains text, some antecedents of Milton's drama, and a few critical essays.

KROUSE, F. MICHAEL. *Milton's Samson and the Christian Tradition.* Princeton, N.J.: Princeton Universtiy Press for the University of Cincinnati, 1949. Essential background in the literary and theological bases of Milton's drama.

PARKER, WILLIAM R. *Milton's Debt to Greek Tragedy in Samson Agonistes.* Baltimore: Johns Hopkins University Press, 1937. Still important pioneer study in the dual tradition, Greek and Judeo-Christian, from which Milton forged his drama.

# Index